™

Traveling the Ohio River Scenic Route

Through Southern Indiana
including Cincinnati, Louisville, and Owensboro

Douglas Wissing

Guild Press of Indiana
Carmel, IN 46032

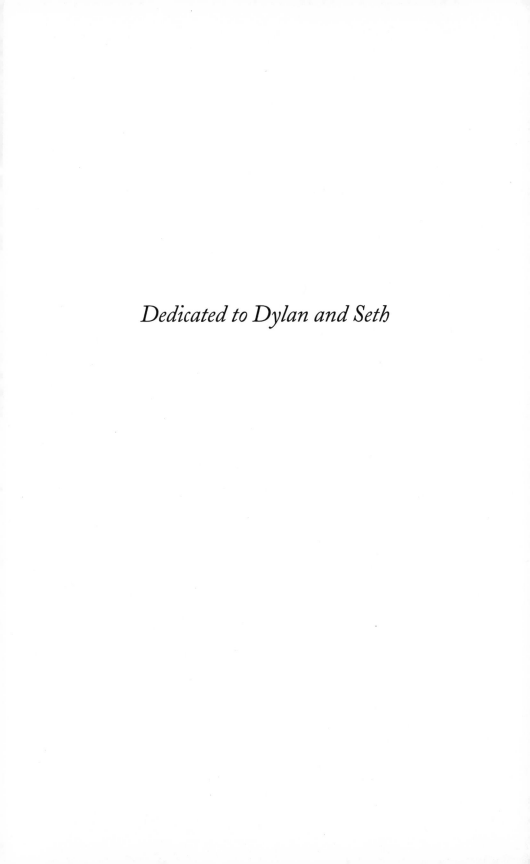

Dedicated to Dylan and Seth

Contents

Prologue

"The river is within us."
– T. S. Eliot

I grew up beside the rivers of southern Indiana—the Wabash and the Ohio—and never ceased to be entranced by the flow. "You can't step in the same river twice," my grandfather used to tell me, and I've spent part of my life figuring that wisdom out. I've wandered the globe's streams: the Mekong, Missouri, and Mississippi, the Rhine and the Red—both the one in Arkansas and the one in Hanoi. I've stalked along the Yangtse and peered into the mighty Columbia; rafted like some post-modern Huck Finn down Thailand's jungley Mae Klong; spit in the Tiber and danced across the Seine; mused on mortality beside Lhasa's Kyichu before traveling hundreds of roadless miles to the sacred mountain in Tibet from where the great rivers of Asia come tumbling down. But I never really left the rivers of southern Indiana. They stayed in my head and they stayed in my heart, and I like to hope they stay in yours.

"A graceful ribbon of blue," an early traveler called the Ohio. He knew what the Americans who came before him knew, that the river is a beautiful sight. The name itself comes from the Iroquois word for beautiful, "Oyo." The first French explorers called it "La Belle Riviere"—the beautiful river. When the late sun angles down though the valley's puffy clouds and tints the river the color of hammered silver, and the reflections of a thousand things play on the surface of the water, it's easy to understand how the names came to be.

The river is a looking-glass, catching the passing colors in its stream. Sometimes it's delicate blue as the rising sun pours down the valley, and the cries of waterfowl drift in the cool air. Other times it is the color of old pewter as glowering storm clouds gather overhead. Or a rich coffee brown as it flows past the golden banks on the Kentucky shore, or vendure green as it passes grapevine-hung islands and forested banks.

It's a special river, part of a unique ecosystem. The Eastern Woodlands is a temperate, relatively southern, forest region. Only China's upper Yangtse valley with its vast rhododendron forests is equivalent. The Ohio's location creates a complex verdancy—southern Indiana along the Ohio is part of what naturalists call the Golden Triangle, where the ecosystems of the North, South, East, and West converge, creating an exceptionally rich bio-diversity. The blue herons that flourish in the cypress swamps of the Wabash wetlands are more reminiscent of Louisiana, while the sprawling hardwood forests of the Hoosier National Forest are the last great remnants of the Eastern stands. The dense forests and verge create a vast reservoir for the country's threatened songbird population, 270 different species in all. Over two hundred species of flowers bloom in the hills and hollows. Northern pines and wildflowers from the plains prosper in the various habitats. The river itself is in the best health its been for generations, with 125 species of fish swimming its waters.

Nearly a thousand miles long, the Ohio stretches from the Alleghenies at Pittsburgh down to the muddy junction with the Mississippi at Cairo, Illinois. The light filtering through the portentous clouds and the abundance of water nurturing the lush forests and fields lends an air of possibilities— a protected, homey paradise where creatures can live out their possibilities.

Ancient mound-builders built their amazing towns and monuments along its banks, the only riverine culture in the Americas that matches the great river civilizations of the Ancient Middle Eastern World. The Ohio was the first great highway for the continent, the passage for Indian tribes and French explorers, pioneers and settlers, warriors and pacifists, utopians of a dozen stripes, nascent industrialists and gimlet-eyed empire-builders. It echoed to the cries of war parties, bawdy flatboatmen songs, and the shrill calliopes of the steamboats tethered to the banks.

Today, there's a lost world quality here. Log cabins still pepper the forested highlands above the river. Anchored by columned mansions, remnant nineteenth-century Greek Revival towns still overlook the river as though waiting for the steamboat's call. During the flatboat and steamboat eras, the valley was a cradle of the industrial revolution, creating some of America's richest towns. Tributary valleys are German-Catholic enclaves where the locals still sing-song to an accent called 'dutchie,' descended from colonies founded 150 years ago. An ancient Devonian reef formed miles of rapids and chutes at Clarksville, the only impediment on the entire length of the Ohio, creating the node of culture at the Falls Cities—Clarksville, New Albany, Jeffersonville, and Louisville. Early in Indiana's history, this was the most populous and prosperous region in the state, a great center of the steamboat age. But the same railroads which stilled the steamboats' whistles, also sent the region into a deep somnolence. To a certain extent, it saved the valley, preserving a paradise of natural wonders, grand historic architecture, and small town life.

While there are twenty-five million people in the Ohio Valley today, the stretch along the southern Indiana shore is primarily pastoral countryside. The Scenic Route traverses the Hoosier National Forest from Artists' Point to German Ridge, part of a vast quilt of state and national forests that stretches almost forty miles to the north, providing hundreds of camping, fishing, hiking, picnicking, and swimming spots.

"We share our land with a lot of wild creatures," Art Stewart said, looking out to the forested hills of his Needmore Buffalo Farm near Corydon, dark green in the dimming light. "There's geese and ducks that stayed, beavers down in the stream, wild turkeys—there must be dozens—coyotes, hawks. I guess we all like it too much to leave." When one of his buffalo sauntered over for a head scratch, Art's grizzled beard and thick, dark hair looked oddly akin.

The people along the route celebrate tradition, living in a world still akimbo to malls and suburbs and interstates. Crawford County just added its first stoplight. Families are still tight. Ted Huber is a towheaded man with a sun-busked face. He proudly tells visitors to the six-hundred-acre Huber Orchard and Winery in the high Knobs area near New Albany that his son is the seventh generation of Hubers to live on the farm. "The fourth, fifth, sixth, and now seventh generation, we're all living here on the farm here together," he said.

So this is the tale of the river and the culture that grew along its banks. It's about the rising and the flooding, and the commerce that floated down the waterway. It's about us—where we came from, where we are going. We understand now that if we turn our back on the river, we'll pay the price, forgetting our heritage and losing our tether to the natural world that ultimately defines and enriches us.

One summer day I sat on Elmer Cooper's screened-in porch looking out at the river. Cooper is one of the few commercial fishermen left on the river, a sinewy guy with a ready smile. Snapshots of his mud-caked living room from the 1997 flood sat on the table. "The river's the boss," he shrugged. A river breeze rustled the cottonwoods outside his windows as the Ohio flowed eternally by. "I just like this river," he said, walking to the screen. "I can't walk past this window without looking out at the river. See what it's doing."

Recognizing the extraordinary legacy of southern Indiana along the Ohio, the U. S. Department of Transportation declared the 320-mile-long Ohio River Scenic Route one of the first National Scenic Byways in 1996, along with roads like the Natchez Trace Parkway, the Blue Ridge Parkway, and Route One, Pacific Coast Highway. There are now fifty-nine of these routes scattered across America, chosen for their outstanding scenic, natural, cultural, archeological, or recreational qualities.

Southern Indiana's Ohio River Scenic Route skirts the broad Ohio through a land of green corrugated hills and running streams, running through micro-ecologies and cultures as distinct as Darwin's finches. From the Greek Revival havens in the east to pioneer communities near Gentryville to an ancient mound builder city near Evansville to the Utopian community of New Harmony on the western border, there's a wealth of diversity.

Traveling the Ohio River Scenic Route is organized thematically, flowing downstream just like the river, from the Ohio border down to Illinois. Each chapter will open with an essay on the dominant natural and cultural motif of the region through which the Scenic Route is passing. A road tour, covering that section of the route, follows with points of interest presented in greater detail. Alternate driving loops of the Scenic Route are included in several chapters. Visitor information follows each chapter, including local visitor offices and recommendations for food, lodging, camping, and additional reading. An appendix at the conclusion of the book includes organizations to contact for additional information, regional festivals, a guide to the architectural styles of the valley, and a listing of other U.S. Scenic Routes.

I hope you enjoy the trip.

Douglas Wissing
Bloomington, Indiana

Recommended Reading

Indiana: A New Historical Guide, edited by Robert M. Taylor, Jr., Errol Wayne Steven, Mary Ann Ponder, Paul Brockman, Indiana Historical Society, Indianapolis, 1989, is an invaluable guide to the entire state, a vast compendium of the state's history.

The Indiana Way, James H. Madison, Indiana University Press, Bloomington, IN, 1986, is an overview of Indiana history written by one of the state's most respected historians.

The Old Northwest, R. Carlyle Buley, Indiana Historical Society, Indianapolis, 1950 won the Pulitzer Prize. It's still a stirring story.

That Dark and Bloody River: Chronicles of the Ohio River, Allan W. Eckert, Bantam Books, NY, 1995, is rip-roaring popular history.

Always A River: The Ohio River and the American Experience, edited by Robert L. Reid, Indiana University Press, Bloomington, IN, 1991, is a mix of lyrical essays and scholarly historiography attempting to place the river in a temporal and global context.

The Natural Heritage of Indiana, edited by Marion T. Jackson, Indiana University Press, Bloomington, IN, 1998, is beautiful exploration of Indiana's extraordinary natural diversity.

Natural Areas in Indiana and their Preservation, A. A. Lindsay, Purdue University, Lafayette, IN, 1969, is the groundbreaking study of remnant natural regions in Indiana.

Indiana's Wildlife Viewing Guide, Phil T. Seng, Falcon Press, Helena, Montana, 1996, showcases eighty-nine of the best wildlife viewing spots in the state.

Historic Indiana 1997/98: A Guide to the Indiana Properties Listed in the National Register of Historic Places, published by the Indiana Division of Historic Preservation and Archeology, Indianapolis, 1998, is a great source of information on Indiana's architectural heritage.

Courtsey Richard Fields

Ohio River island at sunrise.

Courtesy of Madison Area Convention and Visitors Bureau

The Eleutherian College sits on a high ridge seven miles north of Madison, the first college in the U.S. where African-Americans and whites of both sexes could study together.

Classical Indiana

Cincinnati, Ohio, to Madison, Indiana
Ohio River Scenic Route 122 Miles

THE OHIO RIVER SCENIC ROUTE officially begins at the weath-
ered stone marker on U.S. 50 that has stood at the Indiana-Ohio border since
1838. One can imagine prosperous, bushy-whiskered civic leaders inaugu-
rating the monument, sweating in their dark wool suits beside the bustling
river. At the time, Cincinnati, twenty miles upstream, was the entrepôt of
the burgeoning Western Empire, the largest city west of Philadelphia. The
city's public landing at the foot of Broadway was a hive of activity. Steamboats crowded the wharves with the river pilots high in their pilot houses.
Chanty-singing roustabouts toted salt pork and flour, household goods, furniture and whiskey up the packets' gangplanks. Most of the cargo was bound
for the lower South's Mississippi River plantations, too busy growing cotton
for the English market to waste time raising comestibles.

Founded in 1788 when the first settlers stepped from their boats, Cincinnati prospered as a busy intersection in the wilderness. The rivers to the
north all drained toward the crossing, and Licking River on the southern
shore led deep into the already well-settled Kentucky Bluegrass. Initially,
Cincinnati was the site of Fort Washington, located near an ancient mound
built by pre-Columbian Native Americans. Following the Revolutionary War,
American militia sallied forth from the fort several times to do battle with
the Ohio tribes and then fled back in disordered retreat. In 1792
General Anthony Wayne arrived to drill his troops relentlessly beside the
mound until they were sufficiently trained to march into battle. The subsequent campaign broke the power of the Ohio tribes, and Indian wars moved
further west, hastening the European settlement of the valley.

Cincinnati grew from five hundred people to fifteen thousand in the five
years from 1790 to 1795, bulging with settlers drawn by the promise of the
Western Empire, floating down the Ohio from the East on flatboats,
keelboats, even rafts. By 1811 the first steamboat, the *New Orleans,* arrived
at the landing, and by 1825 provender floated down the Miami and Erie Canal from the newly settled interior Ohio valleys. Cincinnati was the largest
pork-packing center in the world by 1850, even known as Porkopolis for a
while. Up to the Civil War, Cincinnati and the Ohio River towns one hundred miles downstream to the Falls of the Ohio, got first crack at the com-

merce of the entire Western Empire.

Lawrenceburg, Rising Sun, and Aurora, the Indiana cities just downriver, were part of this mercantile network—trading and manufacturing towns that served markets similar to Cincinnati. Further down the Ohio, the Swiss town of Vevay and the proud industrial city of Madison also preened in the new wealth. They all exhibited their new prosperity by building sturdy Federal-style structures, often designed in the popular Greek Revival style that resonated the ideals of democracy and citizen participation. The esthetic was so prevalent in the first half of nineteenth century that it became known as the National Style. The same pediments and columns and entablatures that graced the Capitol Building in Washington were writ small across the built landscape of the new cities of the trans-Appalachian West.

However, the whistle of the railroads played a dirge for mercantile domination of the river towns. By 1860 Chicago passed Cincinnati as the leading pork center. The Civil War destroyed the southern markets. Even haughty Madison was left to bask in the Indiana sun with an incongruous architectural grandeur, as the main lines of the railroads went elsewhere. In the passing decades, it struggled along as just another Indiana market town, albeit graced with a imposing legacy.

But poverty and thrift are often the great preservers. The Indiana river towns from Lawrenceburg to Madison spent the next century in a genteel poverty, with just enough money to reuse and maintain, but not enough to tear down and build new. It is as though a glacier of commerce and democratic ideals and classical esthetics came over the Appalachians and ground relentlessly down the Ohio Valley, leaving behind the small cultural moraines of these Indiana towns. Luckily, a group of doughty preservationists organized in the 1960s before prosperity could tear holes in the architectural fabric, saving many historic structures throughout the region that might have gone the way of the wrecking ball.

The waxing and waning of prosperity and the determined grassroots preservation movement has maintained the Scenic Route from the Ohio border to Madison as a rolling architectural history lesson. Hugging the river's edge through a verdant bottomland, the route is punctuated with farms and towns that look like full-sized models of nineteenth-century carpenters' style books—harmonious pastiches of Federal, Italianate, and Gothic Revival styles, leavened with Queen Anne and vernacular carpenter/builder houses.

So let's explore the Ohio River Scenic Route. Because of the strong connection to Classical Indiana and the other towns downriver, we'll begin at the public landing in Cincinnati. The official scenic route begins twenty-three miles to the west at the state line.

Mileage

Please note: The official start of the Ohio River Scenic Route is at the Indiana State line, twenty-three miles downstream. So we will count down mileage to the border, which will be mileage point 0.0.

(23.0) **Cincinnati, Ohio. Public Landing** is located at the river at Broadway and Mehring Way. This is the site of the settlement Losantiville, which means "town opposite the mouth of the Licking." Thankfully, General Arthur St. Clair promptly changed it to the more classical name, Cincinnati, in honor of the Roman soldier-farmer who returned to his plow after leading the victorious Roman armies. The last of the original floating showboats, the *Majestic,* is moored nearby. As it has for many decades, the *Majestic* continues the tradition of drama, comedy, and musicals on the river. This is also the docking spot for the steamboats *Delta Queen* and *Mississippi Queen* when they dock. Three blocks north at Third and Broadway streets, there is a marker for **Fort Washington**, one of the first forts north of the Ohio.

The **Serpentine Wall** follows the river's edge to **Yeatman's Cove Park** and **Bicentennial Commons at Sawyers Point**, approximately a four-mile walk from Public Landing to the amphitheater at the east end. Bicentennial Commons was developed in 1988 as part of the city's 200th anniversary. It features a whimsical gateway sculpture by Andrew Leicester, with steamboat smokestacks topped by dancing winged pigs, celebrating Cincinnati's history of river trade and pork packing. The commission of the sculpture created such a stir that city council chambers were packed with angry citizens asserting the sculpture would make the city a laughing stock, and proponents wearing faux pig noses and ears, stroking their pet pot-bellied pigs. A scale model of the river from Pittsburgh to Cairo winds under the sculpture. With the fifty-two locks and dams on the river today, it is essentially eighty very long lakes stretching to the Mississippi. The **Tall Stacks Festival** is held every four years, drawing packet palaces up the rivers to Cincinnati. In 1988 fourteen boats arrived at the river front, and nineteen of them in 1995. The next festival is scheduled for 1999. Bicentennial Commons also includes a timeline of the 440 million year history of the Ohio Valley that follows the river front.

Mount Adams looms to the northeast, topped by large brick building and steepled church, formerly a Catholic monastery. Each Good Friday the pious continue to climb the eighty-two steps of the Immaculata Church, pausing to say a prayer at each step. Today Mount Adams is a trendy neighborhood of boutiques, bars, and artists' galleries, particularly on Pavilion Street, an ideal area for sauntering. The **Rookwood Pottery**, 1077 Celestial Street, at the crest of Mount Adams, no longer produces the world-famous ceramics as it did at the turn of the century, but patrons can dine in the enormous kilns.

At 2950 Gilbert Avenue, the nineteenth-century **Harriet Beecher Stowe House** was this famous woman's Cincinnati home from 1832 to 1850. It was where she received her inspiration for *Uncle Tom's Cabin*, an incendiary pre-Civil War novel that has enjoyed a recent revival. Her father, Lyman Beecher, was an influential abolitionist at the Presbyterian Lane Seminary until pro-slavery sentiment in Cincinnati caused him and half of the student body to relocate to Oberlin College, where abolitionism was held in higher esteem. Stowe's *Uncle Tom's Cabin* was reportedly the true story of Eliza Harris, a fugitive slave who fled across the Ohio to freedom from the slave catchers. For many years, tiny towns along the Ohio shore vied with one another as the true spot of Eliza Harris' crossing. "She gazed with longing eyes on the sullen surging waters that lay between her and liberty," Stowe wrote. "If they can get to Cincinnati," one runaway wrote to his still-enslaved wife, "they can get liberty." The era will be commemorated with the **Underground Railroad Freedom Center**, a state-of-the-art museum to be opened in 2002 at a riverfront location.

The magnificent 1933 art deco **Union Terminal**, 1301 Western Avenue, houses the **Cincinnati Museum Center**, a consortium of the **Cincinnati Historical Museum**, the **Museum of Natural History and Science** (whose first employee was the naturalist-artist John James Audubon), and the **OMNIMAX Theater**. The **Rookwood Ice Cream Parlor** in the terminal is a complete Rookwood Pottery interior, a fantasy of 1930s ceramic butterflies, flowers and flitting dragonflies. The museum complex is an ideal introduction to the history and ecology of the valley. The history museum has entertaining multi-media exhibits covering the early and emerging days of the Queen City. The Natural History Museum is famous for its Limestone Cave and Ice Age Exhibit.

Back at the downtown river front, the **Roebling Suspension Bridge** spans the Ohio with a harmonious grace, as it has since it was built in 1866. It was designed by the engineer John A. Roebling, famous for building the Brooklyn Bridge. Twelve years prior to his work on the Brooklyn Bridge, Roebling pioneered his ideas of suspension bridges at Cincinnati. It was here that he perfected the concept of twisting thin strands of wire together to form cables of high tensile strength, essential for the design of the New York bridge. The bridge is still used for traffic today.

Across the bridge, the historic town of **Covington, Kentucky** is a respite from the bustle of Cincinnati. There are fifteen National Register Historic Districts in the city, encompassing more than forty-seven hundred buildings. Just over the bridge, the **Riverside Historic District** boasts a lovely riverside promenade, ante bellum homes, and a lineup of floating restaurants, including Mike Fink's, a sternwheeler on the National Historic Register. There are riverboats based on the waterfront that offer cruises of the river, from one-hour sightseeing trips to seven-day excursions. Several B&Bs are scattered through the district, making it a historic base to explore the area.

To continue on the Ohio River Scenic Route from the Public Landing, take Mehring Way west along the river through an industrial landscape of scrap piles and recycling mills to River Road and on to U.S. 50W. Architecture varies from moldering, narrow river houses to restored Victorian piles in Sayler Park. Grain elevators and oil storage tanks are signs of the barge commerce that moves incessantly down the river.

(15.7) **Anderson Ferry Road.** Turn south to a working toll ferry across the Ohio. The small barge and old white tug churns across every day but Christmas, as the ferry has since 1817. Cincinnatians use it as a short cut to the airport. Foot passengers get a price break at twenty-five cents.

(9.2) **North Bend, Ohio.** North Bend was founded in 1798, the fourth oldest town in Ohio. While it never shared the prosperity of nearby Cincinnati, it prides itself as the birthplace of one U.S. President and the long-time home of another. At the corner of Symmes and Washington, a thirteen-room log-and-frame house was the **Home of William Henry Harrison** (1773-1841).

His grandson, Benjamin Harrison (1833-1901) was born in the house and raised in a family country home a few miles away. He moved to Indianapolis in 1854 and rose to the rank of Brigadier General during the Civil War. After serving in the U. S. Senate, he was elected the twenty-third President in 1889.

South on Harrison Avenue, the fourteen-acre **William Henry Harrison Memorial State Park** overlooks the Ohio. The park is dominated by the sixty-four-foot sandstone obelisk that is the tomb and memorial for Harrison. The monument is a guide for riverboat pilots, and for many decades it was customary for them to honor the President with a low whistle as they passed. Harrison was born a son of the landed aristocracy in Tidewater Virginia in 1773. At the age of eighteen, Harrison moved to Fort Washington and joined General Wayne in his successful campaigns against the Ohio tribes. He was named Governor of the Indiana Territory in 1800 and negotiated numerous treaties with the Indians from Grouseland, his grand plantation-style home in Vincennes. But it was outdoors under the famous Council Tree that Harrison had his fateful negotiations with Shawnee leader, Tecumseh.

Speaking for a coalition of Midwestern tribes that included Miami, Delaware, Wyandotte, Potawatomi, Ottowa, Kickapoo, as well as Shawnee, Tecumseh argued that the Americans needed to respect the boundary lines already established. "Brother," he told Harrison, "they want to save that piece of land. We do not wish you to take it. It is small enough for our purposes." Harrison said he would pass Tecumseh's words on to President Madison, but there was little chance Madison would accede. Tecumseh sadly replied that Madison "is so far off he will not be injured by this war; he may sit in his town and drink his wine, whilst you and I will have to fight this out."

The wars between the Native American tribes and the European settlers pouring over the Alleghenies were nothing more than two distinct cultures battling for control over land—the Native Americans to continue their traditional lives; the Europeans for farms and empire. The impasse between them culminated in the 1811 Battle of Tippecanoe near Lafayette, Indiana. While hardly a resounding military victory, the battle contributed to the decline of the tribes' military power in Indiana. More importantly, the victory spawned a generation of war heroes who parlayed their battle records into political careers. William Henry Harrison was swept into the Presidency in 1840 on a platform of "Tippecanoe and Tyler Too," the first modern-style political campaign, replete with free hard cider and rousing, torch-lit political rallies.

Harrison, however, was fated to have the shortest administration in history. He caught a cold at the inauguration and succumbed a month later to pneumonia, "worn out by the excitement and the importunings of office seekers," as one historian wrote. The ultimate result is the obelisk on the banks of the Ohio.

(4.5)   Turn south on Brower Road to the road that parallels the river. Turn east 3.5 miles to the site of **Fort Finney**, where government commissioners, including George Rogers Clark, negotiated the purchase of two-thirds of Ohio from the Wyandotte, Delaware, and Shawnee tribes in 1785. These treaties were among the many dubious agreements signed in the period. In some cases the Indians who attended the meetings ceded lands to which they had no claims. In others, the warriors who made their marks were, at best, minor chiefs. When the Shawnee arrived at Fort Finney, they threw down a belt of black wampum, signifying war. Clark angrily brushed it from the table and ordered them out. Later in the day, the Shawnee returned with a white wampum belt of peace.

Continue east 3.7 miles to a junction, turn to a second junction. Up this lane 4.4 miles is the early-nineteenth-century brick **Boyhood Home of Benjamin Harrison.**

0.0   **Indiana-Ohio State Line.** The hand-carved marker was erected in 1838 to set in stone the boundary line established in 1837.

2.0   **Greendale/Lawrenceburg, Indiana.** (Henceforth, unless noted, all destinations are in Indiana.) While **Greendale** wasn't platted until 1883, the two towns have grown together with time. They have long been joined by more than proximity. The scent of fermenting mash has hung over this part of the valley since the town's early days, as the area is known for whiskey production. The region's abundant grain and clear, cold well water stimulated whiskey production as early as 1809, when the pioneers discovered the ease of transport and profitability of the distilled elixir versus raw grain. As late as 1941, there were still three major distilleries in town. The gargantuan **Joseph E. Seagram and Sons Inc.** is the only remaining distillery to continue the tradition. The plant began operations in 1933 on the site of the old Rossville Distillery, which began distilling in 1847, and continued till a 1932 fire. The Seagrams operation is considered the largest distillery in the world, but it is not currently open for tours.

In Greendale, turn .5 miles north on Nowlin Street to the **Greendale Cemetery.** The cemetery was founded in 1867 on land given to Colonel Zebulon Pike in 1803 for service in the Revolutionary War. His son, Brigadier General Zebulon Montgomery Pike, was the one-armed explorer of much of the West and the Grand Canyon. Pike's Peak is named for him. A monument at the entrance celebrates their memory. Note the headstone at the western edge of the cemetery with a carved railroad train, dedicated to George H. Dunn, who brought the Lawrenceburg and Indianapolis Railroad to town.

Lawrenceburg was founded in 1802, the fourth oldest city in Indiana. The town was the terminus for the Whitewater Canal, which extended north to Cambridge City. There is a historical marker at High and Elm streets. The turning basin for the keelboats was at the foot of Elm Street and extended two blocks northeast to the end of St. Clair. The canal was completed in 1839, the first in the state. Unfortunately, railroads spelled the same demise for canals as they did for river traffic, and the canal boom that stitched the state with trenches, ultimately bankrupted Indiana and precipitated a new state constitution.

In the heyday of the steamboat era, Lawrenceburg was a favorite port of call. Carousing captains and crews frequented the dives of Gamblers' Row, a vice district famous from Pittsburgh to New Orleans. The area, like Cincinnati, depended on Southern trade and, accordingly, was a hot-bed of Southern sympathizers, known as Copperheads. When the Confederate John Hunt Morgan invaded Indiana with twenty-five hundred troops in July 1863, he expected the most active of the pro-rebel Hoosiers, the Knights of the Golden Circle, who were scattered through southern Indiana, to arise and help him seize Indianapolis. Instead, the Knights laid low, and Morgan's Raiders were reduced to a hurried pillage through Indiana before they were captured or dispersed in Ohio. Morgan's Raid took him through Dearborn

County, including Sunman, New Alsace, and Dover.

The architecture of Lawrenceburg is still a remarkably homogeneous example of the nineteenth-century commercial center. In 1984 the entire downtown district, bounded by Charlotte, Tate, William, and Elm streets and the railroad tracks, was added to the National Register of Historical Places.

An architectural stroll of downtown Lawrenceburg is a good introduction to the styles of the valley. A primer on architectural styles is in the appendix. Among many in Lawrenceburg, **The Dearborn County Courthouse** on High Street is an exceptional example of Indiana Greek Revival architecture. It was built in 1872 by architect George H. Kyle, a student of the preeminent architect of the valley, Madison's Francis Costigan. It features towering Corinthian columns, and a small county museum is inside. At 508 W. High Street, the **Vance-Tously House** stands as one of the oldest houses in Lawrenceburg, a Federal-style structure built in 1818 with plans brought from England. Until the magnificent Lanier Mansion in Madison was built, this was considered the finest house between Cincinnati and Louisville, a resplendent vision from the river.

The small Italianate house at 13 W. High Street was built in 1844. The 1818 **Jesse Hunt** three-story brick building at Walnut and High was considered Indiana's first "skyscraper," an awe-inspiring sight to the pioneers. The Romanesque Revival Masonic Temple at 12 E. High Street was built in 1893. An important group of Federal row houses, currently endangered by the neglect of the current gaming corporation owners, are located at 124-136 E. High Street. At 133 E. High Street, the 1818 Federal/Italianate house has been gussied up with additions through the years, including the bay windows and Victorian moldings.

At 124 Short Street, the fire station with the prominent tower is an 1884 Queen Anne style structure. In the next block at 229 Short Street, the **1882 Presbyterian Church** is also Queen Anne. This was the first congregation ministered by famous abolitionist Henry Ward Beecher, the brother of Harriet Beecher Stowe, author of *Uncle Tom's Cabin*. Beecher was ordained here in 1837 and served as its minister until 1839. After he left for his influential pulpit in New York City, he and his congregation contributed to the construction of this church.

The American Legion at the corner of Second and Short streets has the **Flying Red Horse "Peggy"** in a glass case outside the club. She is a customized Model T Ford, built by two WWI vets who wanted a parade vehicle. Peggy's giant wings flapped as she reared on her hind wheels and spun at American Legion parades all over America from 1936 to 1972. She was put out to her glass pasture in 1994.

The **First Southern Baptist Church** at 31 E. Center Street is an 1850

Greek Revival. The commercial Italianate building at 316-318 Walnut was jacked up one story in the nineteenth century, a common occurrence. Indeed, Chicago's entire inventory of buildings in the Loop was raised ten feet in the same period, while business went on as usual. There is a small 1880 Second Empire commercial structure with a bracketed cornice at 317 Walnut.

In all, there are at least thirty significant buildings in the downtown area. In 1997 a three-block section of downtown Lawrenceburg was added to Historic Landmarks Foundation of Indiana's list of eleven most endangered historic sites. A Las Vegas gaming corporation, Golden Nugget, bought up the properties in the mid-1990s, with the thought of developing a major entertainment destination—a post-Modern Gamblers Row. But they failed to get the casino license that went to Argosy Casino and in 1997 put the properties back on the block at a stiff price. They are attempting to sell the entire parcel for twelve million dollars, twice to three times what they paid, refusing to sell them individually. In early 1998 the buildings stood vacant, and the first three-story building in Indiana is rapidly deteriorating.

The Eads parkway and city park honors the memory of local inventor and engineer **James Buchanan Eads,** who invented and patented the diving bell in 1842 for his river salvage business. He went on to build fourteen armored river craft for the Union in the Civil War, and built the 520-foot central span Eads Bridge across the Mississippi at St. Louis in 1867.

East of the town on U.S. 50, there are signs for the **Argosy Casino** on Argosy Parkway. The immense Las Vegas style complex has the world's largest floating casino, 408 feet by one hundred feet: big enough to hold thirty-four full-sized mobile homes, according to the casino press release. Nearly four million people crossed the gangplank to gamble in 1997.

The Indiana riverboat casinos that dot the Ohio River from border to border are part of nationwide explosion of legalized gambling in the 1990s. In 1993 the Indiana State Legislature approved casino boat gambling in counties where there was navigable water, and a countywide referendum approved gambling. As of 1998, there are eight gambling-boat casinos open or under construction along Indiana's Ohio River and Lake Michigan shores. The Ohio has casinos at Lawrenceburg, Rising Sun, Harrison County, and Evansville, with one license yet to be awarded.

In the northern part of Dearborn county, **Chateau Pomije** offers a European-style winery in the rolling hills near New Alsace. Opening in 1973, Chateau Pomije is part of the revolution in wine making that improved the quality and popularity of Indiana wines. Their well-crafted vintages can be tasted in the charming restaurant located in a reconstructed hundred-year-old barn overlooking sixty acres of vineyards. To reach the chateau, proceed further east on Route 50 to the junction with Indiana Route 1, where the landscape to the north resembles the rounded hills of Vermont's Green Mountains. You'll be following part of the route of Morgan's Raiders as you travel north to the town of Dover. At Dover, turn right on North Dearborn Road and look for Chateau Pomije signs.

When you are ready to roll on down the Scenic Highway, return to Route 50W.

4.0   **Aurora** was founded in 1804 on a picturesque bluff above the river bend with a broad view down the river and over to the gray-green Kentucky hills. The downtown street names of Importing and Exporting are a clue to Aurora's mercantile past. Industry and river trade have been the mainstays of the town from the beginning. In its heyday, steamboats pulled to the public dock to disgorge passengers and load the manufactured goods of the town: foundry work, whiskey, furniture and caskets.

The town name sprang from a rivalry with the nearby town of Rising Sun. Town father Jesse Lynch Holman influenced the post office to name the town. He reportedly wrote, "The Aurora, the Roman goddess of dawn, comes before the Rising Sun."

In 1992 the downtown, bounded by Importing, Water, Market, Fifth, and Exporting streets was recognized as a National Historic District. The downtown still reflects its zenith in the nineteenth century. There are several exceptional examples of Gothic Revival structures in Aurora, commingling with other nineteenth century styles. They include the 1878 St. John's Lutheran Church at 214 Mechanic Street. At 113 Fifth Street, the mid-1870s First Evangelical Church also reflects the esthetic. Two nearby houses, at 318 Fourth Street and 403 Judiciary, are residential examples, the latter a Queen Anne hybrid built between 1870 and 1890.

The crown of Aurora is at the end of Main Street, where the grandiose **Hillforest House** looms like an overly decorated wedding cake. "We say it is Italian Renaissance meets Steamboat Gothic," Hillforest Director Sue Small said. The circular porches wrapping the semi-circular front, the roof-top cupola resembling a steamboat pilot house, the slender columns, and arched windows, all add to the effect. It's as though the largest and fanciest of the grand elephant packets somehow ran aground high on the hillside.

It is a three-story house, topped by the bellevedere that commands an amazing view of the river and surrounding hills of three states, with builder Thomas Gaff's brass telescope still standing in the room. Hillforest was built of the finest materials of the day: Circassian walnut paneling, parquet floors, elaborate plaster borders cast from Italian molds. The house has many original rococo furnishings and French wallpaper. The gardens and grounds on the hillside above the house are underlain with a complex system of drains and cisterns to insure the longevity of the landscape plan, which included formal gardens, terraces, serpentine promenades, and gazebos. It is the oldest extant man-made landscape in the state.

The house was built around 1850 by industrialist Thomas Gaff, who left Philadelphia during a financial panic to make his fortune in the West. Gaff eventually had thirty-three businesses scattered through Aurora and the valley and even overseas, ranging from banks and breweries to mills, cotton plantations, and compressed yeast factories. He eventually moved his headquarters to Cincinnati and became one of the nation's first commuters, taking the train a half-hour each way daily. Hillforest is a National Historic Landmark, owned and operated by the Hillforest Historical Foundation. It is open to the public April through December.

Even higher on the hillside, the landmark 1810 **Veraestau** displays nearly two hundred years of Greek Revival enthusiasm. The house has been owned since its original construction by two families who maintained the original style through two major renovations. It is currently operated by Historic Landmarks Foundation of Indiana and is available for tours and events by appointment only. Call 812-926-0983 for more information. Take Market Street at the west edge of town .7 miles to Glenmary Lane.

Take Route 56W out of Aurora.

8.5   **Riverview Cemetery.** Laughery Creek is at the southern end of the cemetery, where Mohawk leader Joseph Brant and one hundred warriors attacked and soundly defeated Colonel Archibald Lockry and 107 Pennsylvania volunteers in August 1781. The troops were en route to join George Rogers Clark. Lockry and approximately half of his troops were killed with the suvivors taken prisoner. There is a memorial to the **Lockry Massacre** in the cemetery and another at the south end of the new Laughery Creek Bridge. (The creek name was misspelled when it was recorded and was never corrected.)

According to a survivor of the massacre, the warriors attacked from a wooded overhanging bluff while the troops were engaged in cooking a bison they had shot. Other warriors attacked from canoes in the river. The troops fought back until their meager supply of ammunition was exhausted. When they attempted to reach their boats at the mouth of the creek, low water and their weakened conditions prevented their escape.

Following their surrender, the warriors killed Lockry and several of his men, but the slaughter was stopped by Chief Brandt. Later he apologized for the massacre, saying it was difficult to control his warriors who wanted to avenge the murder of Indian prisoners on the Muskingum a few months before.

The skirmish played out aspects of the Revolutionary War in the Ohio

Valley. The British-allied warriors came from several tribes, including the northern Six Nations who laid claim to the Ohio Valley. George Rogers Clark and his Virginia troops were pioneering in the Kentucky Bluegrass. Lockry came from Pennsylvania, which vied with Virginia for control of the lands drained by the Ohio. The prisoners were taken to tribal villages in Ohio and later transported to British forts at Detroit and Montreal, where the British commanded their few Redcoats and many tribal allies against the Americans. And, of course, the massacre was another aspect of the vortex of violence on the frontier.

It was months before families in Pennsylvania learned of the disaster. General George Washington received a letter in late 1781 that read, "These misfortunes throw the people of this country [Pennsylvania] into the greatest consternation and almost despair, particularly Westmoreland County, Lockry's men being all the best men of their frontier." Laughery Creek is the border of Ohio and Dearborn counties. The old **Laughery Creek Bridge** is the only structure in Ohio County on the National Register of Historic Places. Built in 1878, it is an extremely rare iron triple-intersection Pratt through-truss span; the "Triple Whipple Bridge" as it is known in the county. **Ohio County** is the smallest county in the nation in both population and size: 5,315 souls in the 1990 census living in eighty-seven square miles.

Half a mile further down Route 56 is the turnoff to the hamlet of **Hartford**, formerly a bustling stagecoach stop.

15.0   **Rising Sun.** "If this isn't Mayberry," resident Linda Voelker said, "then I don't know what is." Platted in 1814, Rising Sun boomed in the 1830s and the 1940s with as many as twenty-five hundred people thriving in the town. Each spring three hundred to four hundred flatboats left Rising Sun daily, headed downriver. There were eight factories, two steam-powered mills, three potteries, a newspaper, a clutch of churches, and a seminary for teachers. There were also six taverns, including Red Hell and Blue Ruin. A tavern may even have contributed to the town name. Accounts range from the town founder's being struck by the beauty of the sunrise across the river in Rabbit Hash, Kentucky, to Rising Sun's being the name of a steamboat that called on the town, to its merely being the name of the first tavern.

Today the population is about the same: 2,311 in 1990. And it does indeed have a Mayberry air. Kids toss the football in the middle of Main Street; strollers hail friends sitting on their porches. There is still a plethora of churches in town, one for almost any denomination, either in town or out in the county. And there are still a lot of places to get a drink, from the Riverview Liquors housed in a double-wide trailer on Main Street to the sprawling **Grand Victoria Casino & Resort by Hyatt** that sits a few blocks to the east of downtown, connected by a newly constructed Riverwalk. The casino has a riverboat, a two-hundred-room hotel, and a thousand-seat showroom for acts like Tom Jones and Wayne Newton. Unlike the *Argosy* casino boat, the *Grand Victoria* boat actually cruises down the river for about a mile and a half before turning. Rising Sun is on a particularly wide part of the river which allows the turning radius. The casino boat itself has the air of a vintage gambling palace, albeit a highly turned-on and plugged-in one. The interior is decorated with elaborate turned and gilded corbels, and there is easy access to the outside decks and windows.

The Grand Victoria casino opened in October 1996 and sparked a flurry of development in the sleepy town, both with the revenues the boat returns to the counties and towns, and private funds. Downtown Rising Sun has gone through a renovation. The streets are repaved, and some have curbs for the first time. There are a number of interesting accommodations in the tiny town: the 1816 Empire Hotel and nine B&Bs in restored vintage homes at last count, including a group that are at the riverfront in restored 1820s Federal row houses.

An hour-long saunter will introduce the traveler to the charms of this leafy little town. There is also a tourist trolley that transports visitors around the town. The **Ohio County Historical Society Museum**, located in the old Clore Plow factory at 212 S. Walnut, is a good starting point. It is the Grandma's attic of Rising Sun—a collection of quilts and farm implements, diverse and sundry music machines, and the town pride: the famous 1920s "Hoosier Boy" speedboat. Be sure the tour guides tell you about Smith Riggs, a local blacksmith who invented the first modern electric chair. Riggs decided to improve the comfort of the chair for the intended users, reclining the seat and replacing the metal arm and leg clamps with leather ones. There is no documentaion on customer satisfaction. Riggs kept a version of his improved chair in his Rising Sun hardware store for many years. The last versions of the chair were in Michigan City, Indiana, and Elgin, Illinois, prisons.

A 1960s turquoise Ford Falcon sat outside the **Ohio County Courthouse** the day I visited. When the Greek Revival structure on Main Street was built in 1845, the forty-by-sixty-foot brick building had no central hall, which meant the second-story courtroom and all of the other offices were reached from the outside until a 1980s addition. Large round pillars support a classic pediment, and open stairs rise to the second floor. At 316 Fourth Street, the 1840s Federal/Greek Revival-style house is the site of the **Presbyterian Seminary**, which originated in 1827 as the Rising Sun Seminary. Grant Wood would have loved the Gothic Revival house at 510 Main Street, built in 1860. Front Street has a remarkable lineup of Federal and Greek Revival buildings, including row houses, the restored 1816 **Empire House** hotel, and

Indiana's first **Masonic Temple**.

Take Route 156S out of Rising Sun. The road runs through the flood-plain along the Ohio with cabin cruisers and coal barges coursing down the pale pewter river. Sand and gravel quarries dot the road side.

19.0   **Switzerland County Line.** Switzerland County was separated from Dearborn and Jefferson counties in 1814, at the behest of Swiss-French settlers who migrated to Indiana to pioneer wine production in America. Viticulture in Indiana is as old as European settlement—the French in Vincennes were growing grapes to make their beloved *vin* by the mid-1700s. However, production was small-scale. In 1802 French-Swiss entrepreneur John James Dufour petitioned Congress for *"une petite exception."* He requested the government grant him land on the Ohio at Vevay in what is now Switzerland County to grow grapes and publicly disseminate wine knowledge.

Dufour's ten thousand vines caused such a stir that Napoleon sent an emissary to check it out, fearing the impact on the French wine industry. Henry Clay was an aficionado of Vevay wine and ordered a dozen bottles sent to him in Kentucky. When he served his prized wine to his distinguished guests, they discovered the bottles were filled with whiskey. He soon found that his son, James, also appreciated Vevay's product and had substituted bourbon after he drank the wine.

The Vevay vineyard prospered, becoming the first commercially successful vineyard in the country. In 1826 Dufour published *The American Vine-dresser's Guide,* the first viticulture book specific to American soil and climate. Thomas Jefferson, smitten with French wines from his ambassadorship to Paris, proclaimed Dufour "one of the wisest, most far-seeing, most unselfish men he had ever known." By 1828, however, the Austrian traveler Karl Postel found the Swiss vines degenerated and the wine an "indifferent beverage. . . . The town is in a decline; it has a courthouse, and two stores very ill supplied. The condition of these, and the absence of lawyers, are sure indications of the poverty of the inhabitants."

By the mid-nineteenth century, over thirty thousand acres of grapes were in production along Indiana's Ohio River shore, from the eastern border over to the Falls of the Ohio at Louisville, which became known as "The Rhineland of America." By 1880 Indiana was a top-ten grape producer in the nation, but black rot, phylloxera, and the inevitable death knell called Prohibition devastated Indiana production. The industry was moribund till passage of the Indiana Small Winery Act in 1971, which permitted wineries to sell directly to the public. A small, passionate movement has grown since then. Currently there are nineteen wineries scattered through the state, visited by over 425,000 people in 1996.

Not surprisingly, the Ohio River region is still the main wine-producing part of the state, with well drained sandy soils, good aspects to catch the southern sun, and mild climate. Fully a third of the state's wineries are clustered along the Ohio from Cincinnati to Louisville. Beyond the unmistakable lure of the micro-climate and soil for the grapes—what the French call *terroir*—the wineries have situated themselves in the most beautiful and historic part of the state, where visitors can mingle relaxing ambiance with their wine tastings.

"There's been a revolution in our industry over the last ten years," Madison wine maker Steve Thomas said, "about how we grow grapes, about how we make wine." The Indiana wine makers today are vinting consistent, well made wines. Lighter whites and reds are still the mainstay, but Indiana wineries are now capable of growing and making reds of increasing complexity and finesse.

Historically, wine never supplanted the American taste for whiskey. As the decades went by, the fertile soil of Switzerland County began to yield more potatoes than grapes. The price per hundredweight was about the same, and potatoes were a lot easier to grow. Timothy, hay, and tobacco became the main crops by the late nineteenth century. River traffic declined through the nineteenth century, and the railroads and major highways passed Switzerland and Ohio counties by. The same lack of modern transport prevented the growth of large industries and preserved the historically agrarian feel of the region. When an architectural survey of Vevay was taken in 1980, it was discovered that eighty-six percent of the structures in the town were over fifty years old, and nearly two-thirds were built before 1883.

The county sits at an elbow of the Ohio, a land of steep and rolling hills, one of the loveliest places in Indiana. In 1900 there were 11,840 people in the county. By 1990 the population had dwindled to only 7,738. People migrated to more economically vibrant areas as the soil showed signs of depletion and the river markets dried up. As late as the 1940s, the role of the river in transportation was still apparent along this stretch of the valley. One 1940s guidebook noted, "White-painted arms of river signals and lanterns stand beside the highway on the banks of the curving Ohio. At filling stations and on village porches are old men who can recall the long-gone steamboat days when the valley was black with the smoke of proud sternwheelers."

20.2   On the right side of the highway, the Federal-style brick **Merit-Tandy-Tillotson House** sports a balustraded widow's walk on its roof, a somewhat incongruous folly for a one-story cottage. It sits in a stretch of countryside known as Mexico Bottoms, which commemorates the Mexican-American War veterans who returned to clear the bottoms of the giant trees.

23.0   **Patriot** has a woebegone look, with trailers and derelict buildings along the road, as befits a town that has suffered numerous catastrophes. A sad-faced young girl with red hair stood watching the cars pass when I drove through. There are still a number of structures scattered through the village, however, that recall Patriot's palmy days. At one point Patriot had several mills and distilleries and substantial river traffic. The T. W. Pate Distillery alone produced seven hundred thousand gallons of whiskey at the turn of the century. There are several Queen Anne buildings from that period in town. There are also a couple of vernacular buildings worth noting: the tiny whitewashed old stone jail at 106 First Street, and the nineteenth-century tavern on Fifth and Front streets. A fire in 1924 destroyed most of the commercial district. The disastrous 1937 flood swept away the wharf, bank, boats, mills, and distilleries, and the town never recovered.

Floods have plagued the riverside communities from their founding. Up and down the river, one can see lines painted on levees and old buildings, showing the high water marks of various years. Lawrenceburg is illustrative. Zadok Cramer's 1814 edition of *The Navigator,* the Ohio River guide that every captain and keelboat pilot used to navigate the river, stated about Lawrenceburg, "It is at very high floods more or less subject to inundation, which may injure the progress of the town." In 1832 Lawrenceburg had flood waters six feet above High Street, sixty-five feet high. The town also flooded in 1847, precipitating the construction of levees along the river. In 1882 the levee broke and the town flooded, as it did in 1883 and 1884, when the seventy-one-foot waters came over the levee. During the catastrophic five-hundred-year flood of 1937, the water rose over eighty-two feet. On January 31, 1937, the river reached the highest mark ever recorded. Entire valley towns and cities were inundated, with hundreds of people drowned. Coast Guard cutters cruised the avenues of flooded towns. Refugees from along the river were evacuated to northern Indiana, where they were cared for in hospitals, public buildings, and private homes. The 1997 Ohio River floods caused thirteen Indiana counties to be named federal disaster areas.

At the junction of Route 156 and 250, there is a marker to Patriot native **Dr. Elwood Mead,** "the engineer who made the desert bloom." He built the Hoover Dam and his namesake, Lake Mead.

Traveling south on Route 156, the lowland is called **Egypt Bottoms** because the fertility of the soil yielded corn crops of biblical proportions. It is an area of upright I-houses (named because they are most often found in states that start with I—Indiana, Illinois, and Iowa), hand-hewn rock walls, and clapboard Country Gothic churches.

34.0   **Florence,** founded in 1817, was at one time the home of the Anti-Swearing Society, which fined its seventy-five members for profanities. The legacy of the society in the current hamlet is unknown. Given the numbers of marinas in the area accompanied by the requisite number of fishermen, it is unlikely the tradition lives on. A touch to the south of Florence, the brick, green-shuttered Armstrong House was built in 1880. The Scenic Byway is through a Burma Shave and Mailbox Tobacco-signed bit of Americana.

38.5   The **Markland Locks and Dam and Generating Station**, constructed in 1956 and 1963 near the village of Markland, are a few miles south. The dam is 1,416 feet long, with two parallel locks on the Kentucky side of the river that are 110 feet wide. One is six hundred feet long, and the other is twice that length. At times, traffic jams of elephantine proportions back up as enormous strings of barges await their turn through the locks. The dam created a flood pool that extends ninety-five miles upstream. The Markland Generating Plant is the largest in Indiana. Across the bridge in Kentucky, an observation tower overlooks the locks. An information center presents a history of the Army Corps of Engineers projects that dammed the Ohio. Markland is six hundred river miles below Pittsburgh, and is at 455 feet above sea level. By the time the river reaches Louisville it is at 420 feet, and is down to 358 feet at the Newburgh dam. In 1930 the river carried twenty million tons of freight. By the mid-1980s 160 million tons of material moved down the Ohio, more than through either the Panama or Suez canals.

40.0   **Vevay** (That's pronounced *vee' vee*, by the way. The name may look French, but this is Indiana, after all.) It's another river town that deserves a stroll. It is as tidy as a Swiss-French village, filled with lots of ornate, well-kept nineteenth-century buildings. The **Knox House**, at 302 W. Main, adds to the French flavor, with its New Orleans-style iron grillwork, as does the **Grisard-Sieglitz home** at 306 E. Main. In 1868 the *United States* and the *America*, two of the most luxurious boats afloat, collided nearby with a loss of more than seventy lives. The Knox family sheltered renowned violinist Ole Bull who was a passenger of one of the boats.

But Vevay is as Hoosier as can be. There is a lineup of big American pickups in front of the defunct Phoenix Hotel, poignant with papered-over windows. When I stopped at the Lawson Family Diner for breakfast, a bunch of guys with John Deere "gimme" (as in "gimme one") hats sat at the counter discussing politics while country music twanged on the radio. Breakfast set me back $1.50 for eggs, biscuits, and a big slice of country ham. The lunch specials were already on the board: country-fried steak, pork chops, and ham steak.

At 209 W. Market Street, the **Ulysses P. Schenk House** was built with the best elevations facing the river, the important arterial of the day. Schenck was called the "Hay King" from his success in dealing timothy hay from the Switzerland County fields down river on flatboats. It is, as the 1941 WPA guide to Indiana calls it, "a free translation of the Georgian style." Many of the prominent homes in Vevay were built by George A. Kyle, who marked his work with an engraved silver plate on the newel post. The **Dufour Cottage** to the east is one of several houses in Vevay built by Jean François Dufour. The unusual, fish-scale-shingled **Vevay Christian Church** on Market was built as a Unitarian Church in 1863. The 1817 **Morerod Homestead** on Arch Street still has a five-hundred-gallon wine cask in the cellar to vint the grapes from builder Jean Daniel Morerod's extensive vineyards. The clapboard **Armstrong Tavern** at 201 W. Market was built in 1816. Slaves were ferried over daily from Kentucky to work in the tavern in the early days. The **Edward Eggleston and George Cary House** at 306 W. Main is on the National Historic Registry, as is the Old Indiana Theater at the corner of Ferry and Cheapside. The Eggleston house was the boyhood home of noted turn-of-the-century novelist Edward Eggleston, most famous for his unflattering depiction of backwoods Hoosiers in *The Hoosier Schoolmaster*. His novel *Roxy* is most associated with Vevay.

But Vevay's most unique entry in the Historic American Buildings Survey is the **Switzerland County Courthouse Privy**. It is an hexagonal brick outhouse, built in 1864 with a louvered cupola. The courthouse is very nice, too, a Greek Revival structure. The basement has a deep cellar that served as a waystop on the Underground Railroad.

The magnificent **Benjamin Schenck House** sits on a hill overlooking the town. It was built in the 1870s by the son of the "Hay King," but he died before the thirty-five rooms were completed. It boasts the finest furnishings of the day, including walnut tin-and-copper-lined bathtubs. Down at the end of Market Street, The **Rosemont Inn** B&B is another restored merchant prince home, lavishly furnished with period antiques. At the west end of town, the contemporary Ogle Haus Hotel is a good place to sit on the terrace and watch the river traffic. The tall stacks of the Markland Generating Plant and the endless lines of passing river barges are a reminder that the Ohio is sometimes known as "America's Ruhr." It is the most heavily trafficked river in the world.

The **Switzerland County Historical Museum** is in a hundred-year-old Presbyterian Church at Main and Market. Its collection includes a Muzio Clemente piano, reportedly the first piano in Indiana. The piano belonged to Mary Wright, daughter of an aristocratic but impecunious English family who settled a land grant in 1817. Her noble-born English beau deserted her when she moved to the frontier, and Wright lived the rest of her days in a fragile and disoriented state. Local legend has it that Wright gave weekly piano concerts for her rough pioneer neighbors. Each performance, she descended the ladder from her father's cabin loft dressed in court dress and jewels, and proceeded to play her entire repertoire. She then retired back to the loft without exchanging a word with her guests, who silently departed. For forty years, Mary Wright assuaged the loss of her betrothed with her weekly performances. The dress grew tattered and the jewels tarnished. The piano became increasingly discordant and her repertoire increasingly dated as she never added a new composition. But determined Mary Wright played on, without a word.

56.5   Lamb is the home of Indiana's oldest existing brick house. The **George Ash House** was built at the turn of the eighteenth century. Ash grew up among the Indians and had a reputation as a river pirate. For over a hundred years, he and his descendants ran the ferry to Carrollton, Kentucky. Turn left at the town sign and proceed a quarter mile to the dead end, then turn left .3 miles along the river. The upright little house is on the north side of the road.

65.0   Cedar Cliffs parallel the highway. They afford a twelve-mile view down the river for those hardy enough to make the climb. On the other side of the road, marinas, RV trailer parking lots, and ship yards with rusting tugs resting on their sides like abandoned children's toys line the river bank.

69.3   Bachman House at Eagle Hollow, home of Chapman Harris. Look for an old, rusting red crane on the north side of the highway. The roofless, two-story fieldstone house on the hill above is the Bachman House. The Underground Railroad came through here, as it did many places along the river, sheltering the refugees following the North Star. "Wade in the Water, Children," the old Southern spiritual went, and the fugitive slaves followed the coded instructions to the shore of the Ohio.

People—black and white alike—told me of Chapman Harris, an ex-slave who was a minister and blacksmith. During the day, he'd preach of the evils of slavery and the joys of heaven for the righteous. Come nightfall, Chapman Harris would go to his anvil on the river shore. As his hammer rang across the wide black waters, the fugitives on the far bank knew it was safe to cross to the other side, and the skiffs set out on the voyage to the promised land of Canada.

At Eagle Hollow, where the Reverend Harris rang his anvil, the night sky still flares with the guiding ember of the North Star, and the Ohio's waters still lap endlessly on the shore. But the hollow is overgrown, and scraggly trees surround Chapman Harris' small, windowless house.

69.8   Madison. Some call Madison "Queen of the Ohio," others say she is "The Williamsburg of the West," but not Madison preservationist Kim Franklin. "This isn't Williamsburg; it's not a museum," she said, "It's not perfect. It's a small town." There are enough pediments and columns and elaborate cornices in Madison to start a toga fad, with Italianate, Gothic Revival, and Queen Anne buildings to lighten things up. But most of the nineteenth-century buildings in the 133 blocks of the National Historic District are in everyday use. Federal row houses with decidedly unchic porch accouterments sit next to grand B&Bs decorated to Martha Stewart standards. The laundromat is on Main Street among the lovingly preserved structures, as is the preservationist tinsmith. Old farmers in coveralls tuckpoint their nineteenth-century houses. It is preservation woven into a living community.

During World War II, Madison was such an archetypal American town that the Office of War Information filmed a movie here titled, "This is What We're Fighting For." It was translated into thirty-two languages and shown around the world. The downtown district, bounded by the river, the Madison Country Club, Lonesome Hollow, and the Madison State Hospital, was listed as a National Historic District in 1973. Four years later, Madison was one of the three pilot cities for the Main Street Program that is now part of two thousand communities' urban planning. Over the last five decades, a remarkable spate of work has preserved Madison as America's premier collection of Federal-style architecture. "Put a fence around the entire town," one curator counseled when he surveyed it in 1950, "and don't let anyone touch anything in it."

Luckily, the town didn't take his advice, embarking on a grassroots preservation campaign that integrated preservation into the town fabric. "We've got the best of both worlds here," John Galvin, president of Historic Madison, Inc., said. "We've got an old town along the river. Up on the hill, there's industry and subdivisions and fast food. We need all of it to prosper." The historic district in Madison benefited by being clearly defined by the massive bluffs behind the town. The modern development happened up on the hill. Increasingly, the old town is drawing young retirees, artists, and people seeking a new start in a small, nurturing town. Even the suburbanites who fled the old town in the fifties and sixties are returning.

While much of vintage Madison is in private hands, there are several outstanding historical buildings open for tours, including the 1844 James F. D. Lanier mansion, considered the finest house on the Ohio. Even the bars and cafes are historic in Madison: the **Historic Broadway Hotel and Tavern** at 313 Broadway is Indiana's oldest family tavern, serving customers since 1859. The beautifully restored **JWI Confectionery** at 207 W. Main serves candy and ice cream made with the same equipment that was used when Valentino and then Elvis were the big stars. The town is rich with B&Bs in lovely old homes. "Madison is a nice small town, the kind of place where people sit on their front porches and talk to strangers. We tell our guests, *Just go walk around,*" innkeeper Mark Balph said.

The town was founded in 1810 in a bend where the Ohio curls the farthest to the north. Zadok Cramer, in the 1814 *The Navigator,* saw that Madison and its setting "altogether form a scene highly pleasant to the imagination, and one that is mixed with something of the romantic." When Indiana became a state in 1816, Madison was already the largest town. The Treaty of St. Mary's in 1818 opened lands north of Madison to settlers, who used Madison as their provisioning center as they made their way to their new homes. They followed the Michigan Road, Route 421 today, the first highway north to the Great Lakes at Michigan City. An ambitious state project, the road was started in 1828.

By 1839 the pioneering **Madison-Indianapolis Railroad**, the first railroad in Indiana, conquered the high bluffs and reached the town of Vernon. The 311-foot climb over 1.3 miles was the steepest standard gauge track in the world. Initially, horses and teams of oxen pulled the rail cars up one-by-one. They were replaced by locomotives that used a cog-wheel to climb the bluff, followed by the million-pound "Reuben Wells" that hauled the trains up the hill until 1905. The incline can be seen at the corner of Main and McIntire. The locomotive can still be seen at The Children's Museum in Indianapolis. The matrix of river, rail, and road funneled the region's raw goods into Madison for manufacture and processing and trans-shipment out into the larger markets.

In a brief period the town became a bustling industrial city, with brick smokestacks belching and dozens of products being produced: wagon, tack and spoke factories, shipyards, six wharves, castor and linseed oil factories, distilleries and breweries. The **Schroeder Saddletree Factory** was one of a dozen saddletree factories in town, operating from 1878 to 1972. Saddletrees are the wooden internal structure of leather covered saddles, generally crafted from gum, beech, or oak. Today, the factory is being restored as a museum of industrial architecture and archeology, offering a unique view into the republic's growing commercial might in the mid-nineteenth century. The Schroeder factory exported internationally, from Brazil and Hispanic America to Europe, as well as across America.

Madison was a major pork-packing center, rivaling Cincinnati. One plant, the Jenny Lind Pork Packing Plant, memorialized the Swedish Nightingale's Madison performance in 1851, held in a whitewashed slaughter house with an improvised stage, where the opera singer's trills replaced the pigs' squeals for an evening. The event was impresarioed by none other than P. T. Barnum. According to local accounts, the audience found her off-key and distressingly chubby.

In 1850 Madison led the state in manufacturing capital and total number of products shipped. Fortunes were made. Banks, mansions, stores, and stately churches rose where only wilderness existed a few decades before. The commercial possibilities of the West drew gentry from the Eastern Seaboard, including an inordinate number from refined cities like Newport and Baltimore. They brought with them not only their business acumen but also their tastes for fine things and the latest styles of architecture. The result is Madison today, a national treasury of Federal and Classical Revival architecture. The entire town is considered the premier destination for fans of nineteenth century architecture in the Midwest. Indeed, there are few places in the country that present such a complete and intact portrait of an early and prosperous industrial community.

The brick commercial architecture of the downtown area was constructed during Madison's heyday, from 1830 to 1850. After that, new railroads linking Louisville, Indianapolis, and Cincinnati de-emphasized river traffic, sending Madison into a slump. A burst of economic activity in the 1870s "modernized" Main Street with cast-iron fronts that added Italianate touches like elaborate cornice brackets.

Madison is worth a full day's stop to soak up the ambiance. The first destination should be the **Madison Area Convention and Visitors Bureau**, 301 E. Main Street, for materials. In the west part of town, the 1818 **Jeremiah Sullivan House** at 304 W. Second Street is considered one of the finest examples of Federal architecture in the old Northwest Territory. It is open to the public, as is the **Schofield House** at 217 W. Second Street. The 1820 **Talbott-Hyatt House** has extensive restored gardens and outbuildings.

At Poplar and First streets, the **Shrewsbury House** radiates the austere grace of classical antiquity, designed by Madison's resident architectural genius, Francis Costigan. Costigan, a native of Baltimore, was influenced by the work and writings of Benjamin Latrobe, the architect who brought Classical styles to America. Latrobe is best known for the design of the United States Capitol building in Washington, D. C. Magnificently proportioned, the Shrewsbury House has a spectacular spiral staircase that rises through the house's three stories, unsupported except by its own thrust. The period furnishings are evidence of the evolved taste of the owners, John and Anne Windle, the guiding lights of Madison's preservation movement from the 1940s. John Windle, now deceased, was the author of the landmark study of Madison architecture, "The Early Architecture of Madison, Indiana." Anne Windle remains the doyenne of Madison and the hostess of Shrewsbury, her home and museum.

At 511 W. First Street, the grand 1844 **James F. D. Lanier Home**, also designed and built by Francis Costigan, overlooks the broad Ohio. It was considered the finest house on the Ohio in its day. Neo-Corinthian columns soar thirty feet to the fifty-foot-long portico. The interior reflects the lifestyle of one of America's wealthiest men, a luxurious haven of the finest of the day's decorative arts. Lanier was a banker, merchant, and speculator who eventually moved his security business to New York. During the Civil War, Lanier loaned a million unsecured dollars to Indiana, preventing a second state bankruptcy. The house was given to the state of Indiana in 1925 and opened to the public a year later as Indiana's first historic site. It recently went through an extensive, historically correct restoration, returning the home to its mid-nineteenth century splendor. The extensive gardens and grounds are also going through a period restoration. In the summer, a public archeology project allows volunteers to help with the archeological work to recreate the site.

The charming **John Eckert Cottage** at 510 W. Second Street, behind the Lanier house, was built by a local tin-smith in 1872. It is sided with tin panels that are wrought to resemble cut sandstone, perhaps in flinty emulation of the cut stone of the Lanier Mansion, albeit on a lower budget. The octagonal building at 615 W. First Street was **Madison's railroad terminal**, and now houses a museum. The Costigan-designed **Holstein-Whisett House** at 718 Main Street is a Greek Revival structure built in 1840, reminiscent of the townhouses of Salem and Portsmouth. The renowned architectural historian Roger Kennedy declared the 1849 **Francis Costigan's Residence** at 408 E. Third Street "the finest small house in America." It is a jewel box of proportion and scale shoehorned into a twenty-two-foot-wide lot.

Main Street has a fine collection of mid- and late-nineteenth-century commercial buildings, many with Italianate facades. **Hinkles Hamburgers** wears the stainless steel armor of a 1930s diner. It's a great place to catch up on Indiana basketball and eat skinny White Castle-style hamburgers, fondly known as "sliders." They've sold over a hundred thousand on Madison Regatta weekend alone. The Greek Revival **Jefferson County Courthouse** was built in 1854-55. At the corner of Walnut and Main, the **Jefferson County Jail** was built in 1850 to incorporate the latest in penitentiary design. It was a cross between George Orwell's *1984* and something out of Dickens' England, a dark two-story pen designed so everyone could be watched by one jailer. It was used until a Federal order very late in the twentieth century prompted the county to build a new jail. Across the street, the **Fair Play Fire House** is Indiana's oldest volunteer fire department. The fire house was built in the 1880s. Note the weather vane of "Little Jimmy," a folk-figure who turns whimsically with the wind.

Mulberry Street has a remarkable collection of unaltered 1830s commercial buildings. North of Main Street, on St. Michael's Street, **St. Michael's Catholic Church** was designed and built by Costigan in 1839. The rectory is modeled on the Pope's garden house in Rome. Between Third and Fourth streets on Mulberry, the **Christ Episcopal Church**, built 1847-48, is an example of English Gothic style. The 1835 **Second Presbyterian Church** at Third and West is the headquarters of Historic Madison, Inc., the guiding light of preservation since 1960. A half-block west, the Federal-style **Dr. William Hutchings House** is a mid-nineteenth-century doctor's office, with the instruments and lifestyle of the day.

There are three wineries in Madison. "We're having a ball here," wine maker Steve Thomas said in his **Thomas Family Winery**, 200 E. Second Street. In 1995 Thomas moved his wine-making business from Indianapolis to Madison in search of a small-town lifestyle, and the town is richer for it. He purveys a variety of wines and a cider from an 1855 renovated brick carriage house.

A few blocks away and a few feet lower, the owners of the **Lanthier Winery** at 123 Mill Street are well aware that Madison is a river town. The intense flooding of March 1997 inundated the early fort that is their tasting room with eight feet of water. They were able to open in late September during the annual Chautauqua Days, because thirty-seven neighbors pitched in to save the wine and wine making equipment.

Up on the bluffs four hundred feet above the town at 1456 E. 400N, the **Madison Winery** vines are basking in the ambient air, far from the flood waters. Steve and Sandy Palmer are into wine for the long haul, putting together a package of vineyard, wine, and marketing that reflects the continuing maturation of the Indiana wine industry.

The Eleutherian College sits proudly on a ridge seven miles north of Madison. "Can you feel the spirit?" local historian Elbert Hinds asked. "There is a spirit here—a mystical Utopian feeling of education and shared purpose. Can you see it in the straightness of the structure?" The tall, three-story fieldstone structure was the first college in the U.S. where African-Americans and whites of both genders studied together. It was founded by New England Baptist abolitionists who settled the Lancaster area in the 1830s. By 1839 they founded the Neil's Creek Anti-Slavery Society in spite of the nearness of slave-catchers from Kentucky and Copperhead Southern sympathizers just over the ridge. The college was constructed fifteen years later. Local legend has it that two of Thomas Jefferson's grandchildren by Sallie Hemmings studied here. To reach the college, travel north on Route 7 for six miles. Turn west on Route 250 a mile to the village of Lancaster. The college building is on the south side of the road.

Three main lines of the Underground Railroad passed through the area. The Underground Railroad was an informal route that coursed up from the Deep South all the way to Canada, with hiding places every ten to fifteen miles. Slaves from the plantations of Alabama and Mississippi used Indiana and Ohio as part of their escape route. Quakers, Covenanter Presbyterians, and New England Baptists were most often associated with the Railroad. The Grand Central Station of the Underground Railroad was at Levi Coffin's House in Fountain City, and Lawrenceburg was a stop for that route. Jefferson County has several Underground Railroad stops, including the Banta house near the college on Route 7, where a cavern under the house could only be reached by diving in a pool and surfacing in the hiding spot. After the Fugitive Slave Act of 1850, work on the Underground Railroad was totally illegal and subject to the violence of the slave-catchers.

It is easy to focus on the heroism of the abolitionists without recalling the inherent racism of much of southern Indiana. It is part of the Butternut region that stretches through the upland South, so called from the color of the southern yeoman settlers' clothing that was dyed with walnut (butternut) oil. The white southerners migrated from the upland South, unable to compete economically with slavery. While over twenty percent of Kentucky's population was slave in the pre-Civil War era, there were only small numbers of African-Americans north of the Ohio, primarily because most of the white Hoosiers didn't want them there.

The racism was codified into the Indiana State Constitution of 1851 which prohibited migration of freed African-Americans into the state, imposed a fine on anyone who employed a black newcomer to the state, and also required the existing African-American populations to register with county officials, creating the infamous Indiana Negro Registers that were tallied from 1852 to 1865. "Difficult," local African-American historian Frank Inskeep said. "Life in Madison was very difficult for black people." The African-American community still celebrates the integration of the local lunch counter by three brave young women in the 1950s.

Leave Madison on Route 62W. At the west edge of Madison, **Clifty Falls State Park** has a rugged terrain of deeply cut canyons, waterfalls, and scenic walking trails. It was given to the state in 1920. The nearby **Clifty Creek Generating Plant** was opened in 1955, the largest steam-powered generating plant in the world. It was built by a consortium of fifteen power companies to provide electricity for the Portsmouth, Ohio, Gaseous Diffusion Plant that manufactured weapons grade enriched uranium. Ironically, in 1984 the construction of Jefferson County's controversial Marble Hill Nuclear Power Plant was stopped because of environmental and safety concerns.

77.0   **Hanover College** is the oldest private college in the state. The Presbyterian institution is noted for its Classical architecture on a bluff over the river. It includes the oldest continuously used college building in the state, the small 1832 gothic church.

The site of **Graysville**, a former African-American settlement, is located two miles north of Hanover, near the intersection of Interstate Block Road and Grange Hill Road. There are few remains from a village of 129 people in the 1830s. The cemetery looks strangely empty, with only a few gravestones. The other markers were wood and have long since joined the deceased in the earth.

Continue on Route 62W. The road climbs out of the river bottom up onto broad open fields, a tableaux of corn and tobacco fields and green forest. The lineups of logging trucks and tractors on the road speak of the area's commerce. Abandoned cars in front of tiny houses, old pickups with people riding in the back, and lounges and liquor stores with peeling paint speak of the area's prospects.

83.0   Turn south on Route 62.

90.9   Turn onto Marble Hill Road and proceed 4.5 miles through a rolling landscape of old farms and ponds and fields of volunteer cedars to the unearthly sight of the **Marble Hill Nuclear Power Facility** erupting from the ground like an alien presence. The facility was never opened after a decade of construction and equipment purchases totaling $2.1 billion. It was similar in design to the ill-fated Three Mile Island nuclear power plant. There were additional concerns about the safety of the construction. When the closing was announced in 1983, it devastated the local economy and tax base. Today, it is a very large, very high-tech salvage yard, as the owner PSI sells off millions of dollars worth of unused, like-new, nuclear power equipment. Need a reactor, cheap?

93.4   The general store at **New Washington** inexplicably has "Leghorn," the giant cartoon rooster, painted on the side of the building. "I say, I say, the Corner Grocery is open," the sign reads. Turn south for eight miles to the village of **Bethlehem.** "It's a spiritual journey out to here," Debbie Llaña, Executive Chef at the Inn at Bethlehem, said. "People rediscover themselves, their marriages, their companions." It is a trip along bluffs and creek beds, fields and farm—a winding passage back through time. The Inn is in a two story brick Federal House built in 1830 alongside the Ohio. Debbie's lodge, where she serves gourmet fare, is in a refurbished barn. Both she and her inn-manager husband, Lawrence, are refugees from the frantic Florida corporate world.

Visitor Information

Greater Cincinnati Convention and Visitors Bureau, 300 W. 6th St., Cincinnati, OH 45202-2361, 513-621-2142, 800-GO-CINCY.

Dearborn County Chamber of Commerce at 790 Rudolph Way, P.O. Box 344, Lawrenceburg, IN 47025, 812-537-0814.

Rising Sun/Ohio County Tourism and Visitors Bureau, 218 S. Walnut St., P.O. Box 112, Rising Sun, IN 47040-0112, 888-776-4786.

Switzerland County Convention and Visitors Bureau, P.O. Box 149, Vevay, IN 47043, 800-HELLO-VV.

Madison Area Convention and Visitors Bureau, 3101 East Main St., Madison, IN 47250-3536, 800-559-2956.

Recommended Reading

Greek Revival America, Roger G. Kennedy, Stewart, Tabori, and Chang, New York, 1989.

Indiana Houses of the Nineteenth Century, Wilbur D. Peat, Indiana Historical Society, Indianapolis, 1962.

The Early Architecture of Madison, Indiana, John T. Windle and Robert M. Taylor, Jr., Indiana Historical Society, Indianapolis, 1986.

Recommended Regional Dining

Mike Fink's, at the Roebling Suspension Bridge and Riverside Drive, Covington, KY 41011, 606-261-4212, offers riverboat dining with a view of the Cincinnati skyline.

Gold Star and Skyline Chili parlors are ubiquitous in Cincinnati, with the unique Middle-Eastern-spiced chili that is gastronomically synonymous with the River City.

Applewoods is on the river at 215 Judiciary St., Aurora, IN 47001, 812-926-1166, with steaks and ribs as a specialty. During the 1997 flood, the owner visited the inside of her restaurant by boat.

Bien's Coffee Haus, 110 4th St., Aurora, IN 47001, 812-926-0396, is a friendly spot for excellent coffees and lunch.

Gallimaufry's Riverwalk Cafe and Bakery, 135 Front St., Rising Sun, IN 47040, is located in an 1820 row house. While known for their pastries, they serve a full menu including steaks. Regionally produced micro-brews are available in the downstairs bar.

The Lawson Family Diner, Route 156, Vevay, IN 47043, is the place for down-home Hoosier cooking with a smile.

The Ogle Haus Inn, Route 56W, Vevay, IN 47043, 800-545-0360, offers a bit of German Switzerland on the Ohio, with dining rooms, bars, and terraces offering great river views.

JWI Confectionery, 207 W. Main St., Madison, IN 47250, offers old-fashioned sweets and new-fangled light lunches in Maryanne Imes' salubrious surroundings.

Turchino Pécora, 104 E. Main Street, Madison, IN 47250, 812-273-4888, serves artisanal Italian fare from their wood-fired oven.

The Upper Crust, 209 W. Main St., Madison, IN 47250, 812-265-6727, reflects Chef Nick Izamis' Mediterranean island heritage, spiced with an American touch.

Campgrounds

Lake in the Pines, 10412 N. Dearborn Rd., Sunman, IN 47041, 812-623-2136, is located about twenty minutes north of Lawrenceburg.

Clifty Falls State Park, 1501 Green Rd., Madison, IN 47250, 812-265-1351, has both Class A and C campsites available.

Recommended Bed and Breakfasts

The Amos Shinkle Townhouse, 215 Garrard St., Covington, KY 41011, 800-972-7012, built in 1854, was the home of the Roebling Suspension Bridge's owner. It is a Greco-Italianate two-story house with a frippery of iron work across the front.

The Rising Sun Courtyard Suites, 127 Front St., Rising Sun, IN 47040, 812-438-4035, has five redecorated suites in historic 1820s row houses.

Rosemont Inn, 806 W. Market St., Vevay, IN 47043, 812-427-3050, is an 1881 mansion that overlooks the river.

Schussler House, 514 Jefferson St., Madison, IN 47250, 800-392-1931, is a commodious 1849 Federal/Greek Revival home tastefully redecorated for the visitor's delight.

The Crescent House at 617 W. Main St., Madison, IN 47250, 812-265-4251, offers a guest suite with sumptuous furnishings and Egyptian cotton sheets for $110 a night, including an afternoon tea on MacKenzie-Childs china.

Inn at Bethlehem, Walnut and Riverview, Bethlelem, IN 47104, 812-293-3975, is a bucolic rural treat in a tiny village on the banks of the Ohio.

Madison's Shrewsbury House reflects the elegant grace of the town's golden decades.

Courtesy of Madison Area Convention and Visitors Bureau

Photo by Richard Fields

Foot-powered wine-making at the annual Vevay Wine Festival.

Courtesy of Clark/Floyd Counties Convention and Visitors Bureau

The Culbertson Mansion, part of New Albany's Mansion Row Historic District, is open to the public.

Fossil Beds and Steamboats

New Washington to New Albany 22 miles

Nearly four hundred million years ago, this drifting bit of earth we call Indiana was down by the equator, covered with a tropical sea. Millions upon millions of marine creatures thrived in the warm, fertile waters, forming immense coral reefs. As time moved on, so did the continent, drifting north to its current location. The glaciers came and the glaciers went, and twenty thousand years ago the last retreating ice sheet covered Indiana with a deep layer of sediment. It was through this blanket of glacial drift that a great river—the Ohio—scoured out its valley with the relentless erosion of its water, eventually exposing the fossilized reef. And the great coral reef, which was created so many hundreds of million of years ago, became a vast limestone barrier on the river: the Falls of the Ohio.

In the Ohio's 981 miles from the Allegheny Mountains to the Mississippi, the Falls of the Ohio were the only obstacle, with the river dropping twenty-four feet in two turbulent miles. The Ohio raced over the falls in a series of rapids and chutes and waterfalls for thousands of years until canalization and damming in the nineteenth and twentieth centuries subdued it. This immense natural barrier created a node of ecology, history, and commerce: a ganglion of culture for over twelve thousand years.

Mastodons and mammoths grazed at the falls. Millions of bison pounded out the broad Buffalo Trace across Indiana as they migrated from the Illinois prairies to the falls, crossing the river to the Kentucky salt licks. It created the territory's first natural highway, followed by both Native Americans and pioneers. For thousands of years, Native Americans lived at the cascades, gathering food and hunting the large game and buffalo herds that came later. According to some sources, twelfth-century Welshmen—"white Indians"—made the falls vicinity their home.

George Rogers Clark and his Kentucky adventurers camped at the head of the falls on Corn Island, beginning their epic Revolutionary War conquest of the Northwest Territory by shooting the rapids during a portentous eclipse. In 1803 Clark's younger brother William and his compatriot Meriweather Lewis started off on their journey to the Far West from the falls. Four years later, Aaron Burr used neighboring Jeffersonville to plot his conspiracy to form a new republic in the West, launching the campaign from the riverfront. The naturalist-artist John James Audubon haunted the shores of the falls, searching for new specimens and sketching the birds that became part of his folios. "The rumbling sound of the waters as they tumble over the rock paved rapids," he wrote, "is at all times soothing to the ear."

When European settlement of the valley began, the falls disrupted shipping, forcing boats to pull to shore to obtain the services of a pilot. Depending on water levels, freight had to be portaged around it. "From the great danger in passing the rapids," Zadok Cramer's *The Navigator* advised in 1814, "the courts of Louisville and Jeffersonville have been very careful to appoint experienced and trusty men as pilots, who can be had at a moment's warning to conduct boats and vessels over them; and from a little ambition shown by the pilots of both places to excel in their occupation, accidents, arising from the want of either skill or care, seldom happen."

The resulting commerce created the metropolitan complex of Louisville, Kentucky, and the Indiana cities across the river—Clarksville, Jeffersonville, and New Albany—collectively known as the Falls Cities. The Falls of the Ohio neatly divided the river into the Upper and Lower Ohio. East to Pittsburgh was the Upper; from the falls west to Cairo, Illinois, at the junction with the Mississippi, the Lower.

Until a canal was built on the Louisville side in 1830, boats pulled to the Indiana side at Silver Creek, or Beargrass Creek on the Kentucky side, to secure a pilot. Cramer recommended the passage along the Indiana side—the "Indian Shute"—as the safest, except in the highest of waters, when the boats could rip over the shelf at thirteen miles an hour. It was a momentous passing that fired the imagination of boatman and poet alike. Walt Whitman wrote after shooting the rapids in 1848, "Notwithstanding proposals for blasting rock ledges out of the river, Ohio Falls unchanged roared on. Even after the opening of the Louisville and Portland Canal, some bold skippers shot the Rapids. Our captain with Western hardihood determined to go over the 'boiling place.' The bottom of the boat grated harshly more than once on the stones beneath, and the pilots showed plainly that they did not feel altogether as calm as a summer morning."

A few years later a youthful Mark Twain passed downriver on an ancient tub named the *Paul Jones*. "We reached Louisville in time—at least the neighborhood of it," he wrote. "We stuck hard and fast on the rocks in the middle of the river, and lay there four days."

The fossil beds of the falls were a source of wonder and mystery in the republic's early days. Thomas Jefferson collected specimens sent to him from the beds, speculating on their origins. Over six hundred different species of fish, coral, and other sea creatures have been identified from this fossil bed, four hundred of them "type specimens," seen for the first time, forming one of the bulwarks of the republic's early geological study. On a Clarksville, Indiana, bluff overlooking the river and just off the busy interstate, the Falls of the Ohio Interpretive Center's stratified brick and limestone exterior mirrors the layers of fossils below. One of Indiana's newest state parks, the center presents a multi-media glimpse of life at the falls as well as spectacular views of the Louisville skyline. Nature hikes allow visitors to walk on the largest exposed Devonian-era fossil bed in the world.

As commerce developed in the nineteenth century, the enormous need for portaging, provisioning, and hospitality made the Indiana Falls Cities a prosperous place. The number of flatboats passing through the falls doubled in the 1820s alone. Equally astonishing, the population of the new state increased six hundred percent between 1820 to 1850. New Albany was the biggest city in the state from the 1830s to 1850.

Boat-building increasingly dominated the economy of the area. Between 1834 and 1940, the Howard shipyards launched over a thousand vessels into the deep water off Jeffersonville, including the fastest ship on the river, the City of Louisville. Below the falls, New Albany shipyards produced over 350 steamships during the Golden Age of river travel, including posh gambling palaces like the *Robert E. Lee.*

The first steamboat came down the Ohio in 1811. However, it wasn't until 1820 that steamboats had enough power to travel against the current. Even after the Louisville and Portland Canal bypassed the falls in 1830, Jeffersonville and New Albany prospered as ship-building centers. The canal could handle only boats shorter than 182 feet. Many of the packet palaces were well over two hundred feet. The steamboat *Louisville,* for instance, was 235 feet long with a water-wheel thirty feet in diameter. In addition, the deep water below the falls seldom froze, allowing year-round construction and repair. The ships launched by the Indiana shipyards had a reputation for speed, durability and, importantly, shallow draft. The *Louisville* drew only three feet of water. The *Indiana,* built in 1900 by the Howard Shipyard, drew even less: thirty inches. "Those Howard boats can sail on the morning dew," the river saying went. (Today, the canal, expanded with the McAlpine Lock and Dam, handles more tonnage than the Panama or Suez canals. The lock is the biggest on the Ohio.)

The golden age of river travel is celebrated at Jeffersonville's Howard Steamboat Museum, housed in the Howard family's 1894 High-Victorian brick mansion. Models, tools, photographs, documents, and memorabilia of the Great Steamboat Era are exhibited in the museum's twenty-two rococo rooms, amidst the stained glass, chandeliers, and intricate woodwork of an industrialist's dream home.

Be forewarned, the Indiana Falls Cities are a labyrinth of neighborhoods and dead-ends and generally confusing routes, as befits an area with such a long, layered history. At this date, the Ohio River Scenic Route is not well marked with signs, though state signage is described as imminent. The official route description recommends this path through the Falls Cities: Proceed west on Route 62 to Allison Lane in Jeffersonville, then right on Market Street, left on Walnut Street, right on Riverside Drive, right on Sherwood, left on South Clark Boulevard, right on Harrison Avenue, left on Randolph Avenue, then west on Route 62, left onto Vincennes Street, and right onto Main Street in New Albany. Stay on Main Street, which turns into Corydon Pike. Corydon Pike dead-ends at Route 62. The Route 265 bypass around the Falls Cities can be used to jump from locale to locale.

Mileage

90.1　Charlestown erupted in the 1940s when a gargantuan DuPont smokeless powder plant was built on the outskirts. Population rose from 939 people to between fifteen thousand and forty thousand, housed in a ramshackle collection of trailers and cottages. The **Indiana Army Ammunition Plant**, built at a cost of $85 million, was reactivated during the Korean and Vietnam wars and then was refurbished in the 1980s for large artillery ammunition manufacture. In the post-Cold War era, the sprawling facility is being reborn as a business park.

Charlestown was the home of **Jonathan Jennings,** Indiana's first governor. His grave can be seen at the Charlestown City Cemetery. Jennings' grand niece, **Mary Garrett Hay**, was born in Charlestown in 1857. She was a nationally famous suffragist, temperance reformer, and influential Republican. Her birthplace is now the Grayson Funeral Home at 893 High Street. At 673 High Street, the 1816 **Benjamin Ferguson House** is on the National Register, as is the 1809 **Thomas Downing House** at 1045 Main Street. The **Watson House**, 1015 Water Street, was built in 1900 and is also on the Register.

At the southeast edge of Charleston, turn at the railroad underpass and proceed 1.5 miles; turn left and proceed 2.8 miles to **Rose Island**, formerly a pear-shaped ridge 280-feet high, bounded by the Ohio on one side and Fourteen Mile Creek on the other. The ridge had natural and man-made ramparts. This site is associated with the Mississipian Mound Builder culture and legends concerning **Madoc** and his band of twelfth-century Welshmen.

In 1167, it is said, Madoc was cast from Wales in a fraternal fight for power. He sailed westward with a band of companions, eventually traveling down the Ohio to this natural fortress. The 1582 book by Richard Haykuyt, *Divers Voyages Touching the Discovery of America,* mentioned the Welsh adventurers. Captain John Smith's papers include a reference to "white indians." George Rogers Clark reported that Chief Tobacco told him of a great battle between tribesmen and "a strange race." There is a local legend that brass armor bearing a Welsh coat-of-arms with a mermaid and a harp with a Latin inscription that read "Virtuous deeds merit their just reward" was found along the Ohio in 1799. Historians are increasingly taking the legend seriously. The Falls of the Ohio Interpretive Center has an exhibit on the Welshmen. Perhaps they later went west. The explorer George Catlin claimed that the Mandans on the Missouri spoke several words of Welsh in their dialect, and used coracles identical to those used in Wales.

In the early twentieth century, Rose Island was the site of an amusement park, Fern Grove. The park drew up to four thousand holiday-goers a day, who arrived by scheduled excursion boat, the *America*. The 1937 flood destroyed both the park and the bridge that led over Fourteen Mile Creek, covering them with ten feet of water.

The **Charlestown State Park** was founded in 1996, in an area formerly part of the Indiana Army Ammunition Plant. The 2,100-acre park stretches through the forested terrain along Fourteen Mile Creek, one of Indiana's geologically oldest streams. There are three hiking trails through the park.

The **Clark Maritime Center** is an eight-thousand-acre intermodal transportation hub that is the newest of Indiana's three ports, opening in 1985. It is a complex of a foreign trade zone, an industrial park, and the port.

102.0 **Jeffersonville** was designed by Thomas Jefferson in 1802 with an alternating checkerboard of green spaces and buildings to protect the town from yellow fever and other pestilences that plagued the early settlers. Yellow fever and malaria—known as "ague"—along with "bilious fevers" were thought to be caused by bad air, rising from swamps. Malaria was so common along the Ohio that it was thought to be a fact of life, like death and hard work. Jefferson hoped to reduce the endemic diseases with clean air from the green spaces. Naturally, local speculators devoured Jefferson's "trees and turf" in the public squares by 1817. The traveler Edmund Dana described the town in 1819. "Jeffersonville stands just above the falls, on the west bank of the Ohio. The noise and the sight of the waters tumbling over the precipices below, together with the town of Louisville on the opposite shore, present a scenery at once variegated, romantic, picturesque, and grand."

In 1806 **Aaron Burr**, vice-president from 1801 to 1805, fled west to Jeffersonville after he killed Alexander Hamilton in a duel. Plunging into the social life of the frontier city, he formed a company to try to dig a canal around the falls, but it failed as others did on the Indiana side. (In fact, the second canal company around the falls launched one of Indiana's earliest lotteries, which also failed.) While in Jeffersonville, he plotted his grand Western

Empire, basically a secession of the Western states combined with Spain's holdings, all under his command. Without tipping his hand about his ultimate goal to head his own country, Burr recruited a number of locals to his cause. At the time Spain's refusal to allow free trade on the Mississippi essentially bottled up the Western markets, a source of great frustration to the settlers, who felt abandoned by the indifferent Eastern Seaboard-dominated U.S. government.

Burr convinced his Indiana supporters that he intended to take Mexico for the United States government. Among those who cast off from the shore of Silver Creek on their journey of conquest was Major Davis Floyd, a member of the General Assembly. When the plot was discovered and the expedition foiled in Natchez, Floyd, claiming he knew nothing of Burr's ultimate plans, was fined only $20 and sentenced to three hours in jail. He was the only Burr co-conspirator tried and convicted. A few days later, he was elected clerk of the lower house of the territorial legislature. Floyd County was later named for Major Floyd.

Warder Park at Spring and Court streets has a marker commemorating **Lafayette's visit** in 1825, on a triumphal tour of the nation he had helped to establish. The local ladies erected a grand arbor of beech branches intertwined with roses and wildflowers and served him an elaborate dinner.

The nineteenth-century Old Jeffersonville Historic District was listed on the National Historic Register in 1983. The district is bounded by Court and Graham streets, the Ohio, and Route 65. Within the district, the quirky 1837 **Grisamore House** at 111-113 W. Chestnut and the 1832 **Henry French House** at 217 E. High are on the National Registry. The Grisamore house is a unique American marriage of Federal and Greek Revival styles, as interpreted by a German-born architect builder. The house is currently the southern regional office for the Historic Landmarks Foundation of Indiana.

A few years ago, **Schrimpff's Confectionery**, 347 Spring Street, was named as one of Indiana's seven "Hidden Treasures." Since 1891 four generations of Schrimpffs have sold candy under their old pressed-tin ceiling with patrons sitting in old wire-backed chairs enjoying ice cream from the soda fountain. Since its construction after the Civil War, the Renaissance Revival brick and tile building has survived three floods. The high water marks are painted on the front.

Low-lying Jeffersonville has always suffered the caprices of the river. In the twentieth century alone, the town has flooded in 1913, 1937, 1945, 1983, 1984, and 1997. The January 1937 flood devastated Jeffersonville, the hardest-hit city on the entire length of the river. The river crested ten feet higher than the previous record. The nineteen inches of rain in that month caused over $18 million in the Indiana Falls Cities. Over ninety percent of the town was inundated, with four of five inhabitants evacuated.

The business of government has always been a major part of Jeffersonville. It was the early county seat, and the home of Indiana's second land office. The 1874 **U.S. Quartermaster Depot** at 10th and Meigs was the major dispensary for the armed forces from the Civil War to the Korean, warehousing everything from mule saddles to army shirts. Seventy-one thousand different types of items were stored here. The grounds were designed by Frederick Law Olmstead, the landscape architect best known for New York's Central Park. Since the depot closed in 1957, it has become the census processing center for the country. During the 1990 census, two thousand people were hired to process eighty million returns.

In October 1811, the sleeping citizens of the Falls Cities were roused in terror from their beds by the horror of a whistling, steaming creature at the riverside. Some were convinced that some monster of the deep had inexplicably made its way inland. Rather, it was the *New Orleans,* built in Pittsburgh by Nicholas Roosevelt to steam down the rivers. In 1820 the *Washington* proved she could move upstream against the Ohio's wild, untamed current with her improved horizontal high-pressure engine. Not long after, in 1834, the Howard Family started building boats. Indiana boats were in the first recorded steamboat race: the New Albany-built *Baltic* racing the Howard-built *Diana* through dense fog and a rising river from New Orleans to Louisville in 1858. The *Baltic* won by two hours, taking five days, eight hours, and twenty-two minutes to make the fifteen-hundred-mile voyage.

The **Howard Shipyards** dominated Jeffersonville from 1848 till well into the twentieth century. On the fifty-two acre site along the deepest section of the Ohio, the Howard yards produced over a thousand boats. The output launched in some years exceeded by more than ten percent the total that sailed the Western rivers. Of the more than four thousand boats on the Western rivers—the Mississippi and her tributaries: the Ohio, the Missouri, the Red, the Outchita, the Yazoo and the Arkansas—more than one-third were Howard boats. In some periods in the 1870s, eighty percent of the gilded behemoths lined up at the New Orleans docks were Howard-built. They hauled thousands of passengers and millions of bales of cotton, hogsheads of tobacco and pork, barrels of whiskey, and the lumber of a thousand stands along the stream beds and drainages of the great West. Furniture and manufactured goods floated downstream from the burgeoning factories of Cincinnati. Even jazz moved up the rivers from New Orleans to the North on the decks of Howard boats.

Mark Twain trained to be a river pilot on a Howard boat. He was piloting another, the *Alonzo Child,* when the Civil War broke out. When Confederate General John Hunt Morgan invaded Indiana, he crossed on a Howard boat, the *Alice Dean.* The fastest steamboat on the river, the *City of Louisville,* was launched in 1894. It still holds the record. The powerful backwash from the boat caused problems up and down the rivers, swamping another packet in one instance.

In 1878 the *J. M. White* slid down the Howard ways, the most opulent steamboat ever built. The boat was 321 feet long and ninety-one feet wide. The paddlewheel was forty-four feet in diameter. "It was a lot of lumber to get around a bend," the pilot said. The boat's ten engines produced as much power as most of the ocean-going vessels of the day. The ten-story-tall smokestacks were topped with seven-foot-high acanthus leaves, with a five-tone whistle and a 2,880-pound roof bell announcing the grandeur of its arrival. She could carry eight thousand bales of cotton at $1.25 a bale, helping pay off her $250,000 investment in three years.

The *J. M. White* was a floating, five-star luxury hotel, boasting stained glass in both interior and exterior windows. Gingerbread and elaborate fretwork festooned the outside, and exotic woods, expertly crafted, decorated the interior. Doors leading to the staterooms were made of rare rosewood and walnut burl, while many of the rooms were furnished with matching French-designed bedroom suites. A musician played the tunes of the day on a Chickering grand piano in the lounge.

Guests mingled in the octagonal barroom and rococo main cabin under Egyptian-inspired, gold-plated chandeliers and a thicket of turned and carved wood corbels and brackets, painted in white and gold. Intricate parquet covered the floors. They dined from Haviland china decorated with a likeness of the boat, with Gorham silver engraved with the boat's silhouette and dabbed at their lips with Irish linen napkins monogrammed with JWM. At the end of the salon, a huge mirror with an ornately carved frame reflected the luxurious finery and social performance. African-American servants of the 225 guests lived in a set of cabins on the top deck, called the "Freeman's Bureau."

The *J. M. White* worked the Mississippi in the "Bends Trade," from New Orleans to Greenville. She ended her days as many of the steamboats did—she burned and sank. In December 1886, a blaze started in the cotton bales stored on the top Texas deck and spread to kegs of gunpowder in the forward hold. By morning, the grandest boat on the Western waters was nothing more than a derelict hull and blackened boilers.

The Howard boats were famous for their longevity, though it wasn't much to boast about by today's standards. The average steamboat on the rivers of the West lasted only five years. They were snagged or crushed in an ice gorge, washed to the shore with high winds or steered there by drunken pilots. They burned, afloat or at the wharf. The boilers, located on the main deck, blew up with horrific loss of life. When the *Lansing's* boilers exploded in 1864, the ship's clerk's body landed across the Mississippi on the Iowa shore, while the pilot's corpse flew across Hampton, Illinois, to land on the other side of town. Some boats, like the *Julian Podras,* just plain wore out, limping back home to the Howard docks for dismantlement. The average Howard boat lasted seven years, only two years more than the competitors' boats, but still provided two additional years of profit for the boats' owners.

The record of the river steamboats reads like a regimental listing of the fallen. "*City of Savannah,* sank at Dogtooth Bend, a total loss." "*The Morning Star* burned and was lost in the wharf at Cincinnati in 1922." "*The Henry Harley* lost to heavy winds and ice." "*The Gem,* sank twice and raised, finally burned at Hahnville, Louisiana, with a loss of five lives." "*The Robert E. Lee* caught fire after leaving Vicksburg, September 30, 1882. Completely destroyed with the loss of thirty lives."

Until the Civil War, riverboats were the utilitarian transportation of the West, totally dominating the commerce of the riparian West. At landings up and down the river, farmers and travelers waved lanterns and lit bonfires to hail the packets, which pulled in to load goods and passengers. The steamboats traveled thirty to fifty miles down the rivers before pulling to shore to onload wood, coal, or oil for the insatiable boilers. Traveling upstream in high water, the packets made two to three miles per hour. But a fast boat like the *City of Louisville* could travel at up to twenty-three miles per hour with the current. Having only one rudder, the older style sternwheelers were difficult to steer and dock. The sidewheelers, on the other hand, were highly maneuverable, as the side paddlewheels could be rotated independently.

Steamboats were an integral part of the river life well into the twentieth century. In the early days, the packets literally brought society and culture to the hinterlands, cut off except for water traffic. As the decades wore on after the Civil War, railroads diminished riverboat importance, and by the 1880s the proud palaces were used primarily for luxury travel, entertainment, and recreation.

The steamboats remained inextricably part of the river folklore and culture. The *Robt. E. Lee* and the *Natchez* ran their fabled race in 1870. The last great competition on the Western rivers didn't happen until August 1928, when the two largest sidewheelers on the rivers raced from New Orleans to St. Louis. Mark Twain wrote in *Life on the Mississippi,* "I think that much the most enjoyable race of all races is the steamboat race. Two red-hot steamboats raging along, neck and neck, straining every nerve . . . quaking and straining and groaning from stem to stern, spouting white steam from the chimneys, raining down sparks, parting the river into long streaks of hissing foam . . . this is the sport that makes a body's very liver curl with enjoyment. A horse race is pretty tame in comparison."

Each steamboat's distinctive whistle shrilled five miles into the forests and fields, announcing the boat's arrival, as synonymous with steamboat sound as calliope music. Named after the seventh Greek muse who was noted for her beautiful voice, calliopes are basically thirty-two-note pipe organs under steam pressure. When calliopes were invented in 1855 to replace church bells, few parishioners appreciated the shrill tones on Sunday mornings, exiling them forever to more secular uses. The early calliopes were mechanically attached to the whistles, so an extraordinary amount of hand strength was necessary to operate the solid brass keyboard.

Steamboats ran scheduled routes, much like airplanes today. In 1894 the *City of Louisville* departed the dock at Louisville at 3:00 PM, arriving fifty-seven minutes later in Charlestown. At 6:16 PM she tooted at Madison; she arrived at the final destination of Cincinnati at forty-two minutes after midnight—nine hours and forty-two minutes after leaving Louisville. Frances Howard Kohlhepp, one of the Howard children, remembered, "Quite often, just before five o'clock in the afternoon, Daddy would take us out for a ride in his motorboat so as to meet the waves of the mailboat on her nightly run to Cincinnati. Suddenly, there she was beside us, white and enormous, steaming steadily upstream."

The Howard yard manufactured wooden boats up to about 1910, switching to steel hulls when a WWI wood shortage drove lumber prices sky-high. Initially, they riveted with wooden bolts, then steel rivets. In the 1930s the Howard shipyards began welding steel hulls, a new technology. They were so unsure of the safety that they also riveted the steel hulls every nine inches. By 1893, as the rivers were cleared of obstructions, the Howards began making propeller-driven craft. Well into the twentieth century, the melodious sounds of the Howard bell called hundreds of workers to the yards, where they labored beside groaning oxen pulling the giant engines and boilers to the boats.

In 1898 Howard's Shipbuilding signed their most unusual contract, agreeing to build four wood-burning steamboats to service the Yukon Gold Rush hordes drawn to the banks of Alaska's Yukon River. Owner Ed Howard sent 112 Ohio Valley men to Dutch Harbor in the Aleutian Islands to build the boats. It was a tough fall and winter of construction. On some days, the Eskimo apprentices had to shovel snow off the hulls before they could resume construction. When completed, the 220-foot boats sailed five hundred miles across the Bering Sea to the Yukon where they operated for many years. Reportedly, one of the hulls is still in operation on the river.

At 1101 E. Market, the **Howard Steamboat Museum** brings this world to life with a collection of steamboat memorabilia relating to the Golden Age of River Travel, a wide array of bells and whistles and ships wheels and models, tools, photographs, and documents. The museum is housed in the Howard family mansion dating from the 1890s, built by the steamboat craftsmen who wrapped the Arts and Crafts and Moorish house interior in fifteen exotic woods. Three hand-carved arches are a whimsical array of acorn, ribbon, and abacus designs. Many of the rooms are decorated in high-style Victorian furnishings and elaborate trappings brought from Chicago's Colombian Exposition.

Across the street, the giant **Jeffboat** complex continues Jeffersonville's maritime tradition. Through World War II, the shipyards produced many of the landing craft used in the invasions in both fronts, with thirteen thousand workers laboring in the yards by 1944. Today, Jeffboat encompasses the old Howard shipyards, producing the tugs and barges that are ubiquitous on the river. It also occasionally reverts to the old ways. In 1979 it launched a $20 million floating palace, the *Mississippi Queen*, the only steam-powered stern paddlewheeler built in this century. Jeffboat is America's largest inland shipbuilder.

102.7 Take Riverview Drive .7 miles west to **Clarksville**, the oldest American town in the Northwest Territory, chartered in 1783 by George Rogers Clark on land that the grateful state of Virginia granted him and his Illinois Battalion for their Revolutionary War heroics.

Virginia ceded 150,000 acres to Clark in 1781 as Clark's Grant, with a thousand acres for a town located at the head of the Falls. In 1803 Clark built a cabin at **Clark's Point**, on a rocky point above the falls that overlooked Corn Island and Louisville, which he founded in 1778. Today, Clark's Point, at the intersection of South Clark and Harrison Avenue, is considered the best lookout and picnic spot in the Falls Cities.

George Rogers Clark is another of the Promethian figures erupting from history now and again, bespeaking the heroism of an age, but suffering a tragic fate rather than well deserved accolades. While yet a young man, Clark organized a campaign from Kentucky against the British forces scattered through the West. In one of the most remarkable conquests in history, culminating in the Battle of Vincennes in February 1779, Clark captured the immense territory north of the Ohio River and east of the Mississippi, which later became the Northwest Terrritory.

Clark signed personally for all of the materials that were used in the Revolutionary War campaign, carefully taking receipts. After the conquest of Vincennes, he sent a messenger back to the Virginia capitol at Williamsburg with the receipts for payment and reimbursement. Unfortunately, the state of Virginia never acknowledged their arrival, and Clark spent the rest of his days hounded by creditors. The ensuing legal battles occupied him to distraction, and many say to drink.

A few months after Clark finished his cabin in 1803, his younger brother William arrived to help him untangle his financial mess. It was while William Clark was living there that a letter from Meriweather Lewis arrived, inviting him to join his journey of exploration to the Pacific. Many say the Lewis and Clark Expedition began when Meriweather Lewis arrived from Pittsburgh and the two men shook hands beside the General's cabin. The two embarked on their momentous journey of exploration on October 23, 1803. There is a marker at the location of **George Rogers Clark's Home** west of the corner of South Clark and Harrison Avenue.

Like many war heroes, Clark was ill-suited for peace and civil harmony. He did little to hasten the development of Clarksville. The town suffered a reputation for unhealthiness and was poorly situated on the river without a suitable boat landing. Quickly, the neighboring towns overshadowed Clarksville, and within five years the town was deserted and Clark was living alone in his cabin.

In 1809, befuddled by either a stroke or alcohol or both, he fell into a fire. A few days later, to the sound of a fife and drum playing outside, his leg was amputated. He spent the balance of his days penniless across the river at Locust Grove, living by the good grace of his brother-in-law. Until his death in 1818, Native Americans from the Ohio and Mississippi drainages brought their young braves to Locust Grove yearly to meet Clark, believing that they should have the opportunity to meet the greatest warrior of all.

In one of the great poignancies in the history of the West, the bundle of Clark's receipts was found in the attic of the capitol in Richmond in about 1903. The **Clarksville Museum** in the Town Hall at 230 E. Montgomery has a collection of memorabilia relating to Clark.

In 1808 **Henry Clay and Humphrey Marshall** journeyed across the Ohio from Kentucky to satisfy a matter of honor. A political dispute had escalated into a personal one: Marshall called Clay a liar and poltroon in the furor of debate in the Kentucky House of Representatives. They came to the west edge of Clarksville to fight a duel on the banks of Silver Creek—it was illegal in Kentucky. The choice of dueling grounds was ironic, given the fact that the duel had arisen in part from a dispute relating to Aaron Burr's treason. Silver Creek was the embarkation point for Colonel Floyd's flotilla to join Burr in Natchez. When Clay and Marshall both suffered flesh wounds in the duel, the seconds declared that "honor was satisfied." Five days later, the Kentucky house censured both while commending them for bravery.

Clarkville was also the site of one of the first instances of government privatization. The old Indiana Reformatory for Men was the **First State Prison for Men**, built in 1821. It was built with publicly subscribed funds and then leased to private individuals who incarcerated the prisoners on a per capita basis. The first lessee, Captain Seymour Westover, was killed with Davy Crockett at the Alamo.

The red-brick Romanesque complex was sold in 1923 and remodeled into **Colgate-Palmolive-Peet Company Factory,** South Clark Boulevard and Woerner Avenue, for the production of soaps. It operates today as one of the area's largest employers. The **Colgate Clock** on the building is the second largest timepiece in the world, a horological landmark in the Falls Cities for seventy years. It is forty feet high, with a minute hand that is over twenty feet long weighing one-third of a ton.

The **Car Works** to the west of the Clark Bridge and Missouri Avenue and north of Riverside Drive is a multi-use facility housed in late-nineteenth-century industrial buildings built for the **Ohio Falls Car Manufacturing Company,** where twenty-three hundred workers manufactured railroad cars until the demise in the 1930s.

The most unique aspect of Clarksville, however, is the **Falls of the Ohio State Park,** 201 West Riverside Drive. In 1981 the United States Congress declared the Falls of the Ohio the country's first National Wildlife Conservation Area, a 1,404-acre site that is a favorite of bird-watchers. The conservation area protects the habitat of migrating birds who visit the falls to feed in the wetlands and potholes of the limestone reef. Over 265 species of birds throng the falls area. Blue heron stalk like somber priests while sandpipers race across flats. Bald eagles, falcons, and osprey soar overhead. In the river below the falls, 125 species of fish swim, including the endangered paddlefish.

Importantly, Congress also moved to protect the immense fossil beds, these being the largest exposed Devonian Age fossil beds in the world. The Indiana state park opened in 1990 on sixty-eight acres overlooking the fossil beds and a dramatic view of the Louisville skyline. A few feet down from the park's interpretation center, visitors can hike the 220 acres of fossil beds through a landscape of natural arches and tiny canyons, fossilized coral, and clusters of miniature crinoids and trilobites. Adventurous souls can cross the McAlpine Dam spillway to explore the outer fossil beds.

The sixteen-thousand-square-foot interpretation center encapsulates much of the history of the Falls of the Ohio area. The layered architecture of the center mirrors the geologic strata of the fossil beds below. A multi-screen video explains the epochal geologic story of the falls. There are exhibits on everything from coral reefs and the fossil beds to mastodons and early humans, steamboats, George Rogers Clark, the legendary Welshmen, and the ecology of today's falls. Three aquariums show the varied life of coral reefs and the Ohio River.

109.0 In July 1813 **New Albany** became the first city founded below the falls, as urbanization moved downstream. It is located in a lowland east of the geologic formation known as the Knobstone escarpment, the most dramatic scenery of the state's unglaciated Driftless Area. Three Scribner brothers arrived from New York and bought up the platted land, naming the city after the capitol of their home state. The **Scribner House** at 106 W. Main was built by brother Joel in 1814.

New Albany was at a fortunate spot. River traffic thronged the bustling wharves. The Buffalo Trace, the first graveled road in the state, became known as the Paoli Pike in 1820 and wound "like a white thread among the green hills." By 1800 the mail ran regularly across the state on the trail, arriving in Vincennes in four days. One 1819 traveler on the trail already found the settlers' land-clearing fires to be chastening. "No water, no food fit to eat," Richard Lee Masgrave wrote, "dusty roads and constantly enveloped in cloud of smoke owing to the woods and prairies being on fire for 100 miles."

At New Albany ferries scooted like waterbugs across to Louisville, making it the Middlewestern gateway to the South. From 1830s to the 1850, New Albany was the largest city in the state. In 1850 it was among the top one hundred American business cities. Up to the Civil War, steamboat building was also the primary industry in New Albany, with four to seven shipyards working constantly. Yawls, snagboats, and barges crowded up against steamboats, tugboats, and ferries along the congested waterfront. Foundries belched black smoke while producing goods for the yards and export. The Hill shipyards were located on Water Street between West Fourth and West Eighth, where the record-holding *Robert E. Lee* was built.

With prosperity came the trappings of an urban center. Mansions arose on the boulevards. While the nine churches vied for congregations and social preeminence, the town's numerous taverns jostled for theirs. **Town Clock Church** at 300 E. Main Street was built with a tall steeple in the mid-nineteenth century. The prominent timepiece has been a landmark for river pilots since. The southeast corner of West Main and West First is the site of **Hale's Tavern**, considered the finest tavern in New Albany's early days. A lineup of early-nineteenth-century political luminaries stayed at the tavern, including Henry Clay, Daniel Webster, Aaron Burr, Andrew Jackson, Martin Van Buren, and William Henry Harrison. Some of Burr's conspiracy was undoubtedly planned here.

New Albany's Mansion Row Historic District was named to the National Register in 1983. It includes Main bounded by State and Fifteenth, and Market Street between Seventh and Eleventh. It is a redoubt of stately homes that range in style from Federal to Italianate to French Second Empire. Among many fine examples, the **Culbertson Mansion** at 914 E. Main is a state historic site open to the public. The Victorian French Second Empire was built in the 1860s at a cost of $120,000.

Nearby, the **James Collins House** at 917 E. Main is the home of the Indiana's first cookbook author, Maria Lorraine Collins. She published *Mrs. Collins*

Table Receipts: Adapted to Western Housewifery in 1851. "Our generous and prolific clime affords a bountiful supply of nutritious fruits and vegetables, and the forests and hillsides abound in excellent game," she wrote. Many dishes are easily recognizable today: "pease" and asparagus soups, and recipes for tomato catsup and ham. Others speak of another day, Calf's head soup, for instance. "Get a Calf's head with the skin on, take out the brains and wash the head in cold water several times . . . " The frugal housewife could use the leftovers for the recipe for brain balls, a kind of forcemeat. A recipe for whortleberry sauce is there, along with succotash á la Tecumseh. River trade and shared culture is evidenced by recipes for oysters and curry and a disconcertingly bland gumbo.

Numerous educational institutions rose in the city, including colleges destined to flower elsewhere. The New Albany Theological Seminary was founded in 1852, later becoming Chicago's McCormick Theological Seminary. The Indiana Asbury Female College subsequently became DePauw University in Greencastle. One institution that lived its full life in New Albany was the Christian College, founded in 1833 by Dr. John Cook Bennett for the purposes of medical education, Indiana's first. However, the first degree was issued only forty days after the college opened. Based on that, it appears that the school either attracted particularly advanced prodigies or was a diploma mill.

At the southwest corner of Lafayette and Market streets, the Anderson Female Seminary and Anderson Collegiate Institute for Boys were founded in 1841. The Confederate general John Hunt Morgan attended the latter. The college's founder, Colonel Anderson, became affiliated with the Pennsylvania Railroad in later years, with a subordinate named Andrew Carnegie. Anderson afforded Carnegie the use of his library and extolled the virtues of education. The advice bore fruit as industrialist Carnegie later gave most of his large fortune to the establishment of public libraries.

A couple of notable lynchings happened in New Albany. The southeast corner of State and Spring streets is the site of the **old county jail**, where a mob hanged the **Reno Gang** in 1868. The Reno Gang terrorized southern Indiana from 1864 to 1868, perpetrating the nation's first train robbery in 1866. In 1868 they robbed a train in Scott County of over $96,000. When the long-suffering citizens of Jackson County learned that the gang members were housed in the New Albany jail, they organized a vigilance committee. On a cold December evening a group of men wearing red bandannas descended from a one-car train running without a headlight, traveling from an unknown location to the north. Within a short time, the sheriff was wounded, and three gang members swung from the jail's iron staircase.

The **Hole in the Wall Tavern** stood at the northeast corner of East Main and

East Fourth streets. It was infamous for the desperadoes who frequented the establishment. One day a man reportedly was hung from the third story window, though the record on the offense is unforthcoming.

The Floyd County Museum, 201 E. Spring Street, offers paintings from regional artists, both historic and contemporary, as well as the Yenawine Diorama, an animated, hand-carved expression of early Indiana life.

As with Jeffersonville, the Civil War destroyed New Albany's commerce with the Deep South. However, glass manufacture took up the slack, beginning in 1867 with America's first plate glass factory. By 1881 it was among the nation's largest glass centers, with over two thousand workers laboring in twenty-five acres of riverfront property. Several of New Albany's mansions have plate glass between layers of the walls for insulation. The king of New Albany was Washington C. DePauw, who, along with the glass concerns, owned roads, banks, utilities, mills, and insurance companies. In 1866, when the average workman made $100 a year, DePauw made $64,000. He provided substantial funding for DePauw University, thus its modern name.

The 1890s gas boom in northern Indiana moved the glass industry north. Increasingly, lumber and veneer products became the mainstay of the twentieth-century economy. Today, the town's economic base contains both industry and retail, with a large part of the labor force working across the river in Louisville, Kentucky.

An alternate loop to the Ohio River Scenic Route. To continue on the Scenic Route, follow Route 62W. For the alternate route, take U.S. 64 across the **Sherman Minton Bridge** to Louisville, Kentucky. Sherman Minton was a native of nearby Georgetown, Indiana, an ardent New Dealer who was a Senator and later a Supreme Court Justice. Founded by George Rogers Clark in 1778, **Louisville, Kentucky,** nestles in a bend of the Ohio, a bastion of Northern mercantilism tucked below the Mason-Dixon line. Though still tempered with the Deep South's *joie de vivre*, Louisville hardly moves at a languid pace. Rather, it's a sprightly place touched with a whimsical grace, like an eccentric aunt wearing a bit too much lipstick and her hat slightly cocked as she heads somewhere, fast.

Louisville citizens and visitors celebrate river history with the ***Belle of Louisville***, 401 West River Road, the nation's oldest operating Mississippi-style sternwheel steamboat. She began life in 1914 as just another packet, working the river trade. As other forms of transport undercut the freight, the boat became an excursion craft, at one point running trips from a Louisville amusement park to the amusement park at Rose Island. She stalwartly towed barges through the war years, though not really designed for blue-collar work. From 1949, she was a gypsy boat, traveling the rivers of the interior, from Omaha to Nashville. In 1962 the city of Louisville bought her at an auction, sadly derelict, and rehabilitated her as Louisville's own boat. She is registered as a National Historic Landmark. Through the summer months the *Belle* offers excursions down the river. Tours begin at the end of the Fourth Street Wharf. While at the Belle, don't miss the **Andrew Broaddus**, also listed on the National Register. The 1929 Coast Guard vessel was retired in 1972 and now serves as the wharfboat and offices for the Belle. **The Portland Museum**, 2308 Portland Avenue, trumpets the days when Portland was a bustling river port, vying with Louisville for predominance. It offers a sight-and-sound show about the river and the culture that coalesced there.

Louisville's architecture still speaks of the commercial successes of the nineteenth century, with Main and Market streets handsomely refurbished and filled with prosperous shops and businesses. Vintage residential neighborhoods like Old Louisville and Highlands are rapidly gentrifying, dotted with trendy cafes and Bed and Breakfasts. Award-winning architecture like the Humana Building testifies to the continued corporate commitment to the downtown.

West Main Street is a great walking street, with nineteenth century cast-iron store fronts restored and thriving with unique businesses. The **Kentucky Art and Craft Gallery**, 609 W. Main Street has an excellent selection of regional handmade work, including artists from southern Indiana. **The Louisville Slugger Museum and Bat Factory** at 800 W. Main Street is easy to find. Just look for the giant baseball bat outside. Along with great exhibits on our nation's pastime, the museum also offers multi-media interactive excitement. You can stand behind a plexiglass screen and have a virtual reality Roger Clemons hurl a ninety-mph fastball at your knees or walk through a mock locker room onto a playing field. The 1869 Italianate **Brennan House** at 631 S. Fifth Street is the last remaining downtown mansion from the days of river nabobs and imposing family homes. It is filled with the global treasures of the Brennan family and is available for tour.

Locust Grove, at 561 Blankenbaker Lane, is George Rogers Clark's final home. The fifty-five-acre National Historic Landmark is anchored by a restored 1790 Georgian home. Visitors can tour the home, the vintage gardens, and visitor's center, which includes a video. **Farmington**, 3033 Bardstown Road, is a Thomas Jefferson-inspired Classical home with fourteen-foot ceilings and octagonal rooms. The house retains its period gardens and decorative arts, which Abraham Lincoln may have seen when he visited in 1841. The house is part of the three-state Lincoln Trail and is available for tours. Near the Victorian Old Louisville neighborhood, the **J. B. Speed Museum**, on the campus of the University of Louisville at 2035 S.

Third Street, is recently remodeled and houses an exceptional regional collection of European decorative arts and Old Masters.

No visit to Louisville is complete without a trip to **Churchill Downs** at 714 Central Avenue. The horse track has been the home of 123 Kentucky Derbies and has a full spring and fall racing schedule. **The Kentucky Derby Museum** at the track offers three floors of memorabilia and exhibits on the "greatest two minutes in sports."

Return to New Albany via U.S. 64.

Floyd County, Indiana, was named for Major Davis Floyd, the only co-conspirator tried and convicted in the Aaron Burr case. A good vista of New Albany can be seen by driving up State Street to the village of **Floyds Knobs**. The Knobstone Escarpment is Indiana's most prominent phsysiographic feature, rising nearly six hundred feet from the valley below. An 1816 traveler, David Thomas, spoke of the awe that early travelers felt about the knobs. "My mind had thrilled at the name of the Knobs . . . . But these heights would interest without the aid of philosophy."

The Knobs area above New Albany is a long-time truck farming area for the Louisville market. For many generations, the mostly German farm families hauled berries and melons to the Louisville wholesale market. Tobacco was also a major crop in the high ground. Today, it is the center of a several modern amalgams between small scale agriculture and family entertainment, the area's largest tourist draw.

The **Starlight** area is a center of the farming/entertainment. **The Huber Orchard and Winery**, established in 1843, is at 19816 Huber Road. Either take the Hamburg exit off of U.S. 65 or take Navilleton Road off Route 150. The Huber complex is particularly well marked. Nearby, **Stumler's** also has a business complex including restaurant, party barn, petting zoo, and farm market. The **Joe Huber Family Farm**, 2421 Scottsville Road, has over fifty varieties of fruits and vegetables for sale and a farm restaurant rated four-star by *The Louisville Courier-Journal.* The nearby **Forest Discovery Center**, 533 Louis Smith Road, celebrates the role of Indiana forests in the state's ecosystem and economy with interactive displays and tours of Koetter Woodworking, Inc.'s sprawling factory.

North of Louisville a few miles on Route 150, **The Mary Anderson Center**, 101 St. Francis Drive, Mount St. Francis IN, is a nationally renowned artists' retreat, the sixth largest in the country in terms of the number of artists it serves. The center is focused on providing a haven for creative work. Their goal is "to provide time and place where artists can concentrate and work." The artists who utilize the center range across the creative spectrum: textile artists to painters, performance artists to clothing designers, book makers to playwrights. The facility is located on four hundred acres of rolling forests a few miles north of New Albany and Louisville. Trails wind through the property and wildlife sanctuary. The facility includes studios for visual artists, live/work spaces for writers, and kilns and presses for potters and printmakers.

Up to six residents can be housed in the sturdy eleven-room, red-brick house. All meals are provided or are reimbursed. The center costs $30 a day, though several fellowships are available for poets, photographers, writers, and visual artists. The average length of stay is one month, though many stay for shorter periods. "The time here was a godsend," writer Leatha Kendrick said. "It restored me to the heart of my work and, I think, forever altered my relationship to my writing life."

To the north another seven miles, Greenville is the home of the nationally celebrated **Capriole goat's milk cheese**, P.O. Box 117, Greenville, IN 47124, 812-923-9408. Trendy shops from New York to San Francisco offer their Wabash Cannonball and Old Kentucky Tomme, a firm country cheese, along with cheese disks wrapped in brandy-soaked chestnut leaves. It's a working farm, so drop-ins are very disruptive. Their cheeses are available in Louisville at Lotsa Pasta, 3717 Lexington Road, 502-896-6361.

Five miles west of New Albany on Indiana Route 64, **Georgetown** was the birthplace of Supreme Court Justice Sherman Minton, along with historian R. Carlyle Buley, who won the Pulitzer Prize for his two-volume work, *The Old Northwest*.

115.0 On Route 62W (the continuation of New Albany's Main Street and Corydon Pike), the hamlet of Edwardsville is the home of Indiana's longest tunnel, the 4,311-foot **Edwardsville Tunnel**, built in 1880 by the predecessor of the Southern Railroad.

Visitor Information

Southern Indiana Clark-Floyd Counties Convention and Tourism Bureau, 315 Southern Ave., Jeffersonville, IN 47130, 812-282-6654, 800-552-3842.

Louisville and Jefferson County Convention and Visitors Bureau, 400 S. 1st, Louisville, KY 40202, 502-584-2121, 800-626-5646.

Recommended Reading

Before the Dinosaurs: The Mysteries of Indiana's Fossil History, Richard Seltzer, Guild Press, Indianapolis, 1996, is kid-friendly introduction to the big fossil and geology picture.

Life on the Mississippi, Mark Twain, originally published Boston, 1883, Penguin edition, New York, 1984.

Scenes from Memory, Francis Howard Kohlepp, Howard Steamboat Museum, Jeffersonville, IN, 1991. This is a nostalgic look at the last days of the steamboat era by a member of the Howard family.

Recommended Regional Dining

Schrimpff's Confectionery, 347 Spring St., Jeffersonville, IN 47130, 812-283-8367.

Joe Huber Family Farm and Restaurant, 2421 Scottsville Rd., Borden, IN 47106, 812-923-5255, features Hoosier farm cooking—chicken and ham and all the fixings.

The Seelbach Hotel's Oakroom, 500 S. Fourth Ave., Louisville, KY 40202, 800-333-3399, specializes in contemporary regional cuisine by award-winning Chef Jim Gerhardt, including Kentucky free-range chicken with Kentucky ham and pesto stuffing with a Maker's Mark bourbon sauce and creative presentations of an unlikely (and very tasty) regional specialty, paddlefish. Gerhardt utilizes the produce of Indiana's Knobs region in many of his dishes. The upscale restaurant is located in the paneled and colonnaded charm of the Edwardian men's billiard room.

J. Graham's Cafe at the Brown Hotel, 4th and Broadway streets, 502-583-1234, is the place for that Kentucky gastronomic legend, the "Hot Brown." This is the place where the sandwich was first concocted.

Lilly's, 1147 Bardstown Rd., 502-451-0447, also features local produce in Chef Kathy Cary's menus. It's a New American place with dishes that reflect a carousel of cuisines.

Lynn's Paradise Cafe, 984 Barret Ave., Louisville, KY 40204, 502-583-EGGS, is an idiosyncratic Louisville institution, serving highly evolved comfort foods. You can't miss it, just look for the eight-foot-high red coffee pot pouring java into chrome yellow cups in front of a very-retro fifties cafe. Inside it is a turquoise, pink, and aqua flea market gone mad. The place hums with energy.

Campgrounds

Deam Lake, R.R. 2 Box 568, Borden, IN 47106, 812-245-5421, is part of Indiana's Clark State Forest, located about twenty miles northwest of New Albany. Take I65 north to Route 60W. The campground is about nine miles north.

KOA Kampground, 900 Marriot Dr., Clarksville, IN 47129, 812-282-4474, is about one mile from the river.

Recommended Hotels and Bed and Breakfasts

Honeymoon Mansion and Wedding Chapel, 1014 E. Main St., New Albany, IN 47159, 812-945-0312, 800-759-7270, is a sybaritic retreat for getaways in a restored Queen Anne—"Southern Indiana's Most Ornate," as they claim.

The Seelbach Hotel, 500 S. Fourth Ave., Louisville, KY 40202, 800-333-3399, is a 1905 wonder, lovingly maintained with impeccable service. Italian and Swiss marble columns and oak paneling grace the lobby, with vintage murals overhead celebrating the history of the river city. The downstairs Rathskeller is the last surviving Rookwood Pottery room in the world, a large charming vaulted room of glazed tile and ceramic pelicans. Given the period splendor, it's logical that F. Scott Fitzgerald placed the wooing of Daisy in the Seelbach.

The Old Louisville Inn, 1359 S. Third, Louisville, KY 40208, 502-635-1574, is a ten-thousand-square-foot mansion built in 1901 for a local telephone magnate in the shady environs of the Old Louisville neighborhood. Eleven sumptuous guest rooms are decorated with period antiques.

The Louisville skyline stands as a friendly neighbor along the Ohio River.

Canoeing, hiking the fossil beds, and birdwatching are some favorite activities at the Falls of the Ohio State Park, the country's first National Wildlife Conservation Area.

The Joe Huber Family Farm and Restaurant is one of the area's biggest tourist attractions with plenty to do for the entire family.

The site of many a heated debate, the 1816 Capitol Building in Corydon is a state historic site.

Thunderbolt of the Confederacy

Morgan's Raid in Harrison County
New Albany to Corydon 18 miles
Route 11 Alternate Loop 30 miles
Route 135 Alternate Loop 60 to 85 miles

In 1804 the imperious governor of the Indiana Territory, William Henry Harrison, purchased land at the confluence of the Big Indian and Little Indian creeks. Son of Tidewater Virginia, Harrison ruled the territory from his gracious roost, Grouseland, in the territorial capitol at Vincennes. Harrison hoped to transplant the Tidewater culture to the Northwest Territory, bringing slavery and plantations to the newly opened West.

Like many Virginia land speculators, he held the land around Indian Creek for a brief time, selling the property in 1808 to Harvey Heth, who laid out the present town of Corydon. But Harrison himself named the town Corydon, after a shepherd character in a lachrymose song entitled, "The Pastoral Elegy." A local girl, Miss Jenny Smith, sang the dirge to Harrison many times when he visited her father's house in the town.

Ironically, Corydon became the locus of opposition to Harrison's plans. The region to the east and west of the Falls of the Ohio attracted thousands of Kentucky yeoman families, fleeing economic competition with slavery. In 1813 the Indiana Territory legislature, expressing the burgeoning political power of the yeomen, voted to abolish slavery, expand suffrage, and diminish the power of the governor. And they voted to move the capitol of the territory to Corydon, closer to their power base. The original choice was Madison, but Harrison wrested Corydon as a compromise from the legislators, since he still owned land in the surrounding county.

In 1816 forty-four delegates gathered in the torrid heat to discuss and debate statehood. They eventually concurred and, by December of that year, Indiana joined the Union as the nineteenth state. The prim blue limestone Federal-style building that Dennis Pennington built a few years before as the Harrison County courthouse became the first state capitol. From 1816 to 1825, Corydon was the state capitol, alive with the bustle of a large governmental seat. Tradesmen busied themselves in their shops and stables. Legislators debated in the capitol and in the taverns. Lawyers, who called themselves "squires," minced nattily around the square, with their eel-skin-wrapped hair queues hanging three feet down their backs.

When the capitol moved north in 1825 to the miasmic swamp that the legislators named Indianapolis, Corydon deflated. It became another county seat, albeit graced with some substantial architecture, dozing for almost forty years until a shrill Civil War alarm awoke the countryside.

On July 9, 1863, Governor Oliver P. Morton issued a proclamation to all citizens in the southern half of Indiana, urging them to immediately prepare to defend themselves. "It is hereby ordered and required that all able-bodied white male citizens of the several counties south of the National road forthwith form themselves into companies of at least sixty persons, elect officers and arm themselves with such arms as they may be able to procure. Said companies will perfect themselves in military drill as rapidly as possible and hold themselves subject to further orders from this department. It is desired that they be mounted in all cases where it is possible."

From Indianapolis south, fire whistles shrilled and church bells clanged, sending the alarm into the boiling summer air. In every town and village, militia commanders tacked up orders requiring all soldiers on leave and convalescents to report for duty, commandeering all railroad and telegraph for military uses, ordering curfews on all businesses except printing, telegraph and post offices, drugstores, and livery stables. Housewives threw their silver into wells and cisterns. Farmers led their prized livestock and horses deeper into the country. Bankers as far north as Indianapolis loaded their bullion and currency onto express trains headed to Chicago. Citizens scanned the horizon for telltale clouds of white dust, the portent of invasion by dreaded Confederates.

Contradictory reports stuttered down the telegraph wires and across the split rail fences that snaked through the southern Indiana hill country. Confederate General John Hunt Morgan with forty-eight-hundred cavalry had crossed the Ohio on July 8, headed north to free five thousand Confederate prisoners in Camp Morton. He was aimed for New Albany and Louisville, for Paoli, for Lawrenceburg and Cincinnati. He had eleven thousand men; he had three thousand. His troops had seven cannons; they had four. They marched under a black flag, taking no prisoners and giving no quarter.

The news unleashed consternation in a state fixed on the great battles raging to the east and west. In the rolling hills near Gettysburg, Pennsylvania, the great armies of Generals Lee and Meade had commenced their butchery a week before. In the West, Grant ended his long siege of Vicksburg and secured the Mississippi and West. By noon of July 11, there were fifteen thousand Hoosier militia in the Indiana fields and parade grounds, sixty-five thousand within another few days' travel. Union troops marched south from Michigan; ammunition steamed west from Washington; armored gunboats patrolled the Ohio. Five regiments slept in the Indianapolis State House yard.

General John Hunt Morgan, the "Thunderbolt of the South," was a progenitor of the lightning wars that followed in the next century. With plumed snap-brim hat, insouciant eyes, a rakish mustache and Van Dyke goatee, Morgan affected the air of a gallant Southern cavalier. A son of the Bluegrass, he cut a raffish figure, known more for his foppish militia outfits and mercurial disposition than military rigor.

In battle, however, Morgan displayed a genius for crisp analysis of military situations and rapid decision-making. Nature blessed Morgan with "gifts that she very rarely bestows, and which give the soldier who has them vast advantages; a quickness of perception and of thought, amounting almost to an intuition, an almost unerring sagacity in foreseeing the operations of an adversary and in calculating the effect of his own movements upon him, wonderful control over men, as individuals and in masses, and moral courage and energy almost preternatural," one of his brigadier commanders, General Basil Duke, wrote. Morgan gathered around him some of the best young men of the region. Most of his Kentucky force was under twenty-five years old, intensely loyal to Morgan. His cavalrymen were reared in the saddle, capable of traveling forty miles a day, tested and hardened in internecine warfare of the border states.

Morgan was an innovator. He threw away the cavalryman's emblematic saber, replacing it with rifle and revolver. His style was boldly offensive, in a Southern command that was cautiously reactionary. Morgan's Raiders were, in essence, a highly mobile infantry—flashing to the point of engagement, dismounting for combat, and returning to the saddle to attack the next objective before their opponents could regroup. Morgan understood the value of disinformation. His battle retinue included his personal telegraph operator, "Lightning" George Ellsworth. Ellsworth delighted in tapping into Union telegraph lines, listening to other operators to copy their idiosyncratic styles, and then promulgating wild rumors throughout the land before cutting the wire. He was the source of much of the conflicting information about the size of Morgan's force and his movements.

Morgan crossed the Ohio and threatened Indiana against the orders of his commander in Tennessee, General Braxton Bragg. The raid began when Morgan crossed the Cumberland River into Union-held Kentucky. His orders were to invade Kentucky, drawing large numbers of Union forces to ease the pressure on Bragg's Confederate forces deadlocked with Union General William Rosecrans in the Tennessee campaigns. Morgan succeeded admirably, taking Columbia, Lebanon, and Bardstown, and destroying large amounts of Federal stores. The raid quickly attracted a pursuing army commanded by General Edward Hobson. But when Morgan crossed into the rich, unsullied land of Indiana in July 1863, he was on his own, without recourse to reinforcements or supply, or even the support of his superiors.

Morgan's plan was to range across Indiana and Ohio, disrupting the rear of the enemy, and pillaging as he went. As Morgan left Tennessee, General Lee's great army was moving to the North. After his raid, Morgan hoped to link up with Lee in Pennsylvania. Alternately, he would ford the Ohio east of Cincinnati to return to Confederate lines.

Morgan's raid was not the first Confederate incursion during the summer of '63. On June 18, 1863, Captain Thomas Hines, one of Morgan's most trusted men, led sixty-four men on a reconnoitering raid across the Ohio, landing near Rome, Indiana, in Perry County. Dressed in plain clothes, the men portrayed themselves as Union soldiers, searching for deserters. Hines was particularly interested in linking up with Southern-sympathizing Copperhead Democrats and the secret society, the Knights of the Golden Circle. Accordingly, they aimed north for Orange County, the home of Dr. William Bowles, the owner of the French Lick Springs Hotel and head of the Knights.

By 1863 there was deep dissension in the Midwest about the war. Defeats at Fredericksburg and Chancellorville had demoralized the North. The trade ties to the South, as well as familial ones, made the war onerous in some quarters. Increasing enlistments, as well as a recently passed draft law and resulting draft riots, added to the peace proponents' obstinacy. Though Governor Oliver Morton was a staunch Lincoln Republican, Anti-Lincoln Copperhead Democrats won the majority in the Indiana legislature in 1862, which became known as the Peace Legislature.

The name "Copperhead" originated in Republicans' claims that the Democrats' pro-Southern sympathies reminded them of the yellow-headed poisonous snakes. "All Democrats are traitors to some degree," the Republican canard went. The Peace Democrats rebutted by wearing the cut-off heads of copper Liberty cents on their lapels. The debate quickly devolved into acrimony, with all of the political diplomacy of a schoolhouse playground. Morton increasingly extended his powers, decidedly extra-legally, to break the impasse—raising money privately and suspending *habeas corpus*. A scholar of the period, Frank Klement, stated, "A stubborn governor and an ill-mannered legislature brought an end to constitutional government in Indiana." Only a Union victory could sanitize Morton's actions.

The Knights of the Golden Circle were the most radical of the anti-Lincoln forces, a shadowy secret society that promulgated pro-Southern ideas. They dreamed of an empire based on cotton and slaves that included an annexed Mexico. Indeed, they may have been so shadowy as to be almost nonexistent. While some claimed that there were more than fifty thousand members in Indiana alone, others contended that there were virtually no Knights, and the society and the linkage with the Peace Democrats was a clever bit of political footwork on the part of Governor Morton.

At the point of Hines' foray, however, the Confederates were expecting an uprising of the Copperheads and Knights of the Golden Circle to aid Morgan's Raid. "We went up north to stir up some Copperheads," General Basil Duke said.

The day after Hines and his reconnoitering Confederates crossed the Ohio, Hoosiers discovered the soldiers' identities in Orange County and the group was put to flight. The Home Guards of Leavenworth and Corydon eventually trapped the Confederates on an island at the mouth of the Blue River above Leavenworth. Townspeople gathered on the shore to watch the fight, wives ferrying ammunition to their husbands who kept up a continuous fire. Three of the Confederates were killed by cannon and rifle fire, and the balance surrendered waving the only white shirt among them. "Our citizens, though unused to actual war, showed the nerve of soldiers," the *Corydon Weekly Democrat* crowed.

Hines, however, escaped across the Ohio into Kentucky and made his way to the rendezvous with Morgan at the port of Brandenburg, Kentucky, about forty miles west of Louisville. By the time Morgan and his army arrived at Brandenburg on July 8, two river packets stood steaming at the wharf, courtesy of the resourceful Hines, who helped capture them. Hines, a small man with curly hair and impish eyes, was described by those who did not really know as "the most dangerous man in the Confederacy," a master of irregular warfare, plunder, and escape-skills he later used to excel as a lawyer and an appellate judge.

The Confederates captured the *J. T. McComb* when she docked in Brandenburg in the middle of the night. Steaming to the middle of the river, they hung distress signs out and lured the *Alice Dean* to help. Quickly, the ship's captain found himself the distressed vessel, as the *McComb* sprouted guns and forced the *Alice Dean* to shore.

Alerted by Brandenburg citizens who crossed the river to Mauckport, Indiana, a Union commander hailed a passing steamboat and sent it to Lawrenceburg for a six-pound cannon. Unfortunately, the gunners had no experience and were forced into on-the-job training. By the light of forty-foot-high plumes of burning natural gas left from failed oil wells, the men wrestled the cannon into position on a bluff.

At daybreak they let loose a salvo that clipped the *McComb* and killed Morgan's quartermaster. Morgan's artillery, considerably more experienced, responded with a fusillade that killed the cannoneers and drove back the home guard. Under the cover of artillery, the two boats ferried across more than twenty-five hundred men and horses, as well as their four small cannons. After the crossing, the Confederates burned and sank the *Alice Dean* in mid-channel to prevent her use by the pursuing Union forces of General Hobson. With the provision that she sail to Louisville and stay out of military action, Morgan spared the *J. T. McComb* because of the ship captain's life-long friendship with General Basil Duke. When the captain arrived in Louisville, he breathlessly announced he transported forty-eight hundred men, five thousand horses, and four giant cannons "by his own count."

After plundering the village of Mauckport, the first battalion across the river made camp while the balance of the force was ferried over, finishing about midnight. The next morning, the combined battalions of Confederate cavalry moved up the road to Corydon where four hundred Home Guards, lightly seasoned from their victory over Hines at the Leavenworth island, awaited them. They were armed with an arsenal of muskets and squirrel rifles, with a few Henry rifles sprinkled in. Composed mainly of young men and aged Mexican War vets, the Home Guard was isolated because Ellsworth's telegraphic follies convinced the Union to reinforce New Albany, thinking it was Morgan's target.

Morgan sent the vanguard and his own brother, Richard, to charge the barricade, and they leapt it on their Kentucky mounts. The militia beat back the charge, killing eight Confederates and wounding thirty-three. The Confederates soon flanked the breastworks, and artillery was brought to bear. When Morgan purposely overshot the town, some shells inadvertently landed at a farm outside of town, Cedar Glade, where many refugees from town were gathered, putting them to further flight. "These shrieking shells," militiaman J. Edward Murr later wrote, "were quickly interpreted by the militia as an order to retreat and hundreds did from the first."

Attia Porter, a puckish sixteen-year-old Corydon girl, described the Battle of Corydon in a letter to her cousin: "Our home guards skirmished with the rebs from the river to [Corydon] and on one of the hills overlooking the town had a grand *battle*. The battle raged violent for *thirty* minutes, just think of it! And on account of the large number of rebs we were forced to retire which our men did in good earnest everyone seemed determined to get out of town first but which succeeded remains undecided to this day . . . . one of our brave boys run three miles from the rebels, and really run himself to death. He stopped at a house and fainted and never came to. Dident he deserve a promotion?"

In the battle, Confederates killed three Harrison County men and wounded two others. Morgan disarmed and later paroled three hundred militia, with the provision that they not fight again. In all, local historians list ten Harrison County citizens killed and six wounded, including two women who "died of exhaustion" following the raid.

While Morgan questioned prisoners upstairs at the Kintner House where he was headquartered, General Basil Duke chatted with the town's young ladies in the courtyard. Morgan was later dining at the hotel when the innkeeper's daughter walked in and handed him a newspaper. The bold black headline trumpeted, "Glorious News! Vicksburg Surrendered with Over 20,000 Prisoners! The Great Battle at Gettysburg Penn. Between Gens. Meade and Lee—Lee Badly whipped."

Morgan required $1,000 from each of the three mill owners in town, but settled for $2,100. When one mill owner handed him $1,200, Morgan returned $200, saying, "Do you think I would cheat you of one cent?" One mill was burned, probably because the owner failed to submit. The Confederate troopers, used to the war-ravaged South, went on a carnival of plunder, pillaging the stores. One store was lightened of $3,500 of merchandise, punctiliously paid for with $140 of Confederate script. Hardened cavalrymen paraded down the main street with women's bonnets on their heads and blue ribbons trailing from their horses' tails. A couple of playful Confederates convinced two adventuresome young ladies from the town to ride behind them, enticing them with matching ribbons for their hair.

"I never before seen anything like this disposition to plunder," General Basil Duke wrote. "At the same time, anything more ludicrous than the manner in which they indulged their predatory tastes can scarcely be imagined." Though it was a sweltering day in July, one trooper trotted out of town with seven pairs of ice skates around his neck. Another jingled away loaded with sleigh bells. Until an officer made him give up his booty, one cavalryman carried three canaries in a birdcage on his saddle. Another had a chandelier, yet another a Dutch clock. A silver, casket-shaped chafing dish and a green glass decanter with matching goblets were part of the loot, perfect baggage for the well-appointed cavalryman preparing for battle.

Though deep behind enemy lines, in desperate straits, Morgan's Raiders obviously had their sweethearts in mind. The most common articles of appropriation were baby shoes and bolts of calico. Later, commentators told of terrifying cavalry charges, rebel yells piercing the air, and calico snapping from the saddles like the scarves of errant knights. "Some of the columns looked like traveling circuses," one Union officer wrote, "with useless plunder and an excess of clowns."

The main body of the Confederates moved north toward Palmyra later that day, past the wheat-stubbled and corn-tassled fields of mid-summer Indiana, jingling and clanking with their booty. Many of Morgan's wounded were left in the care of the Corydon people, who nursed them until they could return south.

While the Battle of Corydon was a short skirmish, the Corydon Home Guard considerably slowed down Morgan's march, allowing an advance of only fourteen miles in twenty-four hours, buying valuable time for General Hobson's army to gather transports and cross the Ohio in pursuit. In contrast, the raiders advanced forty miles the next day, as they did for many days to come. Obviously, the short June campaign that culminated in the skirmish in Leavenworth against Hines' small reconnaissance force stiffened the Corydon Home Guards' fighting resolve for Morgan, preparing them for their brief moment in the Indiana sun. The Battle of Corydon was one of the few Civil War engagements on Northern soil.

With Lee no longer in Pennsylvania, Morgan's Raid now became a run for the Ohio River crossing at Buffington Island, upstream from Cincinnati. With General Hobson in close pursuit and an aroused state militia rapidly mobilizing, Morgan moved northwest, across the grain of upland Indiana, paralleling the river on an oblique line. For the next four days, until he crossed into Ohio at West Harrison in Dearborn County, Morgan zigzagged for two hundred miles across Indiana, feinting and dissembling in his headlong rush. Many days, his men spent twenty-one hours in the saddle, taking turns leading one another while the other slept.

Cavalrymen covering that much ground had to have fresh horses, and accordingly they de-horsed wide segments of Indiana. By the time they reached Palmyra, the raiders had collected five hundred horses, displaying remarkable ingenuity in ferreting out their hidden locales. Morgan, reviled as the "King of the Horse Thieves," dispatched raiding parties from the head of each of his two or three columns to ride five miles to each side. As they gathered the region's horses, they returned to the rear of the rapidly moving force. In this way, he unhorsed a ten-mile swath along his route. His men were not even appreciative of their booty—"as a rule the horses we took were very inferior to the Kentucky and Tennessee stock that we had brought with us, and which generally had a large infusion of thoroughbred blood. The horses we impressed were for the most part heavy, sluggish beasts, barefooted and grass-fed, and gave out in a day or two, sometimes in a few hours," a soldier wrote.

Morgan continued north to Salem where his advance guard dashed into the town square where the Home Guard was assembled with a small cannon used for holidays. Thoroughly rattled, the cannoneer dropped the live coal as he attempted to fire the cannon and was captured before he could find another. As before, Morgan's men burned railroad bridges, water tanks, and depot to disrupt troop movements. The troops also helped themselves to Salem's stores, "particularly delighted with the style of Salem clothing and the quality of Salem whiskey," the *New Albany Daily Ledger* reported.

Lightning Ellsworth continued to shinny up poles to eavesdrop before sending out his messages of confusion. Between the consternation caused by Morgan's outriders and the false information dispersed by Ellsworth, it is small wonder Union officers were unsure of Morgan's movements. The telegraph was only a few decades old, still mainly confined to one skinny line following the railroad tracks. Even Indianapolis only had one telegraph office. Once Morgan cut the line, it effectively isolated a region. At one point, the New Albany newspapers had to confess that they had no news from the outside because the lines were severed. The lines were cut north of the city, and one of Morgan's raiding parties had circled below Louisville, cutting the telegraph leading south.

Morgan continued to encounter an empty land—houses abandoned, sometimes with bread dough still rising. At one house, the woman had left two warm pies on a table outside the kitchen, perhaps as a propitiatory offering. At Salem, Morgan turned east toward Vienna and Scottsburg in two columns. General Hobson's forces drew increasingly closer, less than seven hours behind by the time Morgan reached Vienna.

On July 11 Morgan's force encountered the first organized opposition since Corydon, a group of militia under a Federal commander at Vernon, Indiana. Morgan called for their surrender, but the commander refused, asking for time to evacuate noncombatants. Behind a screen of skirmishers, Morgan slipped away toward Dupont, leaving the Vernon defenders to fret in the dark. During the evening, defenders along a creek heard a great splashing at the ford below the bluff where they were dug in. Fearing a surprise attack, the militia took to their heels. In the ensuing rout, several men fell from the twenty-foot-high bluff to the stream below, causing numerous injuries. Indeed, more men were hurt in the Battle of Finney's Ford than in any other engagement besides Corydon. Unfortunately, the casualties couldn't be attributed to Morgan's Raiders, who were miles away. The splashing that the militiamen heard was from a herd of cattle being driven to safety by local farmers.

In Versailles the Confederates encountered a group of militia and local citizens. Summarily, the troopers took them prisoners, broke their guns against the edge of the stone courthouse, paroled them, and rode on. The Indiana Home Guard was reduced to felling trees to slow Morgan's advance and bushwhacking and sniping at the passing troops. General Duke later stated that, if the militia had stood and fought, the Confederates could not have forced their way through their greater numbers. However, the Indiana militia were totally untested men against well trained and experienced fighters.

When Morgan arrived in Dupont, his troops roused the sleeping Stout family, and he and his officers slept for a few hours in their beds. An Indianapolis newspaper reported the cavalrymen, riding four abreast, took two hours to pass through the town when they rode out the next morning. Many carried a canvas-covered ham on their pommel, having availed themselves of porcine booty from a large, local packing plant. Eventually, they captured a bit more. The packing house owner's daughter came out to harangue the men as they left with her father's hams bouncing on their saddles. One smitten trooper declared he would return when his war years were over, and make her his. Reportedly he did, and they and their family lived in the Dupont area for generations.

Feinting toward Aurora, Morgan inspired a local Paul Revere to canter the twenty miles in two hours to announce the invasion. The local populace fled to the hills where they waited in vain, as Morgan continued to move east. In Sunman, they stopped for a brief rest, barely more than a few hours. By this time the endless days in the saddle were beginning to exhaust the men. "I'd give a thousand dollars for an hour's sleep," one trooper said. But they had to march on, moving east through Dearborn County—New Alsace, Dover, and finally leaving Indiana at West Harrison on the Ohio border.

Morgan's Raiders never did make it across the Ohio as a cohesive unit. The river had risen six feet since they crossed only five days before. Hobson nipped at their heels. General Judah, stationed in Cincinnati, blocked their escape that direction. Gunboats patrolled the crossings. General Lew Wallace, rousted from a fishing trip on the Wabash, was hurrying with a force from Indianapolis. As the writer William Wilson wrote, "Morgan was no longer a wolf on the prowl; he was now a fox in flight, and the hounds were baying all around him."

Morgan retained his talent for deception, creeping around the outskirts of Cincinnati in the night. He made a beeline for the ford at Buffington Island, but missed a critical chance to escape in the night. By daybreak Judah was hammering him from one quarter, and gunboats prevented the crossing of most of his force. Morgan was half way across the river on a strong horse, escape in his sight, when he realized that the majority of his men were stranded on the northern shore. He turned his horse back to Ohio, rather than leave his forces leaderless.

For the next six days Morgan led the hounds on one last grueling chase. He traversed the eastern half of the state in a continual running game of hide-and-seek. When Morgan finally surrendered in West Point, Ohio, he was on the Pennsylvania border, sixty miles from Lake Erie, the farthest north of any Confederate force. Word of surrender passed among the remaining 364 raiders, and exhaustion overcame dismay. When a Union force arrived a few minutes later to take formal charge of the men, all were sound asleep in the field.

Morgan and his men were taken as common criminals to the Ohio State

Prison in Columbus. Barely four months later, Morgan was on the loose again, escaped with the help of his wily compatriot, Captain Thomas Hines. The Confederates tunneled out of a veritable fortress, and Morgan and a compatriot calmly boarded a train for Cincinnati. A few weeks later, he was back behind Confederate lines. The war ended abruptly for Morgan in Greenville, Tennessee, during his next campaign. He was shot point-blank by a Yankee private as he was trying to surrender. "Surrender and be damned," the private yelled. "I know who you are." As he stood over the body, he said, "I've killed the damned horse thief."

The success and failure of Morgan's Raid has been debated for generations now. On the one hand, Morgan disobeyed direct orders, eliminating his force of twenty-five hundred men as a cohesive organization. On the balance, however, Morgan's Raid had an enormous impact on the North. In contrast with their own small losses, the Confederates captured and paroled six thousand militia and troops, caused six hundred casualties, and kept hundreds of thousands in frantic panic for a fortnight.

At the peak, there were 110,000 men in the field chasing the raiders, including the entire cavalry of the Midwest. The raid immobilized twenty-eight thousand Union troops which could have joined General William Rosecrans in his chess match with Bragg in Tennessee. Morgan caused an estimated $10 million in damage with his destruction of bridges, depots, mills, steamboats, and telegraph lines, in the process totally disrupting the communications and commerce of Indiana. The thousand-mile march through the heart of enemy territory remains a stirring saga of military history. The thirty-two-hour, eighty-four-mile march from Sunman, Indiana, to Williamsburg, Ohio, is one of the longest cavalry marches in the record.

By the standards of military action, it was a remarkably lenient raid. There was only one private house burned in the march, retribution for a cavalryman who was killed by a nearby sniper. Women were respected, with no reports of the brigandage that often accompanies war. Compared to the unrelenting savagery of Sherman's March to the Sea in Georgia, this was a saunter, an early version of "Wander Indiana."

The greatest failure of the campaign, however, may have been the South's complete misjudgment of Midwestern affinities. Copperheads failed to strike, and the Knights of Golden Circle failed to rally. Almost to a man, there was little concrete support for the Confederates. Even by the end of his swing through Kentucky, Morgan realized that he would get little help from the Copperheads and was churlish about it. When a Hoosier identified himself as a Copperhead, Morgan reportedly replied as he took the man's horse, "Good. Then you ought to be happy to contribute to the South." Although Hines and others would try another Quixotic scheme in the summer of '64—

the so-called Northwest Conspiracy to free prisoners at Camp Douglas—it too would fail. While there were many in the North who may have been willing to reconcile with the South, there were few who were interested in submitting to it. Still Morgan's Raid stands as a landmark in Indiana history, and the area along the Ohio which bore the brunt of the raid will never forget it.

Mileage

116.0 Polly's Freeze Outs ice cream stand is a particularly redolent piece of roadside Americana, the vestige of a local man's trip to Florida in the 1950s. The stand has served generations of Hoosiers since.

117.0 Harrison County Line. Harrison County is the axis of the thirteen counties along the Ohio. Organized in 1808, Harrison County is called the "Cradle of Indiana" because the first state capitol was in the county seat of Corydon, as well as the first state constitutional convention. The Scenic Route courses through an open broad valley, part of the fertile bottom land that runs along the river. To the north, the topography is more typical of this section of southern Indiana—rural and rugged and pocked with caves.

118.0 Route 11 South/135 North is a **scenic alternate route to Corydon**, allowing the visitor to follow the path of **Morgan's Raiders**. The alternate route is approximately thirty miles. The Ohio River Scenic Route itself continues on Route 62W to Corydon. Mileage indicated in the left hand column refers to the Ohio River Scenic Route path which stays on Route 62 through Harrison County.

Fifteen miles south on Route 11, the site of **Old Goshen Church** has a memorial slab giving a history of the oldest church in the county (no longer standing), built by relatives of Daniel Boone's family. Many of the descendants still live in the county. Route 211 leads to **Caesar's Indiana** at Bridgeport, North America's largest floating casino, originally scheduled to open in the summer of 1998. Controversy over environmental impact studies and conflict with Kentucky horse tracks have complicated the schedule. The hamlet of **Laconia** was founded in 1816. South of Laconia on Kintner Bottoms Road, the 1837 **Kintner-Withers House** is on the National Historic Register. It was the only working plantation north of the Ohio. Five miles past Laconia, Route 11 rises over a promontory to descend to **Mauckport**, where Morgan's Raiders first landed on Indiana soil. The 1966 **Matthew Welsh Toll Bridge** provides access to Brandenburg, Kentucky.

At one point, Mauckport vied with Madison to be the terminus of the Michigan Road (Route 421). The remnant of the village gives little clue that in 1820 it was one of the twenty major settlements along the Ohio from the

Falls to the Mississippi. The town slumbered until Morgan's Raiders invaded in July 1863. The flood of 1937 basically destroyed the town. Take Route 135N out of town for one mile. A road to the right leads to the **Mauckport Overlook**, which offers a stirring vista of the river.

Route 135 follows the route of Morgan's Raiders north fourteen miles to Corydon. General Basil Duke mentions seeing a house along the route with the doors wide open, a fire blazing in the hearth, and "chickens strolling before the door with a confidence that was touching but misplaced."

The road follows Buck Creek, where there were three flour mills when Morgan's men surged up the valley. The first, Lopp's Mill, was burned when the owner refused Confederate script for food. The second, Squire Boone's Mill, was completely missed by the raiders. **Squire Boone Caverns and Village** is 2.7 miles past the Mauckport Overlook turnoff. It is a recreational complex today that includes the cave Daniel Boone's brother, Squire, discovered in 1790, a replica of the gristmill he built in 1804, and a pioneer village. Many raiders camped at the third mill on the creek, Frake's Mill, but left it unscathed.

Six miles north is **Jordan Cemetery**, burial place of Lutheran minister Peter Glenn. He was killed by the raiders, and his house, just across the road from the cemetery, was burned. It was the only private house burned in the entire invasion, reportedly in retribution for the death of one of Morgan's troopers who was shot by a sniper. About 9.5 miles past the turnoff for Squire Boone's Cavern, the **Haywood Nature Reserve** is a 160-acre park that includes Pilot Knob, a promontory above Indian Creek.

The site of the **Battle of Corydon** is on Capitol Avenue (Old Route 135) in Corydon, a five-acre state historical site and memorial park. See mileage point 150.0 for Corydon.

119.0 Continuing on the **Ohio River Scenic Route** on Route 62W, **Lanesville** was settled in 1792 and was an important stage coach stop on the New Albany-Corydon road. It has a particularly photogenic Mail Pouch tobacco sign on a barn outside of the village.

124.0 The **Needmore Buffalo Farm** is the home of southern Indiana's largest bison herd and their passionate keepers, Art and Jane Stewart. Drive south on New Middleton Road to the New Middleton School to Payton Road. Follow signs to the farm. Visitors are welcome.

127.0 **Corydon** has a pace reminiscent of the fifties—sometimes 1950s, sometimes 1850s. Eventide brings locals out from the old neighborhoods to the charm of Old Capital Square, where they mingle with the tourists staying at the venerable nineteenth-century Kintner House, unwinding to the small town's gentle rhythm. On the corner, Donahue's unrepentantly retro neon sign invites guests in for "Cocktails," as it has since 1936.

Corydon was founded in 1804 at the junction of Big Indian and Little Indian creeks by Territorial Governor William Henry Harrison. In 1813 the same year that the Shawnee chief Tecumseh died in a battle of the War of 1812, and a year after the last battle between the Midwestern tribes and white settlers on Indiana's soil—Corydon became the territorial capital. In part it was to move the seat of government away from the pro-slavery claque centered in the then-capitol at Vincennes, as well as locating the capitol closer to the most settled part of the territory. In 1816, when Indiana finally reached the bench mark population of sixty thousand required by the Northwest Ordinance, the first state constitutional convention was held in Corydon. It was the capitol of Indiana until 1825.

A large section of the town, dating from 1808 to 1865, is listed as a National Historic District, roughly bounded by Summit, Maple, Walnut, Chestnut, Capitol, Poplar, Water, Beaver, and Mulberry streets and College Avenue. The main square has many fine examples of cast-iron store fronts that modernized the buildings in the 1890s. The Mesker Iron Works in Evansville produced most of the fashionable facades. Visitor information can be obtained from the **Harrison County Information Center** at the southeast corner of Elm and Walnut streets. On the north side of Walnut, the **Corydon Capitol State Historic Site Visitor's Center** is next to **Governor Hendricks' House**. Built in 1817 by Davis Floyd, the New Albany luminary who mistakenly joined Aaron Burr's conspiracy, the house served as Governor William Hendricks' residence during his term of 1822-25.

The **Old Capitol** was built 1814-1816 at a cost of $3,000. It is an unadorned, two-story cube of rough-cut limestone, topped with an octagonal cupola, furnished with many period architectural elements harvested from other vintage buildings, including some furnishings from the Old Goshen Church. The building was used as the county courthouse until 1929, when the current **Harrison County Courthouse** was finished at the corner of Walnut and Capitol. The 1873 **Kintner House** on Capitol Avenue is the second hotel to bear that name. The hotel where Morgan received the news of Gettysburg and Vicksburg was located on the northeast corner of Capitol and Beaver. That structure burned after the Civil War. The current Kintner House is a fine B&B and provides tours.

The **Old Treasury Building** at the corner of Walnut and Mulberry served as the state treasury and auditor's office until 1825. The state treasury vault was secured in the cellar. Travel north on Mulberry then west onto High Street to the **Constitutional Elm Memorial**. In the sweltering days of June 1816, the state constitutional convention convened under the vast canopy of this magnificent tree, fashioning the statutes that became the law of Indiana. A nearby spring cooled their libations and lubricated the debate. In the early 1920s, elm disease attacked the grand tree and by 1925 it was dead. Initially, a bumbershoot of roofing protected the remaining five-foot-diameter trunk, but in 1937 a hundred-ton sandstone canopy was constructed by WPA and CCC workers.

West of the Constitutional Elm is the **Westfall House**, the oldest existing house in Corydon, built in 1807. It was eventually owned by Colonel Lewis Jordan, who commanded the Corydon Home Guard during the Battle of Corydon. Continue west to Water Street and the railroad track. Turn left to the **Corydon Scenic Railroad Depot** and the Louisville, New Albany and Corydon Railroad. The railroad has a well-defined mission: since 1883, the train runs the 7.7 mile track to connect to the Southern Railroad at New Albany, the shortest railroad in Indiana, "the Dinky" as it is known locally. They still use the rare stub switch in their yards, which was outmoded even in the Civil War era, rather than install new-fangled switch points. Today they handle over ten thousand freight cars a year for local industries. They also operate the **Corydon Scenic Railroad**, 210 W. Walnut, which hauls passengers on the weekends along the route that Morgan's Raiders took north out of Corydon.

To the east of the depot, turn right on Oak Street to the 1817 **Posey House.** The house is owned by the local Daughters of the American Revolution, who have operated an historical museum since 1925, including artifacts of the Battle of Corydon. The museum was partially financed by the sale of memorabilia crafted from the sawed-off limbs of the Constitutional Elm. Returning to Walnut Street, turn right to Capitol Avenue, then turn right to **Branham Tavern**, built in 1808. The two-story log structure was built by Territorial Governor William Henry Harrison.

The **Battle of Corydon Memorial Park** is located south of Corydon downtown on Capitol Street. On July 9, 1863, 450 local militia and local citizens faced twenty-five hundred Confederate cavalrymen led by General John Hunt Morgan. A monument honors the dead of both North and South. A marker details the battle. At the **Cedar Hill Cemetery**, located back in Corydon on Summit Street, there are gravesites of the fallen, including Confederate soldiers, as well as veterans of every war beginning with the Revolution.

Leaving the cemetery, go north one block to Elliot Avenue and then right two blocks on Capitol. On the right is **Cedar Glade,** where townspeople took refuge during the Civil War battle and where Morgan's errant cannon shots landed. The Georgian-influenced house, also known as the **Kintner-McGrain House**, was built in 1808 and is listed on the National Historic Register. When Morgan's men were foraging for horses, they exchanged their worn-out mounts for fresh ones. One of the Kentuckians' horses was Lady Morgan, a fine thoroughbred mare who became the matriarch of a renowned line of southern Indiana horses known as the Edward Everett horses.

Returning to High Street, proceed west to the 1890s **Lenora Brown School**, perhaps the oldest extant former African-American school in Indiana. Until the 1950s, Corydon African-American grade-schoolers were segregated to this school. Nearby, the 1904 **James Best House** is the childhood home of one of America's icons, the actor who played Sheriff Roscoe P. Coltrain on television's *Dukes of Hazard*.

Corydon is also home of some long-lived companies. Take the street leading west opposite Cedar Glade to the **Keller Manufacturing Company**. Since the nineteenth century, the company has crafted wood products. Initially, it was wagons—250,000 from 1901 to 1935 alone. Their primary product line is now solid wood furniture. They are the largest Corydon employer. On Valley Road off Mulberry Street, the **Zimmerman Art Glass Company** produces entrancing art glass paperweights, as they have since 1961. If you've ever wondered how they got those glass flowers in those clever little objects, this is the place to find out.

Route 135N, which follows **Morgan's route** to Salem, is **another alternative to the Ohio River Scenic Route.** The alternate loop is sixty to eighty-five miles, depending on whether you return to Corydon via Route 135 or loop through the old mineral springs resort valley of French Lick and West Baden.

North of Corydon 12.7 miles, the crossroads town of **Palmyra** obtained a post office in 1823. It was hopefully named after one of King Solomon's rich caravan towns in the Syrian desert. The original land lessor, Hays McCallen, gave up the land because he felt hemmed in by two new towns emerging four and six miles away. Palmyra is at the junction of two of Indiana's earliest roads: the Mauckport Road that became Route 135, and the Buffalo Trace that crossed Indiana from Vincennes on the Wabash to the Falls of the Ohio at New Albany and became Route 150. The trace was pounded out by the millions of bison migrating from the prairies of Illinois to the salt licks in Kentucky. In some places the road was pounded six feet into the earth, wide enough for two wagons to drive abreast. The **Buffalo Trace Park,** .7 miles east of Palmyra, celebrates the historic trail. The 146-acre park includes recreational facilities and primitive camping. North of Palmyra a few miles, Morgan's men camped for the night.

Continue north on Route 135 another thirteen miles to **Salem**, site of a short fight during Morgan's invasion. Salem was the home of attorney Horace Heffren, who was discovered to be the Deputy Grand Commander of the

Knights of the Golden Circle. He was a state's witness in the 1864 military trial that convicted several Indiana citizens of treason, including Dr. William Bowles of French Lick.

When Morgan reached Salem, he was only sixty-five miles from Indianapolis, relatively under-manned and over-populated with Confederate prisoners. Camp Morton was brimming with four thousand Confederate prisoners who could have been armed with guns from the arsenal. Instead, Morgan carried on east to Vienna and Lexington. His decision to turn east at this point may have been a mistake, because within the next twenty-four hours, Governor Morton had mobilized militia and troops, and Morgan was on the run.

A marker on the courthouse lawn commemorates the skirmish where the town's eighteen-inch-long cannon failed to ignite because the gunner dropped his match. Morgan and his men burned the town's depot, water tank, and bridges; pillaging like "boys in an orchard." As the raiders rode out of Salem, they unrolled bolts of calico and gave them to the women and girls of the town.

To return to the Ohio River Scenic Route, you can loop west on Route 56 to **Paoli,** an old Quaker town with one of Indiana's vintage courthouses, up Route 150W to **French Lick,** and visit the magnificent and resplendantly restored **West Baden Springs Hotel**. Then proceed south on Route 145 to Route 62 and the Scenic Route. Or return to Palmyra and Route 150S to follow another leg of Morgan's outriders down the Buffalo Trace. Or, naturally, return on Route 135S to Corydon.

Visitor Information

Harrison County Chamber of Commerce, 310 N. Elm, Corydon, IN 47112, 812-738-2137, 888-738-2137.

Washington County Economic Growth Partnership, 210 N. Main, Salem, IN 47167, 812-883-8803.

Orange County Economic Growth Partnership, P.O. Box 281, Paoli, IN 47454, 812-723-3388.

Recommended Reading

Corydon the Forgotten Battle of the Civil War, W. Fred Conway, New Albany, 1991, is a nice primer to Morgan's Raid.

Recommended Regional Dining

Magdalena's, 103 E. Chestnut, Corydon, IN 47112, 812-738-8075, is renowned for pies and chicken and dumplings.

Granny's Ideal Cafeteria, 221 E. Chestnut, Corydon, IN 47112, 812-738-1644, has the best Hoosier fried chicken in the county, a local favorite.

Donahue's Cafe, 400 N. Capitol, Corydon, IN 47112, 812-738-8954, is the place for libations. They specialize in steaks.

Needmore Buffalo Farm, 4100 Buffalo Ln. SE, Elizabeth, IN 47117, 812-968-3473, serves a not-to-be-missed buffalo burger. They also have lodging available.

Brewer's General Store, 118 W. Walnut, Corydon, IN 47112, 812-738-6047, serves a variety of ice creams, root beer floats, and Amish products in the midst of wooden rakes and Amish rockers, as they have since 1931.

Campgrounds

Wyandotte Woods State Recreation Area, 7240 Old Forest Rd., 812-738-8232, has class A, B, and C class campgrounds.

Recommended Bed & Breakfasts

Kintner House Inn, Capitol Avenue and Chestnut Street, Corydon, IN 47112, 812-738-2020, is a grand old inn, lovingly restored, across from the Old Capitol Square.

Beechwood Country Inn, 8513 Route 56W, French Lick, IN 812-936-9012, is a circus and casino magnate's mansion, opulently decorated with period antiques. There is also a fine dining facility on premises, with a well-chosen wine list.

Courtesy of Harrison County Chamber of Commerce

The Needmore Buffalo Farm is home to southern Indiana's largest bison herd.

Courtesy of Harrison County Chamber of Commerce

The Old Capitol as it looks today.

Marengo Cave has drawn tourists to its magical caverns since the late 1800s.

Caves to Cotton Mills

Corydon to Cannelton 55 miles
Milltown Alternate Loop 30 to 45 miles

Chalk-powder clouds dust a pale blue sky, tinting the river gunmetal and silver. The sycamores' white bark shines in the morning sun, as the Kentucky bluffs glow yellow across from Derby, Indiana. Cries of thousands of waterfowl drift in my open window as towboats pushing football fields of black coal slide inexorably down the stream with a dull thrum. Behind Derby's log cabins, spare white church and tidy homes, the rugged hills rise row upon row like rumpled sheets.

Derby is on the wild, undeveloped section of the river that runs from Corydon to Cannelton, a highland region of steep, eroded cliffs and deep caves. It is on the most isolated section of the river without a power plant or major industry, with more than fifty miles between bridges across the Ohio. Scenic canoeing rivers like the Blue course down from the area's highlands, through glades and bluffs and forests to empty into the Ohio. The hills above the river teem with wild turkey and deer in the patchwork of state parks and national forests. Through this section, the Scenic Route crosses the 188,000-acre Hoosier National Forest, from Artist Point and Buzzard Roost in the eastern part to Rocky Point near Cannelton in the west. The rugged landscape of hardwoods, ravines, outcroppings, and streambeds extends almost forty miles to the north, offering a wealth of camping, hiking, picnicking, and swimming spots.

As in much of the Scenic Route, the people here celebrate tradition, living in a world still mostly removed from malls and suburbs and interstates—Crawford County just added its first stoplight. In neighboring Perry County, the hamlet of Rono changed its name to Magnet a while back—back in 1899. But folks in the area are still partial to the old name, and you're most likely to be directed to Rono as not. It's a place of church suppers and picnics, where neighbors pitch-in to help one another. Time moves at a slower pace; meetings tend to start a little late and digress with a certain charming predictability. In spite of the strong work ethic, the job gets done when it gets done, not when a junior executive declares the just-in-time delivery decrees it. Deer and wild turkey seasons are still big events, with businesses factoring them into their schedules.

The rugged terrain defeated the railroads, and the river was still a main road long after its importance declined at other spots along the river. The people of Crawford and Perry counties have never turned away from the Ohio, and it still figures large in culture, business, and recreation. Bargemen live in the tiny towns, taking the long commute down the river to the Mississippi and Gulf. Uniformed Coast Guards striding down the street of a river town are a strong reminder that the maritime tradition lives on.

"The river's the boss," says Elmer Cooper, a sinewy guy with a tanned bald head, an open smile, and a piece of adhesive tape across the bridge of his nose. Cooper, who lives near Derby, is one of the few commercial fishermen left on the river, catching fiddlers and flatheads mainly. A river breeze rustles the cottonwoods outside his windows as the river flows by. "I can't walk past this window without looking out at the river. See what it's doing." Pictures of the 1997 flood sit on the table, showing piles of mud that lay where we talked. "We had twelve inches of rain in forty-eight hours; river came up in two days. But I can't leave. I just like this river."

You won't find any McDonald's or Wendy's along here. Perched on a scenic aerie above a horseshoe bend in the river, the Breeden Family has served Hoosier fare at Leavenworth's Overlook Restaurant since the 1940s, and the menu remains remarkably the same. This isn't the place for spa food, but you can have some of the nation's best fried chicken, country ham, and pies while enjoying the most spectacular view on the Scenic Route.

This section of the Scenic Route through Crawford and Perry counties is definitely upland country. The southern hill country of Indiana that stretches across the bottom third of the state is physiographically composed of three hilly upland belts, two limestone plateaus, and two lowlands. As the Ohio River Scenic Route traverses west from the Ohio state border, it passes through the sprawling ridges and deep branching valleys of the Dearborn Upland. At Laughery Creek on the border of Ohio and Indiana's Dearborn County line, it descends to the Muscatatuck Regional Slope, a tilted limestone plateau with walled canyons and damp, crawfish-rich flatlands, and drops further into the Scottsburg Lowland, dominated by the wide alluvial plains of the Muscatatuck and White rivers' drainages.

Proceeding west, the topography begins its ascent again, as if it's climbing a flight of tilted stairsteps. First there is the Knobstone Escarpment, the most prominent physiographic feature in Indiana, more than six hundred feet above the Ohio at New Albany. The Knobs are the transition to the Norman Upland, plateau-like here in the south but rumpling into the steep-sided canyons of Brown County further north. The slice of the Norman Uplands are followed by the pocked limestone karst geology and red clay soils of the Mitchell Plain that extends north toward Bloomington.

The Knobs, the Mitchell Plain, and the Brown County Hills to the north are some of America's most rugged terrain east of the Rocky Mountains, acting as a highland rim above most of the surrounding landscape. It is a biologically rich, topographically challenged region, part of the nation's Interior Low Plateaus Physiographic Region that runs from North Alabama all the way to Morgan County south of Indianapolis.

The Chester Escarpment at the western edge of the Mitchell Plain heralds the Crawford Upland, which escaped glaciation as did the Norman Upland. The Crawford and Norman uplands acted as the cleavers of the glaciers, dividing them around these highland islands. At the eastern edge of the Crawford Upland in Crawford County, dozens of caverns course through the porous, Mississippian-era limestone, a world-famous caving area. Indiana, and particularly the Mitchell Plain that stretches to the north, is pocked by hundreds of thousands of sinkholes that drain into subterranean cave systems, over a thousand sinkholes per acre in some areas. There are more than twenty-two hundred known caves in Indiana with more than ten miles of mapped passageways, home of rare animal life including endangered bats, colorless crayfish, and blind white cavefish. But only two, Wyandotte and Marengo, have more than twenty miles of explored passages, and they are here in the Crawford Upland.

Since at least 2200 BC, when Native Americans first mined flint in Wyandotte, humans have used the caves. Aragonite, an easily worked carbonite used to craft artifacts, was mined from 1 AD to 690 AD in Wyandotte Cave, several thousand feet from the sunlight. Settlers and soldiers mined saltpeter for gunpowder from Wyandotte from the War of 1812 to the Civil War. Later, entrepreneurs mined epsom salts from the caverns.

By the mid-1850s, tourists began making their way into the rare and fragile beauty of the mysterious underground. "The myriad miracles in stone whereof we were the witnesses," one nineteenth-century visitor wrote, "were wrought by One to whom darkness and light are alike, and who loves beauty, whether in the tropical forest or the sunset sky, or in the marble halls and crystalline gardens of this deep and lonely cave." For thousands of years, humans have marveled at the ethereal elegance of the stone draperies, the rhythms and harmonies of the tiered stalagmites and straw stalactites, the power of relentless nature in the frozen wonder of the flowstones. Today you too can journey into Indiana's underground at Wyandotte and Marengo caves, both listed on National Registry of Historic Landmarks.

Marengo Cave, with its Crystal Palace, is considered one of America's most beautiful caves, a privately run facility with an education center and other recreational facilities. Wyandotte is a state recreation center, with Mountie-hatted rangers leading tours into the extensive caverns, alternately educating and good-naturedly terrifying their charges.

Many of the trails, structures, and facilities in the Harrison-Crawford State Forest were built as part of the Civilian Conservation Corps program during the Depression. This innovative federal program was one of many, including the WPA, that provided vital employment during the Depression's darkest days. One of Franklin Roosevelt's aides and architect of the program, Harry Hopkins, was warned that the emergency programs wouldn't work long-term. "People don't eat in the long-term," he replied. "They eat every day." Today, the state and nation is left with a magnificent legacy of those programs. Many of Indiana's finest public buildings and facilities are permanent memories of this temporary agency.

Indeed, much of the state and federal land that dominates this region's maps and economies are a legacy of the Great Depression, when the hills were dramatically depopulated. The thin soils and rugged hills of the Crawford and Perry County highlands were always a daunting challenge for the yeomen farmers, who tried to farm a few hardscrabble ridgetop acres and run hogs in the woods. Indiana's broadleaf forests were among the finest of their kind in the world. Late in the nineteenth century, there were still forty-two kinds of trees over a hundred feet high existing in the Wabash valley alone. But during the European American settlement period, the enormous forests were felled and most of the trees dragged to the ravines to rot, mirroring in many ways the deforestation happening in the rainforests of Brazil and southeast Asia today.

By the Depression the forests were gone, erosion had scarred the land, the small fields were "corned out," exhausted from generations of declining crop production. The days of the small subsistence farms were over, and farm after farm lay abandoned through the hills, taxes unpaid, cabins and small houses with their front doors hanging open.

The federal and state governments began the enormous task of reforesting the region, returning it to the mesic forest environment we see today, a mosaic of trees and ferns and wildflowers, massive sandstone cliffs and seeping springs. The springtime floral displays of dogwood, redbud, umbrella magnolia, laurel, firepink and wild geranium can rival the southern Appalachians.

Down Route 66 past Leavenworth, the road twists and turns back down to the river through some of the prettiest forests on the Scenic Route, passing through the sleepy hamlets of Oriole, Dexter, Magnet, Derby and Rome. In the northern interior of the county, villages like Leopold and Siberia maintain traces of the mid-nineteenth-century Belgian, French, and Russian colonization efforts by the Catholic missionaries. As the road reaches the band of level ground along the river, prosperous farms and towns that speak of a wider river commerce reappear.

Perry County is as wrinkled as an old hounddog except for patches of the river valley, mainly from Cannelton to Tell City. This narrow belt is the site of some of the earliest industrial development in the Middle West. In the midst of the dozing shoreside village of Cannelton, a vast rambling sandstone edifice with twin Italianate spires hunkers down, as incongruous as a brontosaurus in your neighbor's backyard. The sprawling building is the remnant of a remarkable nineteenth century industrial concern, the Cannelton Cotton Mill, one of the largest industrial complexes in mid-America in the years before the Civil War. New Englanders built the mill in the 1840s to pioneer steam-driven manufacturing in the western hinterlands, exploiting the nearby cannel coal seams and the New England mill girls who came to Indiana on two-year contracts. Through the decades, the company produced a variety of textiles, from sheets and famous "Hoosier Jeans" to feedbags and beach-set novelties before closing in 1954.

Mileage

133.0 Crawford-Harrison County Line. Crawford County has been described as the poorest real estate in Indiana. The lack of settlement across the river in Kentucky prevented the northward drift of southern uplanders who populated other stretches of the Indiana shore. The high hills in the Indiana hinterlands made pioneering particularly arduous, and conspired to keep the number of settlers low. Crawford was incorporated in 1818 with a few thousand hardy residents. The county's population has long been one of the most nativist in the state with a high number of the original inhabitants being Hoosier-born.

By 1880 Crawford County and neighboring Perry were among the four poorest counties along the lower Ohio River. Today, there are few industries here, and the topography keeps the farm sizes Lilliputian by agribusiness standards. Although poor in dollars, Crawford County is one of the richest in the state in natural beauty, both above and below ground. Half of the county's acreage is forested, with more than thirty thousand acres in state and national forests. Tourism is rapidly becoming an important part of the economy, with the river, the state and national recreational areas, new private resorts, and Patoka Lake, Indiana's second largest man-made lake, in the northern part of the county.

134.0 Wyandotte Caves State Recreation Area is a twelve-hundred-acre facility that includes the world-renowned Wyandotte Cave, home of some of America's largest subterranean rooms and columns. The park rangers offer six tours, from a short introduction tour to an all-day tour with the path leading through Worm Alley and Crawfish Springs. No one with a chest larger than forty-four inches should attempt Jones Discovery.

The Monument Mountain tour takes the visitor past helictites, rare twisted and spiraled cave formations, to the world's largest underground mountain. A half-day tour includes a trip to the Senate Chamber and the impressive Pillar of the Constitution.

The Wyandotte Cave Recreational Area is part of the Indiana State Harrison-Crawford-Wyandotte Complex. Across the road from the caves, the Wyandotte Woods Recreational Area is a twenty-one-hundred-acre facility with one hundred miles of horse trails and ten hiking trails, including the twenty-two-mile-long Adventure Trail. Campgrounds and cabins are available for rent, including the old CCC Camp for large group camping. The recreational area extends one mile along the Ohio shoreline and two miles along the Blue River.

Named for its clear blue, spring-fed water, the Blue River is a meandering canoeing river that courses through the hill country, past caves and bluffs and wooded glades, foremost among Indiana's Natural and Scenic River System. "The Blue is the most natural stream of its size in Indiana," the renowned ecologist Alton Lindsey wrote in the 1960s, and it remains so today. Bullfrogs' basso voices fill the dappled air, calling incessantly, "Jug o' rum, more rum." Raccoons primly wash their dinner, as turtles plop from their logs like animated stones when canoeists pass. Minks still live along the streambed. Catfish, darters, rock bass, perch, and drum swim the water. To add a mild touch of danger, the stream remains the only habitat of the hellbender, a giant poisonous salamander that can reach fifteen to twenty inches in length. The hellbender is a flabby, wrinkled specimen with a wide head that is among the largest salamanders in the world.

141.0 **Old Leavenworth** is located down on the river at the eastern edge of Leavenworth. Look for the road sign for Old Route 62 or Bluff Road and follow the winding road down the bluff. Founded in 1818, the town was once one of the principal shipping ports along the Ohio, with nearly two thousand residents. It served both as a wood yard for the passing steamboats and a shipyard. One shipyard started in 1830 was still operating well over a hundred years later. From 1843 to 1894, it was the county seat, until more centrally located English wrested the honor away.

In 1863 Captain Thomas Hines and a detachment of scouts for Confederate General John Hunt Morgan's raiders were trapped on an Ohio River island about a mile south of the town at the confluence of the Blue. It became a holiday for the townsfolk as they gathered at the riverbank to watch the gunboats and militia shell and shoot the entrapped soldiers. Home guardsmen sniped at the rebels, using the ammunition and provisions brought by their wives. After several of the rebels were killed or wounded, most of the Confederates surrendered, though Captain Hines and a few others escaped across to Kentucky.

Leavenworth flourished in its natural amphitheater, surrounded by high forested hills and bluffs, looking out to the dramatic horseshoe bend of the river. But in the winter of 1937, the full force of the flooding Ohio poured into the natural *cul de sac*, and Leavenworth's amphitheater became an amphibiatheater. Over 111 homes and twenty-one businesses were destroyed or damaged, leaving only eight habitable houses. Faced with the moldering ruin, the town voted to move up on the bluff and, with the help of the Red Cross and government agencies, built a new town—today's Leavenworth.

Old Leavenworth continues to be occupied, a mixture of old, cobbled-together houses, some summer cottages along the river, and a grand old abandoned brick building that was once the water and electric company. In all, it's a place with the air of a slightly raffish yesterday.

142.0 New **Leavenworth** basks in the sunlight up on the bluff, a tidy town of frame houses, most dating from the construction in the 1930s and 1940s. **Stephenson's General Store** on the town square is a combination grocery, gallery, hardware store, and town museum. The **Town Hall Gallery**, open on the weekends through the warm months, offers the arts and crafts of dozens of the area's artists. Three antique and craft shops invite browsing.

Route 62, as it runs from Louisville to the Illinois border, was known earlier in the automotive era as the Wonderland Trail. Old-timers intimate that is was the route for Prohibition-era bootleggers moving hooch from the hills and the German farms to the west to the metroplitan areas. While the Kentucky moonshine industry appears to have had better press relations, since they got all of the infamy, southern Indiana was also a major bootlegging area.

The Overlook Restaurant at the west edge of town has become a landmark since they started serving folks after the town moved up on the bluff. "It's a little bit like Noah and the Ark," the Breedens say. "Everything around here dates back to the time after the flood." Originally, it was a little cafe and grocery on the second floor of the O-Hi-View chicken hatchery—chicks below, fried chicken above. Like many enduring Hoosier cafes, the Overlook kept going by becoming the Greyhound bus stop, providing a steady if small income in the cash-poor small towns of the 1940s and 1950s.

As tourists discovered the view and the food, the Breedens just kept on adding to the place. They now have seating for 225 in the sprawling establishment's multiple dining rooms, all offering stirring views of the oxbow bend far below. In the best bus stop tradition, they serve every day except Christmas Eve and Christmas. Only a fool or a diabetic would miss the Overlook's homemade pies. The coconut cream pie is part rococo architecture, part smile-producing gastronomy.

143.0 **Tower's Orchard, Peach and Apple Shed** at Route 66N is a great place to stock up on munching material and take in the view, should you have failed to satisfy yourself at the Overlook.

Turn north on Route 66N for an **alternate loop** to Marengo, Milltown and Patoka Lake. At Marengo, you can either go east or west to loop back to the Scenic Route. The alternate loop is thirty to forty-five miles depending on whether you go east to Milltown or west to Patoka. The latter is longer. The Ohio River Scenic Route itself continues on Route 62W to Route 66S. Mileage indicated in the left hand column refers to the path of the Ohio River Scenic Route which stays on Route 62W/Route 66S through southern Crawford and Perry counties.

Twelve miles north on Route 66N, **Marengo** is the home of another famous Indiana cave. Discovered in 1883, **Marengo Cave**, with enormous cavern rooms like the Queen's Palace and the Crystal Palace, is one of the nation's most beautiful. Schoolboys from the local academy originally found the cave opening, but plucky fifteen-year-old Blanche Heistand overheard them boasting about their find, and she and her younger brother Orris crawled in first to take the honors of discovery. The farmer who owned the property opened the cave for tourists immediately, and it has been the economic mainstay of the rustic little community since.

There are several tours through the cave, and the cave operators recently added a digitized historical presentation in one of the caverns. The cave facility also offers canoeing, horseback trail riding, hiking, fishing, and a picnic area. The Outdoor Center features courses on cave exploration, a cave simulator, gemstone mining, and a climbing tower. One of Indiana's oldest and largest trees, the **Old White Oak** one-hundred feet tall and sixteen feet in diameter, stands near the cave parking lot.

Milltown on the Blue River is four miles east of Marengo on Route 64. **Cave Country Canoes** rents hundreds of canoes and kayaks for trips down the limestone-bluffed valley. The **Blue River Cafe** is a gastronomic gem, offering gourmet fare in an unlikely setting. If you chose to return south to the Scenic Route, follow the road along the Blue River five miles to an intersection to one of the Crawford County's claims to fame: the **Shoe Tree**, where hundreds of old shoes hang from a bedraggled tree. Reportedly, a pair of basketball star and coach Larry Bird's monster shoes are among them. There is a handmade sign on a utility pole in Milltown pointing the way. After your commune with the old soles, continue south on the road five miles to Route 62 where you rejoin the Scenic Route near Wyandotte Caves.

Proceeding west about eighteen miles from Marengo on Route 64 will take you to the highland region of eighty-eight-hundred-acre **Patoka Lake**,

Indiana's second largest nan-made lake. The $65 million multi-purpose fa-
cility was dedicated in 1980. Besides the lake itself, there are four state recreational areas around the lake covering an additional eighty-eight-hundred
acres; seventy-nine-hundred acres are devoted to wildlife. **The Newton-
Stewart State Recreation Area** on Route 164 north of Eckerty offers nature interpretation in a solar-heated center, along with camping, swimming,
boat launching, and diverse amusements. Take Route 64W for fourteen miles
to Taswell, turn north on Route 145 for three miles to Route 164W to the
Newton-Stewart signs. Near Taswell, **White Oaks Cabins** offers furnished
cabins in the midst of a fourteen-acre wildlife refuge.

At Taswell you can also proceed west under the railroad trestle and proceed to the **Yellow Birch Nature Preserve**, the only place in Indiana where
yellow birch, hemlock, and mountain laurel occur together. Continue south
four miles to **Hemlock Cliffs**, an exceptional natural site of deeply cut sandstone cliffs, waterfalls, and caves of archaeological interest. The nature preserve is particularly magical in the spring when the enchanter's nightshade
and jack-in-the-pulpit are in bloom. Continue south five miles to Route 37
at Grantsburg. Turn south on Route 37 which will cross Route 62 in three
miles and become Route 66, to put you back on the Ohio River Scenic Route.

144.0 Proceeding west from Leavenworth on Route 62, there is a county
road that turns south to **Fredonia,** Leavenworth's longtime rival for ascen-
dancy in the county, one mile past the Route 66N intersection. Through the
nineteenth century, the Crawford County seat bounced among four towns,
beginning in Mount Sterling in 1818. The county seat moved to Fredonia
in 1823, ostensibly because Mount Sterling failed to have an adequate water supply. Fredonia flourished as the county seat and shipping point in spite
of its location high on the bluff, which necessitated a tough tote up from the
river. In 1843 the promoters of Leavenworth succeeded in moving the seat
to their town, and Fredonia never recovered. Remains of the old courthouse
may be seen, and a community center that is a replica of the building. The
county seat settled in 1893 in English, which sat to the north astride the
Southern Railroad.

148.0 Turn south on Route 66 to **Sulpher,** where a general store sells
refreshments, and a never-open antique store has intriguing window displays.
The ghost spa of **Sulpher Springs** is 1.5 miles south, one of the bustling
mineral water spas that flourished in Crawford County at the turn of the
century, when entrepreneurs shipped the rotten-egg-smelling mineral water and a concentrate all over the Midwest. The White Sulpher Spring Hotel,
a three-story structure that served up to 250 health seekers at a time, prospered for years before burning in 1910. As late as the 1940s, Sulpher Springs
was still a popular resort, with cabins and rooms in private homes. A stand

pipe in a pavilion is all that remains.

149.6 **Crawford-Perry County Line.** Named after Oliver Hazard Perry who forced the British navy in 1813 to surrender a squadron of ships on Lake Erie, **Perry County** was formed in 1814. Following the battle, Perry dispatched his oft-repeated bluster to William Henry Harrison: "We have met the enemy and they are ours." Given that the broad Ohio forms the county's border on both the east and south, it was appropriate the forefathers chose a nautical namesake. The river remained a vital transportation link in the county, as the irregular terrain kept railroads away till a small line came to the southwestern corner late in the nineteenth century. The lack of rail transportation isolated the region, providing it with the nostalgic air it has today.

Like Crawford County, half of Perry is forest, with a substantial part of the county in government hands. More than sixty-thousand acres are in the Hoosier National Forest, with five man-made lakes. The riverbottom forms the only flat ground in the county, the location of the prosperous farms and the county's industrial development in Cannelton and Tell City to the west.

The Catholic Church was instrumental in the settlement of Perry County, with missionaries colonizing the interior through the middle decades of the nineteenth century with European immigrants. Grand stone churches stand in tiny villages as a reminder of the pious past and continued devotion. Today, incongruously Gallic and Russian names are painted on rural Hoosier mailboxes and general stores.

153.0 **Oriole** was originally named Chestnut City for the stand of trees that flourished there. It developed late in the nineteenth century as an archetypal rural town, with its grain elevator, post office, school, church, and town doctor. Today, the gable-fronted white clapboard **Oriole Methodist Episcopal Church**, built in 1870, still stands proudly. Nearby, the 1913 **Oriole Grade School** is still there, but in substantially rougher shape. Look for the hand-painted signs for antiques and collectibles and you'll find a quirky trove of well-ordered detritus and occasional treasure.

157.0 Founded in the nineteenth century by French immigrants, **Mount Pleasant** has only a few houses left, but the road to the west leads in four miles to the French-Belgium hamlet of **Leopold**, named after King Leopold of Belgium. The town was platted in 1842 and colonized in the 1840s, primarily by immigrants from Les Bulles, Belgium, later joined by settlers from France, Luxembourg, Ireland, Alsace-Lorraine, and Germany. Scattered along the back roads are examples of Creole-style overhung porches surrounding modest double-pen farm houses, like something out of Louisiana or the French West Indies.

The Gothic Revival **St. Augustinius Church** was built between 1866-1873. During the Civil War, four compatriots from the village, Henry

Devillez, Isadore Naviaux, and Lambert and Xavier Rogier were held prisoner in the South. As they prayed for survival, they vowed to provide a statue for the church when they returned home. Three of the men survived, and they commissioned a statue of the Virgin Mary holding the Christ Child to be carved in Luxemburg. It still stands in the church. Food and libations today can be had at **Good Time Charlie's**, and **Guillaume's General Store** is a friendly haven of small town commerce.

159.0 **Magnet**—Rono, as the locals persist in calling it—is a bucolic little spot on the river, with Kentucky farmland across the way. Rono got its name from the 1830s when steamship wood-yard owner Jess Martin's beloved coon-dog by the same name frequented the waterfront. When the dog died, it was buried in the middle of the docking area, and the name stuck. You've got to love a place that remembers its good dogs. The **Some Other Place** tavern serves whistle-wetters, catfish fiddlers, and other bar fare. The verandah-ed old hotel across the way was built in 1908.

The **Magnet Overlook** north of town is a nice picnic location, affording a long sweep down the river. It is a particularly good vantage point to watch the river traffic, including the giant excursion boats like the *Delta Queen* and *American Queen* when they make their regal way down the stream. A few miles upriver, the U.S. Forest Service maintains **Buzzard's Roost** as a scenic overlook, though sometimes the banks are so overgrown it is more a scenic leaflook. In 1857 a slaughterhouse and commercial smokehouse was built nearby. Since only half of the carcass could be used for smoking, the balance became the provender for the flocks of buzzards who were attracted to the site. Mother buzzards found it so homey that they set up enormous roosts nearby, raising their spectacularly homely broods a short flight from the convenient commissary. Today, it is a good place to spot bald eagles.

The site of **Galey's Landing**, an important shipping point for many years, is about a mile and a quarter from Magnet. The **Prather Family**, renowned horse thieves, lived nearby. The Prathers ran a ring in the 1850s that stole fine horses from Kentucky, corralled them in several spots in the vicinity including a rocky canyon near Mt. Pleasant that came to be known as Penitentiary Rock, and then moved them down the Rome-Vincennes Trace to Missouri for sale. According to the reports, the sons paraded the stolen horses by their rheumatism-ridden father, Robert, as he sat in the breezeway. As he had the best eye for horseflesh, he priced each animal. When the horses were sold in Missouri, the sons returned to the farm to bury the booty.

In May 1858 a band of vigilantes from Crawford and Harrison counties raided the farm and arrested six of the Prathers. The Prathers were sentenced to the penitentiary, where all except one died. According to the reports, the surviving son returned to the homestead after his prison term, dug up a chest of gold coins, and sailed off in a skiff from Galey's Landing. The old farm and Penitentiary Rock have been the site of many a treasure hunt since.

In August 1865 the steamship *Argosy III* was churning home with a roster of mustered-out Civil War veterans, when a storm near Rono hurled the ship against some rocks, bursting the boilers. The blast killed ten Union soldiers returning home after surviving the horrors of war. Local farmers buried them in a mass grave beside the river, forgotten until 1962 when the incident came to light. It wasn't until 1965 that the federal government, on the prompting of local citizens, erected **ten white grave markers** at the grave site. They can be seen, along with a historical plaque, .5 miles south from Magnet along the river. The same local family has tended the cemetery since Clyde Benner cleared the grave site. "It's always been maintained by our family," his daughter Pat Irwin said. "We stop and do whatever needs to be done when we see it needs a cleaning. I look at those names and I think, 'They had a mother, didn't they?' I always ask myself if someone wonders where they are."

167.0 **Derby** was the epicenter of the Catholic settlement of the county. Two Catholic families pioneered here in 1805, attracting a priest, and in 1818, a parish, St. Mary's on the River. The town was laid out in 1835, named after Derby, Ireland. Not surprisingly, a distillery was the first commercial venture.

In the 1830s the Bishop of Vincennes appointed Father Julian Benoit to minister to Perry County's Catholics. Benoit wrote to friends in France, Belgium and Germany, urging Catholics to migrate to Indiana "to spread God's Kingdom." As the immigrants heeded his words, several Catholic missions developed around Derby and later into the interior of the county in places like St. Croix, Siberia, and Leopold.

Derby prospered as a river port, shipping lumber-related products such as barrels, chairs (Perry County's first factory), and railroad ties. In the town's heyday, there were 103 people, three stores, two banks, and two saloons. A disastrous fire in 1893 ended the golden age. After that, the town was a declining spot on the river until an influx of second-homers began to have an impact in the 1970s and 1980s. Today, there are several pristine riverside cabins for rent as well as recreational facilities in the area.

The **Hoosier National Forest** surrounds the area, with eighty miles of hiking trails, five lakes, hundreds of camping spots, and eight mountain biking trails. The entire county is a bicyclist's haven, with hundreds of miles of quiet country lanes and trails to tour. A fine bike-touring map is available. The **Mano Point Boat Ramp** is in constant use, launching craft to cruise the river's eighteen-thousand-acre Cannelton Pool. The unfortunately named **Oil Creek** is a bayou-like canoeing stream, a pristine home to thousands of water fowl. The **Mulzer County Park** in Derby is a shady riverside picnic spot. Should you need supplies of any nature, the **Derby General Store** is adapted for today—beans and spices tucked in with videos, fishing gear, car batteries, and greeting cards. **Ramsey's Derby Tavern** is the hub of the town, locals gathering on Wednesday night to eat spaghetti and solve the town problems.

Derby even boasts a town troubadour, Ed Gluck, who floated two lashed-together canoes into town, carrying himself, a girlfriend, a cat, and a goose "up on the poop deck." He put aside his life as an industrial electrician in Ohio to canoe down the Tuscarora and the Muskigum through old hand-operated wooden locks to the broad Ohio. "Getting on the Ohio, that was a thrill," he said. "It was like being Tom Sawyer." He floated for months down the river, camping on islands and living in caves, until he settled in Derby, where he took a liking to the townsfolk, and they took a liking to him. "They bought me this guitar," he said, his reddish bangs and blue eyes belying his fifty-four years. So Ed set off to write songs about every lady in town, "to keep things even." They are songs of river visions, moonlight rising from the riverside hills, boats bobbing in the current. "You've got those sapphire eyes," Ed sings, and the Derby folk sit back for another night's entertainment.

169.0 **Nancy Alice Martin** returned home to the family farm after her father's death in 1929, after a celebrated career from 1905 to 1925 as Alice DiGarmo, circus trapeze artist. In 1934 hired-hand Ernest Wright argued with her over back wages of $2.75. Evidently the employee conference was not to Wright's liking—he slit Martin's throat with a folding pocket knife and buried her in the barnyard, where her body was discovered a week later. Martin is buried in the Lower Cummings Cemetery two miles to the north. Wright later died in prison.

170.5 Captain Thomas Hines and sixty-four Confederate soldiers landed here on June 17, 1863, as a scouting party for General John Hunt Morgan. The **Hines Crossing Marker** commemorates the landing. He and his men exchanged their worn-out horses for fresh ones from the local farmers under the pretext of being Union soldiers looking for deserters. The Rome-Derby road has long been known locally as the Rebel Road.

173.4 **Rome** was Perry County's first seat of government, founded in 1818. The stately public square that surrounds the classical brick courthouse reflects the town planning as a place of gravity and government. The declining river traffic, and the transfer of the county seat town to Cannelton, sent the town into somnolence. But the bones of the nineteenth century vitality remain in the proud structures that are dotted through the town, and the village retains the air of nobility as it basks quietly beside the river.

The **Rome Courthouse** was built between 1818 and 1822, a Federal-style building based on the new state capitol at Corydon. Built on a high lime-stone foundation, it is a two-story, hip-roofed structure with a large cupola on top. After the county seat moved to Cannelton in 1859, the building served a series of private and public schools, including the area's high school until school consolidations in 1966. Since then, it has served as a town hall and community center. It is listed on the National Registry of Historic Places and is considered the state's oldest existing courthouse. It, and the 1851, two-story white clapboard saltbox **A. Thomas Wheeler Hotel** on Chestnut Street, lend an almost New England rectitude to the public square.

The **Connor** and **Shoemaker Cemeteries** dating from early in the nine-teenth century have exceptional folk-art carved gravestones. The Conner Cemetery is located at the end of the river road to the north of the village. The Shoemaker Cemetery is .25 of a mile to the south of Rome.

Outside of town, the county road runs north 3.2 miles to the **German Ridge Recreation Area,** a rugged landscape palisaded with spectacular cliffs. This was the first campground built by the Depression-era Civilian Con-servation Corps in the Hoosier National Forest. This county road to Ger-man Ridge follows the earliest Indian and pioneer trails in the region, run-ning from Vincennes to the Sinking Creek in Kentucky across from Rome.

177.1 **Route 166** runs down the Tobinsport Peninsula, the earliest settle-ment in the county, dating from 1802. The **Rocky Point Marina and Camp-ground** offers refreshment and various sporting sundries, as well as a camp-ground.

In 1960 a Chicago-Miami flight carrying sixty-three people fell apart in mid-air and crashed into a hillside soybean field. The plane hit the ground at 600 mph, burying the nose fifty feet deep. Parts were strewn from Ger-man Ridge to Gatchel ten miles to the north. Proceed 1.6 miles down Route 166 to Millstone Road. Turn east a mile to the **Air Crash Memorial**. The memorial commemorates the thirty-foot-wide, twenty-foot-deep smoking crater surrounded by trees hung with the passengers' clothing that the first rescuers discovered. There were no survivors of the tragedy. All of the re-mains that could be gathered barely filled two coffins, which were buried along with five empty ones in the Cannelton Cemetery.

There are also few remains of the village of Tobinsport, except for a good B&B. For many years a well-respected Amish herbalist and iridologist, **Reuben Schwartz,** offered his services near the village. Iridology is the sys-tem of diagnosis based on the examination of patients' eyes, almost a codi-fication of the innate sense of health that we discern when we meet some-one. "The eyes don't lie," as they say. Reuben detected digestion, cardiac, respiratory, and gland trouble in the color, texture and intricate designs of the eye. Indeed, most of his patients came to him after medical technology failed them. In 1997 Schwartz moved to an Amish Community near the Kentucky-Tennessee border. His iridology clinic continues in Tell City at "Herbs and Health Care" on Route 37N.

The **Red-Tailed Hawk Inn** is on the river. Proceed past the turnoff for Reuben Schwartz to the Y along County Road 45 to the inn, approximately .75 of a mile on the right.

178.2 Proceeding west on Route 66, the **Lafayette Spring Marker** commemorates the site of Elephant Rock, where the steamboat *Mechanic,* carrying the hero of the Revolution, Marquis de Lafayette, snagged a floating tree and shipwrecked on a dark night in May 1825. As with many things, Indiana and Kentucky have squabbled for decades over which side of the river Lafayette landed, cold and sodden on that rainy night. The ship was precipitously sinking when Lafayette discovered his snuff box was missing. He sent his servant below to retrieve it, as the other passengers fled to the skiffs. By the time he grandly descended to the lifeboat, fully dressed and powder-wigged, the boat was overloaded and unstable in the rough water. Lafayette lost his footing, and he and his wig tumbled into the water. Luckily, a couple of sailors plucked him from the river. He spent the night either under an umbrella on the Kentucky side or in a cabin on the Indiana side, depending on the statehood of the commentator. Either way, the next day found him on the Indiana side, where another steamboat took him upstream to the Falls Cities. The *Mechanic* sank ten minutes after the collision and sits today on the bottom, along with the remnants of the Marquis' carriage, clothing, and about $8,000 of his money.

The river banks begin to flatten in this section of the Scenic Route, and the bottoms are furrowed into rich corn and tobacco fields.

179.0 Replacing three smaller dams upstream, the **Cannelton Locks and Dam** were built between 1963 and 1974 for $99.6 million, taking as much concrete to build as seventy miles of interstate highway. Local resident **Arch K. Boyle** was the civil engineer on the project. The high-lift dam created a vast, 114-mile, eighty-seven-thousand-acre lake that extends to Louisville, the longest on the Ohio. The dam guarantees a nine-foot pool for navigation. The two locks can raise or lower a vessel up to thirty-seven feet by filling and draining more than a million gallons of water in the lock chambers, bringing the boat to the level of the next pool. One lock is twelve hundred feet long, allowing full-sized commercial barges to proceed through the locks intact. The auxiliary lock is six hundred feet long, necessitating breaking the barge trains into two parts. The Cannelton Pool is thirty-seven feet lower than the pool at the McAlpine Dam in Louisville and twenty-five feet higher than the next one downstream at Newburgh, Indiana. Many of the shipping companies that tow (actually the term is a misnomer as the powerful tugs *push* the barges from the rear) the enormous string of barges up and down the river operate like rail lines, picking up a few barges here, dropping off a few there.

181.0 The **Bob Cummings Bridge**, named after a Cannelton newspaperman, leads to **Hawesville, Kentucky**. The **Hancock County Museum,** located in the old railway depot on Water Street, contains displays and artifacts relating to the river, farming, and valley life. It is open Sundays 2-4 PM. **Captain John W. Cannon**, pre-eminent steamship captain, is honored by a memorial at the foot of the bridge. Cannon owned and captained many boats on the rivers, including the *Robert E. Lee.* The **Riverview Restaurant** on Old Highway 60E serves regional fare including quail, froglegs, and bumbleberry pie from an overlook over the locks and dam.

The **Squire Pate House** is located five miles west on Route 334 (River Road) across from Troy, Indiana. In 1827 this was the site of Abraham Lincoln's first trial, following his arrest for illegally operating a ferry into the Ohio at the Anderson River confluence. It is said that Lincoln's success at defending himself encouraged him to attend court proceedings whenever possible and to take up the study of law.

182.1 In 1837 a group of Eastern capitalists formed the American Cannel Coal Company to exploit the easily mined coal near **Cannelton, Indiana,** for steamboats and manufacturers. The town, and neighboring Tell City and Troy, became early industrial sites in the nineteenth century. In 1844 there were only fifteen water-powered grist mills. By 1872 there were fifty steam-powered mills, mainly industrial, located in the flat land along the river.

Cannelton, with two thousand inhabitants, prospered through the nineteenth century with coal mining, pottery and ceramic tile manufacturers, and brick yards. The most significant of the manufacturing ventures was the founding of **Cannelton Cotton Mill** in 1849. The austere sandstone building with one-hundred-foot Italianate spires looms over the town yet today. The five-story building housed steam-driven mills in seventy thousand square feet of space. When the mill was conceived, the intent was to rival the New England textile industry, to become as the prospectus promised, the "Lowell of the Ohio." The investors hoped to make Cannelton the progenitor of industrial development in the Midwest and South. The Cotton Mill was the largest industrial building in Indiana and one of the largest west of the Alleghenies, 280 feet across the frontage and sixty feet deep with walls as much as three feet thick.

New England architect Thomas Tefft utilized finely hewn (ashlar) sandstone from the area for the walls. A two-hundred-foot-high smokestack rose above the surrounding hills to catch the draft needed for the boilers. The twin towers were inspired by the architecture of Lombardy, one housing a fire escape, the other a water tower. The northern spire held a bell used to call the workers to their shifts. Textile mills are always prone to fire and spontaneous combustion because of the mill dust and lint that floats through the air. In spite of open gas lamps in the work rooms, the Cannelton Mill never experienced a major fire. Tefft built lint removers, wide staircases, and a water hose in every room.

By 1851 three hundred spinners, bobbin girls, and lap boys tended 10,500 spindles whirling the cotton of the Deep South into thread and cloth. Most of the workers were young New England women, brought out to the West on two-year contracts. The mill stood at a fortuitous spot. The nearby coal seemed inexhaustible for the raging boilers—coal production was over five hundred million bushels by 1847. The cost of transporting cotton up the river from the Southern plantations was dropping dramatically as steamboats became common. The price of upstream transport dropped from $10 per hundred pounds to $3 during the 1850s. The river offered easy transport of machinery and labor from the East, and transport of manufactured goods back to the markets.

But the mill quickly encountered difficulties: the steam technology was troublesome, cotton suddenly soared in price, and seasonal shutdowns caused by low water created intense labor friction. The investors ran into financial difficulties relating to the co-ownership of the mines and mill. The Civil War totally disrupted the supply of cotton. By 1861 the mill output was dramatically reduced; by 1863 it was closed. In the latter stages of the war, Southern mill workers were sent north to work in the Cannelton factory after the war destroyed the Southern mills. The company survived by manufacturing Union army uniforms, as they did in subsequent wars. Local historians say a Union gunboat threatened the mill with shelling during the war, to insure delivery of new uniforms. Evidently, they must have sailed away looking natty, as no shot was ever fired.

After the war, faced with competition with lower-cost Southern mills, the Cannelton mill turned to the manufacture of cheap sheeting. By 1890 there were 309 employed at the mill, seventy-eight of them men. At the turn of the century, the company was best known for the manufacture of "Hoosier Jeans." The Cannelton Cotton Mill operated under several owners until 1954, making a variety of textiles for the mass market, from sheeting to inexpensive clothing to woven rayon flour sacks, towels, and beach-set novelties. The mill is listed on the Registry of Historic American Engineering Records and the National Registry of Historic Places. In 1990 it was listed as a National Historic Landmark.

The town still bears the mark of the early New Englanders. The **Cannelton Historic District** bounded by Richardson, Fourth, Washington, and Adams streets, includes examples of architecture from 1837-1936. The spare mill building, and the fine ashlar stone houses on Route 66 (Seventh Street), speak of the esthetics and architectural traditions of New Hampshire. Cannelton's first church and cultural institution was the Unitarian Church, started in 1845, the first in Indiana. New England thriftiness is apparent in the reuse of many vintage buildings, including the **Free School**, Indiana's oldest operating school building at the corner of Sixth and Taylor streets. The building has been in use as a school since its construction in 1869. Even the stained glass windows and church bell of the 1845 **St. Lukes Church** at 101 East Third are recycled. The windows are from England, circa 1800, and the congregation salvaged the bell from the *Major Balfour* which sank off of Troy in 1848. The church is listed on the National Registry of Historic Places. The brick **Mason/Sulzer/Newcomb House** next door to St. Luke's Church at 109 South Third Street was built in 1867 for a local judge and was owned in the 1880s by an owner of the Cannelton Cotton Mill.

The **Perry County Courthouse** was built in 1896 of yellow brick and Bedford limestone. Cannelton wrested the county seat from Rome in 1859 and lost it to arch-rival Tell City in 1994. The stately sandstone **St. Michael's Church** on 8th and Washington streets was started in 1858 for the German Catholics in the town, completed twelve years later. The **Sunlight Hotel** at First and Washington was built in 1929.

The 1937 Flood inundated the town, filling some of the buildings with water up to the second floor. At one point, a local man rowed through town, towing a pair of four-hundred-pound hogs behind him. The flood precipitated the construction of the flood wall that eventually was built in 1950.

Visitor Information

Crawford County Tourism Bureau, c/o Wyandotte Caves, 7240 Old Forest Road, Corydon, IN 47112, 888-8GOLD97.

Perry County Convention and Visitors Bureau, P.O. Box 721, Tell City, IN 47586, 812-547-2385, 888-343-6262.

Hoosier National Forest, 248 15th St., Tell City, IN 47586, 812-547-7051, 800-280-2267, for camping information.

Recommended Reading

Caves of Indiana, Richard L. Powell, Indiana Department of Conservation, Indianapolis, 1961, is the classic text.

The Natural Heritage of Indiana, edited by Marion T. Jackson, Indiana University Press, Bloomington, IN, 1998, has a good chapter on caves and Indiana physical characteristics.

Geology of Indiana, Kenneth D. Hunt, Kendall-Hunt, Dubuque, IA, 1989, is a textbook designed for non-specialists.

Recommended Regional Dining

Overlook Restaurant and Lounge, Highway 62, Leavenworth, IN 47137, 812-739-2120 celebrated fifty years of serving guests from their magnificent spot over the twisty Ohio. It is a bastion of Hoosier-style cooking.

Blue River Cafe, Milltown, IN 47145, 812-633-7510. After seventeen years in Chicago and San Francisco, owner Ric Archibald returned home to Milltown to open the Blue River Cafe in a rustic, old general store. He serves some decidedly upscale victuals like Black Angus beef in a garlic, rosemary, and mushroom sauce, and chocolate ganache torte with raspberry coulis.

Ramsey's Derby Tavern, Route 66, Derby, IN 47525, is an institution on that section of the river, serving hearty bar food in a congenial small town atmosphere.

Riverview Restaurant, Old Highway 60 East, Hawesville, KY 42348, 502-927-8417, serves some unusual regional fare on a high bluff above the Ohio.

Recommended Bed and Breakfasts and Cabins

Leavenworth Inn, State Road 62, Leavenworth, IN 47137, 812-739-2120, is a restored turn-of-the-century home filled with antiques. It offers a workout room, tennis court, and a walnut-paneled library with an open fire and lots of *New York Times* best sellers on the shelves. The spacious front porch looks out the Ohio.

White Oaks Cabins at Patoka Lake, R.R. 2, Taswell, IN 47175, 812-338-3120, has comfortable cabins in a forty-five-acre wildlife sanctuary.

Ohio River Cabins, 13445 SR 66, Derby, IN 47525, 812-836-2289, offers a variety of riverside retreats in a peaceful environment.

Red Tail Hawk Inn, HC 65 Box 52A, Tobinsport, IN 47587, 812-547-8889, is on the river in a very quiet part of the world. It is a B&B, but will serve dinner if given notice.

Camping

Wyandotte Woods State Recreation Area, 7240 Old Forest Rd., 812-738-8232, has Class A, B, and C campgrounds available from March 15-December 1.

Patoka Lake, R.R. 1, Birdseye, IN 47513, 812-685-2462, has several campgrounds around Indiana's second-largest man-made lake, including the **Newton-Stewart Recreational Area** along the southern shore closest to the Scenic Route.

German Ridge Recreation Area-Horsecamp, 248 W. 15th St., Tell City, IN 47586, 812-547-7051, has primitive camping, and horse and mountain-biking and hiking trails.

Indian-Celina Lakes Recreation Area, 248 W. 15th St., Tell City, IN 47586, 812-547-7051, offers swimming, boating, and a small grocery.

Hoosier falls make the backroads a phantasmagoric of autumn color.

Courtesy of Vince Vermeulen

A lovely wanderer enjoys a float down the limestone-bluffed Blue River.

Photo by Douglas Wissing

Photo by Richard Fields

The towers of the Archabbey of Saint Meinrad at dusk.

Indiana's Old World

Tell City to Grandview 17 miles
Spencer County-Dubois County Alternate Loop 65 miles

It is 5:00 AM on a drizzly, dark, spring morning, when the monastery bells begin tolling from the belfries. Another insistent clangor rings fifteen minutes later, signaling sleepy townsfolk and guests to shuffle into the Romanesque sandstone abbey. As the bells peal once more a quarter of an hour later, dozens of monks scurry down the hall from the enormous monastery into the church, their cowled cassocks trailing behind them like ravens in a slipstream. Soon, the medieval airs of Gregorian chant mingle with the last tones of the bells, drifting out over the surrounding southern Indiana hills. Nestled below, the tiny town of St. Meinrad is tucked into a tableau of farm, forest, and hillside that looks more Bavarian than Hoosier.

There is a hint of Germany's Black Forest in Dubois, Spencer, and the western part of Perry counties—not surprisingly since it was the home of thousands of immigrants who colonized this part of Indiana in the 1840s. Indiana's Old Country is a place formed by culture and intent, an environment pruned like an immense topiary to a shape that feels just right to the inhabitants. Barely a generation ago, German was the first language in the region's homes, churches, and schools. Today the local accent, "dutchie," still sing-songs to Teutonic cadences. It's a prosperous, scrupulously clean, devout area. At the center of the state's furniture and woodworking industry, the hardworking Indiana Germans export to the world. Family farms are still big business here. Dubois County is a state leader in hog and turkey production. Families are tight. After college, children often return to their hometowns. When Grandma goes to the hospital, it's with round-the-clock family care till she returns home.

From Jasper in the north, down through Ferdinand and Huntingburg to Tell City on the Ohio River, the rural lanes wind through Old Country vistas, ablaze with wildflowers. Villages cluster around the hilltop churches like chicks around a hen. Tractors putter past small, fastidious family farms, baseball-capped drivers offering a minimalist forefinger wave. Roadhouses and cafes serve regional specialties like turtle soup and turnip slaw, bratwurst, brain sandwiches, and wiener schnitzel, with schooners of beer the size of goldfish bowls to wash it all down.

It's a conservative, somewhat insular place. One fifth-generation Spencer County farmer told me the term "Hoosiers" is a bit of an insult down there, referring more to cars on blocks and rusting trailers in other parts of the state than to heroic basketball players. "Yeah, we think those Indiana Hoosier flags up in the bars, they're kind of a joke," he said. Rivalries run deep. The two main towns of Huntingburg and Jasper have an antipathy that runs back to their founding time 150 years ago, with the panoply of slurs refreshed yearly. They both have disdain for the "Hoosier" hill villages like Celestine and Birdseye that dot the area around Patoka Lake. "Birdseye— right," one Dubois County teacher said. "My dad always said they named it after the wrong end of the bird."

Ten twisty miles from the monastery at St. Meinrad, the sprawling brick Monastery of Immaculate Conception at Ferdinand glows rose-red in the late light. A Benedictine convent established in 1867, it is the home for generations of the region's teachers. I asked Sister Sylvia, a white-haired gamin who came to the convent when she was fifteen, why the area is so traditional. "I think a lot of it," Sister Sylvia said, "is they were taught by the sisters. Many of the schools were staffed by the sisters—Catholic and public, both. Of course, now it is lay teachers mainly, replacing the sisters as they retired. But even now, the teachers who teach in the schools were taught by the nuns. So it continues."

Up to a few decades ago, the sisters comprised almost the entire teaching staff of the Jasper public school system, the area's largest town, which made sense, given that substantially more than ninety percent of the townspeople were German-Catholic. Today, the region retains a devotion and respect for their churches that is unusual in our secular times, though the prosperity is attracting non-Catholics. Several people proudly told me about the various denominations that have opened up, including a Morman church in Jasper. The Catholic Church remains the most important cultural and spiritual force, though. A local antique dealer told me, "Whatever the Father says, that's it. It goes."

The comment would have pleased Father Joseph Kundek, who masterminded the colonies in the 1830s and 1840s, envisioning the close-knit German communities that eventually prospered in southern Indiana. Kundek was a Croatian assigned to the few German-speaking families who had already settled in the area. Kundak founded towns throughout the region, and then widely advertised them in German-language publications. The candy-ribbon road, Route 545, follows the trail Father Kundek blazed along the Anderson River, connecting his colonies that were a day's oxen cart ride apart. In 1840 it took three arduous days to get from the Ohio River at Troy to Jasper, a drive of forty minutes today. In a few cases, he was a touch more visionary than candid. Local lore says that the first families who arrived in the village of Ferdinand found the town to be nothing more than a hand-lettered sign tacked to a tree in the forest that read, "Ferdinand."

Yet the Germans came in a steady stream, from the 1830s up to the Civil War. Wracked by the aftermath of the Napoleonic Wars and a rapidly changing economy that devastated their cottage industries, the Germans came to Indiana not to build a new life, but to continue an old one. The Indiana migrations were part of a vast movement of people—*auswanderer* as they were known—out of the German principalities into the larger world, from the steppes of Russia and the mountains of Brazil to the Hill Country of Texas and the banks of the Missouri near Herman, Missouri. It was conservative migration to maintain traditional life patterns, not to pioneer new ones. And 150 years later that conservative propensity continues.

While the area may be devout, it's certainly not dour—the Indiana Germans play as hard as they work. In towns where the streets are sometimes *strassen*, it's natural that the festivals are *fests*—and there are a lot of them. The largest, Jasper's Strassenfest, is held at the beginning of August. It's a riot of activities: an art and craft fair, a parade and beer garden, fireworks and German food, music and dancing, with an accordion player leading the St. Joseph's Church choir in a Polka mass on festival Sunday. Tell City celebrates their Swiss-German heritage with their Schweizer Fest, one of Indiana's longest-running festivals. Huntingburg has its Herbstfest (Harvest Festival) in October. Ferdinand's Heimatfest (Fall Festival) is the last weekend in June. Haysville's Sommerfest is the third weekend in July. Those with more eclectic tastes can attend the Zoar Mosquito Fest near Huntingburg on the first weekend of August. Church suppers are still a center of socialization, purveying hundreds of gallons of turtle soup for parishioners and guests under the spreading shade trees.

Holiday World & Splashin' Safari at Santa Claus, Indiana, is an award-winning theme park. Recently, the park's "Raven" was named one of the world's top three wooden roller coasters. Their Christmas Lake golf course is celebrated, as is the Sultan's Run course in Jasper. Patoka Lake at the eastern edge of the region attracts fishermen and boaters of all stripes. Several state forests and parks offer a variety of recreational possibilities. Jasper's Community Arts Center brings entertainment to the area, including stars like the Vienna Boys Choir, Judy Collins, and Marty Robbins.

Dubois County is a long-time baseball hot spot. Indiana's Baseball Hall of Fame is located in Jasper. In Huntingburg, hometown baseball continues to thrive in the vintage League Stadium, home field for the Dubois Dragons. The movie, *A League of Their Own*, with Madonna and Tom Hanks, was filmed there. Beyond its increasing fame as a movie set, Huntingburg is known as an antiquing destination, with antique shops and malls peppering the Victorian main street. The entire region is a quilt of antique shops, carrying everything from rough country furniture to elegant, high-style pieces that migrated down the river. The region has some of the best bicycling (and scenic driving) on the Scenic Route, through a landscape of rolling hills and shady lanes and villages that feel about as European as you get in America. The best views and the right rhythms are on the old roads that meander along at an agricultural pace through the countryside, like the St. Anthony's Road between Jasper and Ferdinand, the Old Huntingburg Road between Jasper and Huntingburg, or the Ferdinand Road between St. Meinrad and Ferdinand. Give any of them a try. Just take a left turn somewhere onto a twisty little two-laner, take a deep breath, and wander back a hundred years or so.

Mileage

183.0 Tell City was founded in 1858 as a Swiss-German manufacturing community. In 1856 eight thousand Swiss immigrants were dues-paying members of the Swiss Colonization Society, headquartered in Cincinnati. The society was dedicated to purchasing a homestead site where Swiss-German mechanics, shopkeepers, factory workers and small farmers could form a city with a diversified economy and enough prosperity to support a cultured town. The founders sought a location at least one hundred miles below the Falls of the Ohio in a state without slavery, with easy access to Southern markets. For an investment of $20, each settler anticipated receiving two plots of land. In 1857 the Society purchased 4,154 acres of land between Corydon and Troy, which was the site of the first coal extraction west of the Appalachians.

In 1811 an associate of steamboat inventor Robert Fulton, Nicholas Roosevelt (great-uncle of President Theodore Roosevelt), accompanied by his wife, descended the Ohio in a steamboat named the *New Orleans*. Two days after the boat took on coal at Tell City from a coal mine owned by Roosevelt, the New Madrid earthquake rumbled through the Midwest, the most severe quake in American history. The quake was so strong it rang church bells in Boston and redirected the Mississippi River, forming Reelfoot Lake, the Roosevelts just missing the quake. Mrs. Roosevelt delivered her baby somewhere near New Orleans.

The Tell City land passed from Nicholas Roosevelt to Robert Fulton to Fulton's heirs. Judge Elisha Huntington bought the property from them and sold his holding to the Swiss Colonization Society for $85,000, with the first payment of $20,000 in gold being made at Cannelton. The Swiss Colonization Society was active in the administration of Tell City until its disbanding in 1879 when the remaining lots were distributed for schools and parks.

The eighty-foot-wide, two-mile-long Main Street trumpets the ambitions of the settlers. The grand boulevard, wide enough to turn a horse team and wagon, was to be the main thoroughfare for a city of ninety thousand. They laid the city out into four hundred town blocks with seventy-six hundred residential and garden lots. The street names honored their heroes, as well as cultural and economic ambitions: Franklin, Jefferson, and Washington; Mozart, Pestalozzi, Gutenberg, and Schiller; Fulton and Watts. Being European, the Swiss honored an inordinate number of foreign-born Revolutionary War luminaries: Lafayette, DeKalb, and Steuben, as well as Tell Street for their namesake.

By the summer of 1858, there were almost two thousand settlers in town. The Society gave each settler enough materials to build a two-room house to be repaid in three yearly installments. They were expected to build a brick or frame dwelling worth at least $125. The following year, the Society convened in Tell City and voted to finance the most worthy business proposals, among which was the beginnings of the long-lived **Tell City Furniture Company.** The Society also voted to start a shingle factory and buy a wharf boat. Within five years, the town bustled with a flour and grain mill, a plow and wagon factory, a brewery, with the comings and goings reported by the town newspaper that was founded the same year as the town.

In 1866 Tell City shipped forty-eight hundred chairs down the river, along with twenty thousand feet of flooring, hundreds of pieces of furniture, 240 cotton presses, sixty half-barrels of beer, and 300,000 pounds of foundry castings. The burgeoning economy must have kept everyone occupied, because there wasn't even a town jail until the 1870s. The Chair Makers Union of Tell City formed the **Tell City Chair Company** in 1865. For more than thirty years the most popular chair was their Pattern #1, a double-cane, split bottom chair. Over twelve thousand were made annually, with the frames made in the factory and farmed out to cottages around town for caning by women and children.

As the decades progressed and new designs were added, the distinctive seating was sent around the world, including to the White House. Jacqueline Kennedy purchased gilded Tell City chairs for the White House dining room. After many years of labor strife, the company closed its doors in 1996. The 1865 brick industrial vernacular building that was the headquarters is located at 417 Seventh Street.

A block south on Seventh Street, the **William Tell Woodcrafter Building** has **Flood Level Marks** painted on the northwest corner of the building, showing the levels of the 1883, 1884, 1907, 1913, and 1937 floods. The 1937 flood was the final straw—Tell City was the first city in Indiana to erect a flood wall. The wall became a piece of art in 1994, when a mural in Sunset Park at Seventh and Washington was completed. It depicts the early history of Perry County. **The Tell City Industrial Historic District** encompasses most of the south end of the city's business district from Blum to Humbolt and is a collection of industrial buildings from 1860 to the 1960s.

The 1896 brick and limestone **Perry County Courthouse and City Hall** at Main and Mozart was built for $50,000. The three-story building was a tad extravagant for a city hall, but the town fathers anticipated wresting the county seat from next door Cannelton, which they did, but not until a hundred years later and in a new building. Entirely too large for a City Hall, parts of the building were used through the decades as a school, library, church, and town theater. Tell City basketball started on the third floor of the City Hall. During the 1937 flood, it was the headquarters for the Red Cross. Until the 1880s all of the town and court records were in German.

Statue of William Tell and His Son Walther, dedicated in 1974, stands in front of the government building. Based on a statue in Altdorf, Switzerland, it commemorates the thirteenth-century Swiss hero after whom the town was named. According to legend, the expert crossbowman was forced to shoot an apple from his young son's head by the Austrian oppressors. However, it was an early case of Swiss propaganda—the legend is something of a misstatement of the event. The bronze statue almost didn't make it to town for the dedication, as thieves stole the van hauling it from the foundry in New York to Ohio. Luckily, it was found a week later with the statue still inside. Conjecturally, the thieves had little luck with their fencing efforts, as a statue of a medieval Swiss crossbowman has a somewhat narrow market.

The Tell City Pretzel Company is two blocks south at 632 Main Street, the last purveyor of traditional German hand-twisted pretzels. In 1858 a Swiss master baker, Casper Gloor, began baking his pretzels with a secret recipe. After his death in 1912, the recipe passed to his assistant, who in turn passed it to his two sons. Jim Elder purchased the business and the recipe in 1972 and has been twisting away since. The Tell City pretzels are a teeth-challenging bit of yesteryear that are shipped all over the country. Most of the twisting is done in the morning, and you are welcome to stop by and see culinary history.

The Chamber of Commerce and the Visitor and Convention Bureau is located in the old **Southern Railroad Depot** at Main and Blum streets. The brick depot was built in 1915 after the previous one burned. The are several examples of nineteenth-century commercial architecture in town, like the 1885 Italianate **Tell City National Bank** at Main and Pestalozzi. The Neo-classical **William Tell Hotel** at Main and Washington was built in 1890. The Victorian flourishes of Main Street reflect the burst of affluence that followed the arrival of the railroad. The 1950s glass and stainless-steel fa-cades reflect the florescence of the Auto Era, as does the 1955 Frostop Drive-

In at 947 Main. Stop in for a dog and suds.

The Old Stone House at 1239 Thirteenth Street, a double pen constructed of rough-cut sandstone, is the earliest house in town, dating from 1854. It served as an early meeting house and school. Sitting obliquely on a rise above the uniformly level surroundings, the house predates the right-angle planning of the Swiss.

185.0 The eighteen-foot-high **Christ of the Ohio Statue** was fabricated by an ex-German prisoner of war, Herbert Jogerts, who returned to Indiana to practice his art after being incarcerated in Kentucky during WWII. He is responsible for several pieces of monumental religious art in the area. The statue is cast of a durable material composed of Terrazzatine dust and concrete. It has been a landmark for boaters on the Ohio since its dedication in 1957. Across the road from the statue, there were many potteries along the river, including one started in 1837 by the renowned English Staffordshire potter, James Clews, who thought that Indiana clay would be suitable for whiteware. He soon found that not to be the case and closed his pottery the next year. However, other, less picky potters used the local clay for much of the nineteenth century, manufacturing utilitarian Bennington-type pottery.

186.0 Virginian families platted Troy, located at the mouth of the Anderson River, in 1815. It was one of the earliest towns below the Falls of the Ohio. The small, brick, single-pen house that sits between Spring and Main streets on Franklin (Route 66) speaks of an Eastern esthetic sensibility. **The Nestor House** at 300 Water Street is a remnant of Troy's nineteenth-century commercial heyday along the river front. The rough-cut sandstone, Greek Revival building dates back to 1863 and has served as a grocery, tavern, hotel, and now a private residence. Local lore has it that the basement served as a waystop on the Underground Railroad. A Greek Revival house on Market Street at Harrison was built in 1840, as was the gable-fronted Greek Revival in the next block east and the I-house at 525 Walnut Street. Vintage structures ranging from Queen Anne to Craftsman are dotted through the tiny town. **Fortwendel's Hardware Store** on Market Street is a bustling general goods store with crafts among the chicken waterers and electrical supplies located in a well-maintained turn-of-the-century commercial structure.

Troy was Perry County's first seat, but when the county was reorganized in 1818 with expansions, Rome's central location was more appealing to the county's solons. The seat was moved to Rome in 1819. Troy continued to prosper through the nineteenth century as a port town for the road that ran along the Anderson river north into the German hinterlands. **St. Pius Church** is the most visible landmark in the town with its 142-foot bell tower. Built 1881-84 to serve the area's German Catholics, the new church replaced one built in 1847 when the waves of German immigrants were arriving at the waterfront.

Market Street leads to the site of **Camp Koch,** which was built in 1948 to provide summer recreation for handicapped children. The camp closed in the early 1990s, and the buildings are being used as a community center. The bluff affords a thirty-mile view of the river. The hilltop is known as Fulton's Bluff, because Abraham Fulton, Robert's brother, died building a house on the hill when an enormous log rolled onto him. There is a marker to Fulton on the west edge of Troy. He arrived in Troy in 1814 to build a woodyard and manage his brother's coal mine. It is said when the early smoke-belching *New Orleans* puffed past Troy in 1811, the Troy residents took to the bushes in fear. Fulton is buried in the **Troy Cemetery** at the end of Washington Street, the first European buried in what was an old Indian burying ground.

By 1826 the townsfolk were substantially more sanguine about steamboats, as they were a common sight on the river. **Abraham Lincoln** worked in the village, helping out on a ferry boat that crossed the Ohio and picking up extra money selling wood to the steamboats for fifty cents a cord. To add to his income, he built a small scow to haul passengers out to midstream to board the passing steamboats. A Kentucky ferryman allegedly had Abe hauled into court for operating a ferry without a license. Lincoln, seventeen at the time, studied the law and pled his own case before Justice of the Peace Samuel Pate across the river in Kentucky. Lincoln argued that since he traveled only to mid-stream and never crossed the river, the law didn't apply. He won the case, and his success cemented his interest in the law and learning. In some sense, the Gettysburg Address and the Emancipation Proclamation began here on the Ohio. A roadside park at the Anderson River at the west edge of Troy commemorates the event with a roadside marker.

187.1 Route 545N is an **alternate loop** along the Anderson River through the heart of the German colonies. If you want to skip this segment, proceed west thirteen miles on Route 66 to Grandview to stay on the Ohio River Scenic Route. The Scenic Route is through a wooded section of bottoms, with a barge-loading operation five miles down the road. The alternate loop is approximately sixty-five miles long, and passes through the monastery towns of St. Meinrad and Ferdinand and north to Jasper, the region's largest town, returning through the antiquing destination of Huntingburg and the historic theme park village of Santa Claus.

Route 545 follows the trail that the pioneer priest Father Kundek blazed along the Anderson River to the colonies he founded. The towns of Fulda, Ferdinand, and Jasper were laid out a day's ox-cart ride apart.

New Boston is three miles down Route 545, one of the prettiest biking and driving roads in the Midwest. The New Boston Tavern is an old roadhouse, serving regional fare like smoked pork chops, frog legs, and fiddlers on the weekends. At County Road 1290N, follow the red markers to **Huffman's Mill Covered Bridge,** one of the few remaining in Indiana. **Troxel's Fort** was a horseshoe-shaped stone fortification four feet high and two hundred feet in circumference located in a nearby field. Its origins are hazy and attributed to some fairly exotic folks. Some say it was built by one of the French pirate Jean Lafitte's men, who migrated to Indiana. Yet another claims that the fortification was built by that peripatetic twelfth-century Welshman, Prince Madoc, who is credited with the fort at Rose Island near Clarksville. Whoever built it obviously enjoyed the high ground and an easily defended position.

Returning to Route 545, turn north again. In a few miles, the 150-foot steeple of the mid-nineteenth century **St. Bonifacius Kirche Catholic Church** rises from the landscape as if in a fairy tale. The Romanesque interior has sixteen stained glass windows and an 1895 535-pipe organ. Come summertime, the parish puts on a renowned turtle soup dinner, with hundreds of gallons being served in a few hours. Louie's in Fulda is another roadside attraction, regionally famous for their turtle soup.

Be prepared for incredulity as you round a bend and the **Archabbey of St. Meinrad** appears as though air-lifted from the Fatherland. At the behest of Father Kundek, the Benedictine monastery was begun in 1854, and the work continues today. In 1872 the monks began construction of the sandstone complex of buildings you see today. The church with its 168-foot steeples was built in 1899-1907. Local craftsmen and monks carved most of the stone, with the sandstone coming from a quarry a mile away at Mont Cassino. The aforementioned German prisoner of war, Herbert Jogerst, fashioned the statues in the facade when he returned to St. Meinrad after the war.

The church reopened in September 1998 after a $5.2 million restoration that took four years to complete. "The church is very important to us. This is the most sacred place on the hill for the one hundred monks who live here," Restoration Committee Chairman Father Kurt Stasiak said. "It is our home. We pray here four to five times a day. I figured it out once: we're here two to two-and-a-half hours a day—that's a month a year." Stasiak headed the committee that oversaw the restoration, chairing more than one hundred meetings, including thirty with the entire monastery community. "This church is built on as much consensus as you can humanly expect. The process of this renovation renewed the way that we talk with each other," he said. "This is not a renovation for a generation, it is a renovation for the centuries."

The interior is an airy space with Gothic vaults. The six repeating vaults, symbolizing the six days of creation, are echoed by the six marble Stars of David on the floor, composed of thousands of multicolor triangles assembled from Brazil, Greece, Italy, and India by Italian craftsmen. Curls of black marble at the perimeter of the building loop together to represent the Christian fish. The white Italian marble is from the same quarry that supplied St. Peter's in Rome, and the yellow marble is the same as the thirteenth-century cathedral at Siena. Indiana craftsmen made the monks' eighty-two choir stalls, and a local artist designed the lectern and baptistery. An Indianapolis firm, Goulding and Wood, constructed the 3,844 pipe, fifty-five-stop organ that frames the enormous mural of Jesus Christ painted in the 1940s by Belgian monk Brother Gregory. The altar is composed of sixty-eight gilded bronze panels depicting the life of Christ. The only original parts of the church interior are the 1907 Bavarian stained glass windows and the columns of American marble.

Behind the fifty exposed organ pipes in the Blessed Sacrament Chapel, the ornate gilded tower of the original Bavarian Regensburg altar glints in the light that pours in from the nave windows. This is considered the most sacred part of the church, as the Eucharist is kept here, so it requires particular decorum for visitors. The balance of the altar is a floor below, a masterpiece of enamel work. The 1908-09 altar and other ecclesiastic art was removed to storage during the modernization that followed Vatican II in the 1960s. In many churches, pious clergy and parishioners painted over or removed homey religious art that succored generations in the zeal of the post-Vatican II years, like devout Catholic Red Guards. Many of the recent church renovations are an attempt to find a balance between the spareness of the contemporary churches and rococo excess of the Victorian ones.

The monastery at St. Meinrad remains one of the great centers for Gregorian chant, singing that dates back to the Middle Ages. The monks' daily singing of the medieval Gregorian chants rise into the lofts of the vaults, festooning the church's very air with sound, the sustains of the tenors ascending above the sonorities of the bass notes. The monks' daily religious services, from 5:30 AM to Vespers at 6:00 PM, are open to the public.

"It's like the medieval mystic Hildegard von Bingen said, 'I float like a feather on the breath of God,'" St. Meinrad's Gregorian chant scholar Father Columba Kelly said during a class I took on Gregorian chant. Father Kelly teaches Gregorian chant all over the country, as well as teaching the brothers and seminarians at St. Meinrad. "How you say it is how you sing it," he counsels, making Gregorian chant sound much too simple. Gregorian chant is a codified form of tonally conceived speech, devoted to sacred subjects. The melody is totally subservient to the text, decorating it, so to speak.

"You sing a note and let it hang, then sing under it. Can you hear the jubilation?" he said. Modes of quiet compassion, solemn reassurance, inner longing, power and strength came from the chants as Father Kelly deconstructed the medieval tones. Under his expert direction, the class was soon chirbling to the archaic tenth-century musical notations of the monks of St. Gall.

The Archabbey is one of only two in the United States, out of seven in the world. The twenty-five-hundred-acre facility serves as a Benedictine monastery, a seminary for Catholic priests, and a retreat for guests of all denominations. Until recently, the monastery was completely self-supporting with its own farms, smoke house, vineyards, and dairy, but now many of the agrarian operations are being phased out. The town of St. Meinrad was platted in 1861 as a money-making venture of the monks who anticipated sales of the town lots. For many decades since, the monks have supported their operation with the multi-million-dollar Abbey Press, which publishes a variety of gift and book items.

The monastery, with its gracious gardens and grounds and well-tended structures, is mute testimony to the Benedictine vow of "stability of place"— as the monks pledge to live at this monastery for their lifetime. Every nurtured tree, garden, and structure speaks of the love that generations of monks have lavished on this spot. The men who wish to become Benedictines enter the monastery as novitiates, a year-long period of study. A three-year period of Juniorate follows, another period of testing. At the conclusion of this period, the entire community votes on acceptance or denial. If the Juniorate is accepted into the brotherhood, he takes a vow of stability of place, as well as obedience to the abbot and the fifth-century rule of St. Benedict that codifies every aspect of life, from times of prayer to moderation in food and drink. The Benedictine also accepts a conversion of life, devoting himself to a life of community work and community prayer. A few decades ago, most novitiates began their studies in their early twenties, now the age is closer to thirty.

On Route 62, a half mile to the east of St. Meinrad, the tiny sandstone chapel at **Monte Cassino** is a paean to devotion, the site of an annual pilgrimage commemorating relief from an 1871-72 smallpox epidemic. Each January since that date, hundreds of monks, seminarians, townspeople, and other devotees have climbed to the unheated chapel at the top of the hill to offer prayers of thanks for their miracle. "It was twenty-five below zero windchill last January," novitiate Patrick Gallagher said. "There was steam coming out of our mouths as we said mass. It was great." The interior of the church is remarkably well-painted in a naïf style reminiscent of early Renaissance country chapels. The painting was done by German artist Gerhard Lamers in 1931.

Monte Cassino is the site of the monastery's first land, purchased in 1853. It has been a place of veneration since a shrine was erected in 1857. The cornerstone for the present chapel was laid in 1868. The shrine's first hermit died in 1886 and is buried near the chapel. The last hermit, Brother Gerold Ley, died in 1909. The hermits were part of the tradition that dates back to the anchorites in the deserts of Egypt in the earliest days of Christianity, doing "single-handed combat with the demons," as St. Benedict wrote. The nearby sandstone quarry provided much of the stone for the chapel and St. Meinrad, as well as nearby Monastery Immaculate Conception. On the lane up to the chapel, a small stripper oil well continues to provide a small touch of the modern amidst the quietude.

The companion monastery of the Benedictine nuns, **Monastery Immaculate Conception,** is located about ten miles away in Ferdinand. There are two ways to reach it. The scenic back way is down the Old Ferdinand Road that is the county road beside the lane up to Monte Cassino. Follow the road and begin looking to the treeline after five or six miles for the steeples and domes of Immaculate Conception. As in Europe, much of the town placements are steeple-to-steeple. The other way to reach Ferdinand is to proceed west on Route 62 to Route 162, and then turn north to Ferdinand. You'll cross the **Spencer-Dubois County Line** about a mile outside of St. Meinrad. That's pronounced "Doo-boyz´," by the way. It's Indiana, remember, Indiana.

Dubois County was incorporated in 1817, named after the Frenchman Toussaint Dubois from Vincennes who was the Captain of the Company of Spies and Guides and who distinguished himself at the Battle of Tippecanoe. The west half of the county is flat and rolling, while the east is hilly and wooded. The first European settlement was in the north at Portersville on the east fork of the White River near the Buffalo Trace. But the major settlements came in the 1830s and 1840s along the Patoka river as the Germans made their way to Indiana.

Either way that you travel to Ferdinand, it's hard to miss the monastery. The massive, red brick, Romanesque building has stood on the hill since 1915, added to structures that were built in 1883-87. Trimmed in Bedford limestone and Italian terra-cotta, the building is encircled with promenades and Italian-style, curlicue-columned pagodas, with an interior dome rising eighty-seven feet above the floor. The monastery and its grounds were listed as a National Historic District in 1983.

When I joined the sisters for evening prayers, incense perfumed the monastery chapel. A hundred high, thin voices drifted heavenward toward the eight painted angels gazing down from the apse. I was lost in my hymnal, flipping through the pages, when a small hand reached over and found the right one. Sister Sylvia Gehlhausen smiled—another child taken care of—and continued her song. A sweet breeze blew through the doorway as the Benedictine nuns celebrated vespers, as they have since the fifth century.

Elderly nuns in veils and habits mixed with sisters in sport clothes and short, trimmed hair. A young nun in a flowered dress raised her palms to the heavens as she sang. A sister's commentary on Matthew's gospel likened his story of the boat on a stormy sea to their own resolutions of internal storms. Two more hymns and the service was over. A few elderly sisters cut out early to get a head start with their walkers. One nun accelerated her Bravo! electric cart to catch up with a hobbling friend. "Wasn't that lovely?" Sister Sylvia said as we walked through the monastery. "Wasn't that lovely?"

Founded in 1867, the Monastery Immaculate Conception at Ferdinand is one of the lodestones of Indiana's German region, known locally as the "Castle on the Hill." It is home to 234 Benedictine sisters, though only about 130 are in residence at one time. The sisters also follow the Rule of St. Benedict, observing the same cadences and canon as the monks at St. Meinrad. The Sisters of St. Benedict are a teaching order, staffing many of the parochial schools in the region that extends down into the Catholic areas of northern Kentucky, and also sending sisters to schools in Latin America. The Monastery Immaculate Conception is also the home of the Marian Heights Academy, a boarding school for 130 young women, including a number of students from Mexico. The monastery's Kordes Retreat Center provides a haven of quiet for harried people of all denominations. "We see a lot of middle-aged, fast-track people," Sister Sylvia said. "It's like they start asking the question of life: *Is this all?*"

Ferdinand is among the more traditional towns in the region. The 1941 *Indiana: A Guide to the Hoosier State*, written by the WPA's Indiana Writers Project, notes, "Ferdinand is a German Catholic community retaining the language and customs of the Fatherland. English, of course, is understood and spoken, as is a strange admixture of the two languages. Rathskeller signs bear names such as Kunkler, Schnellenberger, and Hoppenjans. Many of the citizens carve and wear wooden shoes, or fashion wooden beer mugs and holders for pretzels."

I've yet to see anyone clomping around in wooden shoes, but the town retains some interesting customs. The Dutchmen (as in "Deutsch") around here are fabled for their thriftiness. You'll go a long way to separate a Dutchman from a dollar. They expect value for their money and they expect to deliver it for the same. Turtle soup and brain sandwiches are still big. The beer drinking can start early, in spite of a work ethic that would burn out a Japanese salaryman. Guys in the taverns play euchre and pound worn leather dice cups on the tables and bar, playing local favorites like Three Horses,

Crazy Trés, and Ship, Captain, Crew.

Jasper, the region's largest town, is thirteen miles north on Route 162. It was laid out in 1830 as the county seat at a good mill site on the banks of the Patoka River, which drains west into the Wabash. A plaque denoting the site of 1820 **Enlow's Mill** can be seen along the river by turning west on Cemetery Road off of Route 164. The marker is in the small park beside the river. The mill stood until 1963 when flood waters weakened it. A desk taken in trade for milling by Thomas Lincoln, Abraham's father, was part of the mill's property for over a century.

By 1841 there were a hundred German families in the vicinity of Jasper. The dense stands of oak that surrounded the town formed the basis of the town economy, as Jasper became the nation's wood office-furniture capitol by the next century. The Jasper Desk Company began in the mid-1860s and is still the nation's oldest operating furniture factory. A plaque on the north side of West Sixth on the courthouse square honors the location of the first **Alles Factory,** the original name for Jasper Desk. The internationally diversified furniture company, Kimball International, Inc., of piano fame, is headquartered in Jasper, as are a number of other well-respected furniture manufacturers.

The heart of the town is **St. Joseph's Church** on Newton Street between Eleventh and Thirteenth. It is a tall, brooding sandstone structure topped by a tower 235 feet high. The Romanesque structure was built between 1867 and 1880 by the parishioners. Scrutiny of the tooled sandstone blocks of the church walls reveals the various styles (and talents) of the early parish volunteer masons. The walls are four to six feet thick, and the foundation is ten feet deep. Initially, the parishioners thought they cut enough sandstone for the entire church from a nearby quarry, hauling it by oxen to the site. But when they finished the foundation, the stone had all disappeared into the hole. Many oxen loads and years later, they had enough stone for the church. The interior stone-clad columns are made of ninety-foot-tall poplar trees, the tallest that could be found in southern Indiana. Swiss stained glass, Austrian mosaics composed of over twenty million individual pieces, carved oak pews, and Italian marble altars grace the interior.

The **Plaza of Pastors** in front of the church on Newton Street honors the three early pastors: Father Kundek, Father Basil Heusler, and Father Fidelis Maute. It was erected in 1944. To the south of the church, the first **Deliverance Cross** was erected in 1848 by George Bauman, who survived a raging ocean storm by promising to erect the statue in exchange for divine intercession. The original was destroyed by a lightning bolt in 1928, and the current cross was erected in 1932.

The Gramelspacher-Gutzweiler House on Eleventh Street between

Newton and Main is the oldest house in town. Built in 1849, the Federal-style, two-story brick building housed everything from the post office to a saloon and a shoe repair shop to a toy store. The sagacious architectural historian Wilbur Peat considered it to be the most imposing structure of this style in Indiana. The stepped gables are a throwback to Jacobean and Flemish buildings, seldom seen on Federal buildings of this age and location as most examples are seventeenth- and-eighteenth-century Eastern Seaboard buildings. The house is listed on the National Historic Register.

On the town square, the site of several Strassenfest activities in August, the **Dubois County Courthouse,** built in 1909-10, is also listed on the Register. The four-story, tan-brick structure replaced an 1845 brick structure. The 1850 **John Opel House**, also known as the **Green Tree Inn,** on St. James Street at the south edge of town on Route 162, is another fine Federal brick building on the Historic Register. Green Tree Antiques, located in buildings on the premises, is one of the best shops in the region. Nearby on Route 162, on the Vincennes University regional campus, the **Indiana Baseball Hall of Fame** honors Hoosier baseball greats. The 1979 dedication was attended by Yankee great, Mickey Mantle.

Another Jasper lodestone is the glockenspiel-topped **Schnitzelbank Restaurant** at 393 Third Avenue (Route 162). Since 1903, the Schnitzelbank has purveyed bier und southern German specialties like beef rolladen, sauerbraten, kassler rippchen, and turnip slaw to locals and visitors alike.

Huntingburg is seven miles to the south on Route 231. It is another small German manufacturing town, with furniture and decorative arts factories. The town is a redoubt of German Lutherans, which some say is the historic root of the friendly rivalry between Huntingburg and Jasper. It was founded in 1837 by Kentuckian William Geiger, who named the town in honor of his successful bear and pigeon hunts in the neighborhood. The many brick homes date from the days when the town brickyards bustled with orders. The brick **William Geiger Home,** 511 Geiger Street, was built in 1854-55. The town's pride is the restored 1866 Italianate **Huntingburg Town Hall and Fire Engine House** at 311 Geiger Street, scene of everything from civic business to wedding receptions. It was listed on the National Historic Register in 1975.

The fine clay deposits attracted **Uhl Pottery Works** from Evansville in 1908. Until their demise in 1944, the plant made over nine hundred different articles, including sixty-gallon pickling jars weighing four hundred pounds. At one point in the 1930s and 1940s, the now defunct **Huntingburg Wagon Works** was the largest wagon maker in the country, marketing wooden wagons to the still-wild Southwest and Great Plains, and down into Mexico.

The Victorian main commercial street has become a string of well stocked antique shops, perfect for a hunting and gathering expedition. The vintage architecture has attracted movie location scouts and is the scene of several movies, including *A League of Their Own* starring Madonna and Tom Hanks, which celebrated the women's baseball leagues of the 1940s; and *Hard Rain,* which inundated the street in a cinematic faux flood, making Huntingburg surely the only southern Indiana town to ever contract and schedule for a flood. The town was also the location for the HBO movie, *Soul of the Game.*

The filming of the baseball movie prompted an extensive restoration of Huntingburg's **League Stadium**, now the home field for the Dubois Dragons. The semi-pro games are held throughout the season from late May to mid-August, a great way to share in small-town life on a balmy summer evening.

Huntingburg was also the home of one of America's largest high school gymnasiums. When Huntingburg's Happy Hunter's basketball arena was built in 1951, it could hold 6,214 howling fans, substantially more than the entire town's population of 5,376.

The gym was part of Indian's high school basketball boom that began in the 1920s and only recently receded. Beginning in the 1920s, over eight hundred high school basketball teams vied for the state crown, playing in barns and quonset huts and vast fieldhouses all over the Hoosier State. Towns competed to build the area's largest gym in order to get home-court advantage for the annual sectional and regional contests. By 1927 over a million Hoosiers could be seated in high school basketball arenas at one time—more than a third of the total state population. The building "contest" has left the Hoosier State with fifteen of the sixteen largest high school gyms in the United States, the lone exception being an arena in Texas.

Ten miles south on Route 231 at Dale, take Route 62E. **Mariah Hill,** four miles east of Dale (see Chapter Six for info on Dale), is another traditional German village with a hilltop church and a thronged summer turtle soup dinner. Turn south on Route 245 a mile east of Dale to **Holiday World** at **Santa Claus, Indiana.** The town was platted in 1846 and the name of Santa Fe was chosen for the post office. However, news arrived around Christmas time that the name was already taken by a town in northern Indiana, so the town gathered to decide on a new name. Local lore has it that in the midst of the village meeting, the door blew open and they all looked out into the starry Christmas night, and the new name came to them: Santa Claus. Being the only town in the country named Santa Claus, the post office prepares for an annual onslaught of millions of pieces of Christmas mail needing the special Santa Claus, Indiana, postmark.

Beginning in 1914, local postmaster Jim Martin began responding to the

"Dear Santa" letters that made their way to Santa Claus. Today, the entire town is involved in the yearly task, responding to up to ten thousand letters from around the world. "Everyone around here is so aware these letters have to be sent out," said Pat Koch, queen mother of the Holiday World and leader of Santa's Elves, the organization that co-ordinates the letter-writing. The local Garden Club, senior citizens, and volunteers from around the region are involved. Letters in foreign languages are sent to the Benedictines at the two area monasteries for reply. "There are some great happy letters and some very sad ones," Koch said. "'I want my mommy and daddy to get back together.' Some are very funny: 'I want a goat, a pig, a horse. I want three horses.' 'I know you're not real,' one skeptic wrote, 'but just in case, I want . . . .'"

Santa Claus Land, the original name of Holiday World, is the first theme park in the world, pre-dating even Knott's Berry Farm's rides by a bit. It began in 1946, when the Koch family established the park. Actually, Santa parks were started even earlier in the 1930s, with a "Toy Town" in medieval-looking buildings, and even a Santa Claus College existed where Santas in training learned to be hearty, cheery, and generally Santa-ly, graduating with Bachelors in Santa Clausing.

The Koch's theme park was renamed Holiday World in 1984 and it boasts the wooden Raven roller coaster, ranked one of the three best wooden roller coasters in the country. State-of-the-art amusement rides share the park with charming vintage rides that are lovingly preserved. The Splashin' Safari water park features a wave pool, water slides, and an action river. The Koch family is still deeply involved with the park, and its pristine cleanliness and friendly staff reflect their concern. "It's been more than half a century since the park opened, and we've held onto the original premise that we want a safe, clean, fun place for families to enjoy together," president Will Koch said. "We are dedicated to creating a special place like no other, where families can come to have fun and enjoy just being together."

The 1880 Duetsch Evangelische St. Paul's Kirche on Santa Fe Road south of Santa Claus is listed on the National Register of Historic Places. Continue south fourteen miles on Route 245 to the junction with Route 66 and the Ohio River Scenic Route, turn west to Grandview and the Ohio River Scenic Route.

Visitor Information

Perry County Convention and Visitors Bureau, P.O. Box 721, Tell City, IN 47586, 812-547-2385, 888-343-6262.
Dubois County Tourism Commission, P.O. Box 404, 610 Main Street, Jasper, IN 47547-0404, 800-968-4578.
Spencer County Visitors Bureau, P.O. Box 202, Santa Claus IN 47579-0202, 812-937-2848, 888-444-9252.

Recommended Reading

Peopling Indiana: The Ethnic Experience, edited by Robert M. Taylor Jr. and Connie A. McBirney, Indiana Histrorical Society, Indianapolis, IN, 1996.
Finding the Grain: Pioneer German Journals and Letters from Dubois County, Indiana, edited by Norbert Krapf, Max Kade Center, Indiana University-Purdue University, and Indiana German Heritage Center with Dubois County Historical Society, revised and expanded 1996.

Recommended Regional Dining

Tell City Pretzels, 632-B Main St., Tell City, IN 47586, 812-547-4631, has been selling pretzels since 1858. They ship their traditional pretzels all over the country. New-fangled ways have entered the place; they also sell chocolate-dipped pretzels.
Capers, 701 Main St., Tell City, IN 47586, 812-547-3333, is located in an 1894 building listed on the National Historic Register. It serves well-prepared pastas, pizza, and po-boys, as well as steaks, chicken, and seafood. They have music on Friday and Saturday nights.
Louie's, Route 545, Fulda, is a 1940s-style road house, with the best turtle soup in the region.
Fleigs, Ninth and Main, 812-367-1310, is also a renowned turtle soup spot, as well as a great place for beer and dice.
Schnitzelbank Restaurant, 393 Third Ave., Jasper, 812-482-2640 has the best in Indiana German cooking, including turnip slaw on the "wunderbar," their prodigious salad bar.
Merkey's Meats, 3994 W. 180 North, Jasper, is an old-style German butcher, specializing in knockwurst, bratwurst, souse, and summer sausage-style German bologna.

The Chicken Place, Highway 56, Ireland, four miles to the west of Jasper, may have the best fried chicken in Indiana. Phone 812-482-7600.

Heichelbech's, 222 E. Twelfth, Jasper, 812-482-4050, is a local favorite, known for their turtle soup.

Fat & Sassy's, 403 N. Jackson, Huntingburg, 812-683-4801, serves gourmet coffee and desserts and an evolved selection of soup and sandwiches, a great respite from a hard day of antiquing.

Recommended Bed and Breakfasts and Cabins

St. Meinrad has rooms at the Saint Meinrad Guest House, decorated in classic 1950s Catholic School style. Call 1-800-581-6905.

The Powers Inn, 325 W. Sixth, Jasper, IN 47546, 812-482-3018, has three guest rooms in a Second Empire style house.

Camping

Patoka Lake, Route 164 and 145, Wickliffe, IN, 812-685-2464.

Ferdinand State Forest, 6583 Route 264, six miles east of Route 162, Ferdinand, IN, 812-367-1524.

Lake Rudolph Outdoor Resort, Route 245, Santa Claus, IN, 812-937-4458.

The Monastery Immaculate Conception, "the Monastery on the Hill" is home to generations of Benedictine nuns.

Photo by John Eicher, courtesy of the Indiana Department of Commerce Tourism Division

Saint Meinrad Archabbey looks as though it levitated from the Fatherland.

Courtesy of Holiday World & Splashin' Safari

Holiday World's *The Raven* is one of the world's top-rated roller coasters.

Lincoln Land: Spencer County

Grandview to Rockport 5 miles
Spencer County Lincoln Land Alternate Loop 45 miles

"I grew up in Indiana," Abraham Lincoln said, and so he did. From 1816, when seven-year-old Abe and his family ferried across the Ohio at Troy, until they rolled down the old buffalo trail by oxen cart to Illinois in 1830, Abe was a Hoosier, by temperament and by training. He grew from childhood to robust manhood on a pioneer farm in the hills of Spencer County, surrounded by the cabins of Kentucky yeomen like his father. Abraham Lincoln felled trees and raised cabins, grubbed the hard earth and helped wrest a living from it, split rails by the thousands to fence the wildness out. It was in Indiana that he lost his beloved mother and the sister who nurtured him. There is no doubt that these losses fed the deep wellsprings of melancholia and empathy that marked his character throughout his life.

He learned to read and write and cipher here. He learned his politics from the log stump hustings and cracker barrel corners of the frontier crossroads stores, and his law from the rough, log cabin courthouses of the early state. It was during his formative Indiana years, when he flatboated trade goods down the rivers to New Orleans, that Lincoln first experienced the travesties of slavery. And it was here he learned to convince his fellow man, melding his power of persuasion and ideas with their own language. He learned the simple, clear, elegant writing of the Bible; the raucous and wry tales of his kinsmen and neighbors, and spiced them with Aesop's Fables. He studied the dense and literary phrases of the preachers and literary preceptors of virtue that Lincoln read as his texts. "There was something native, natural rather than singular, and wholly inexhaustible about him," Woodrow Wilson wrote.

The Spencer County of Lincoln's youth was organized in 1818 from parts of Perry and Warrick counties. It was named after yet another hero of the 1811 Battle of Tippecanoe, Corydon sheriff and tavern owner, Spier Spencer, who died in the battle while leading his company of "Yellow Jackets." Physiographically, the county is part of the southwestern Indiana lowlands that extend west to the Wabash, a region of modest hills and wide valleys, interspersed with low river drainages that harbor a swampy habitat more akin to that of the lower Mississippi valley. Spencer County's broad valleys and rolling hills are the foundation of a rich agricultural heritage that continues today. It is the hottest region in the state, with the longest growing season. In the summer, the heat and humidity can combine into a veritable gumbo of air.

The Lincolns were part of a Kentuckian colony that migrated north of the Ohio. Much of the early settlement was in the western half the county along Little Pigeon Creek, the major stream between the Blue and the Wabash that extended into the interior. In Lincoln's day, the region was, as he said, "a wild region with bears and other wild animals in the woods," with panther screams and the howls of wolves unsettling the night. Even a decade after the Lincolns arrived, the settlers killed nine bears in a community hunt.

The eastern part of the county developed in the mid-nineteenth century when the Germans began forming communities such as St. Meinrad, Santa Claus, and Mariah Hill to the west of the Anderson River. By 1850 Spencer County had the second highest percentage (11.2%) of foreign-born people of any Ohio River county from the Falls of the Ohio to the junction with the Mississippi. "It's still a very rural county," Lincoln Boyhood National Memorial Chief of Interpretation Mike Capps remarked. "It's the first place I've been where you've got to leave the county to find a McDonald's."

Many of the Kentuckians were like Abraham Lincoln's father, Thomas, losing farm after farm in the post-Revolutionary War period to flawed land titles. Thomas Lincoln lost three different Kentucky farms to owners who demonstrated stronger claims to the land. Virginia, which held jurisdiction over Kentucky, required the land holders to provide their own tract surveys. The settlers and land owners depended on marked trees, meandering streams, and movable rocks to form their corners and boundaries, creating a welter of conflicting claims. "In the unskillful hands of the hunters and pioneers of Kentucky," an historian wrote, "entries, surveys, and patents were piled upon each other, overlapping and crossing in endless perplexity."

In contrast, north of the river, the Ordinances of 1784 and 1787 that created the Northwest Territory neatly gridded the land into invisible but indisputable squares laid out by professional government surveyors, dividing the land into sections and quarters. When Thomas Lincoln traveled to Indiana the year prior to moving, he had only to pile brush at the four corners of the quarter section that he chose and build a half-face camp as a habitation to claim it. The next year, after he harvested his first crop, he traveled the sixty miles to the U. S. Land Office at Vincennes to register his claim and make his initial payment of $16 toward the total cost of $320 for his 160 acres.

Thomas Lincoln also moved to Indiana to enjoy another part of the Northwest Territory's Ordinance. "There shall be neither slavery nor involuntary servitude in the said territory," the law read. When Indiana became a state in 1816, the Constitution of Indiana read, "No alteration of this constitution shall ever take place so as to introduce slavery or involuntary servitude in the state." Yeomen like Lincoln, who made most of his living as a carpenter, could not compete economically with slave labor. It was apparent to him that Indiana would never be a slave state.

The Lincolns crossed the Ohio at Troy on Thompson's Ferry and followed a wagon trail that was cut from Troy to Hurricane, the township where Thomas Lincoln had staked his claim. The wilderness road passed within four miles of the Lincoln homestead, and Thomas felled trees the rest of the way to make a path for the wagon. Abraham Lincoln later said he "never passed through a harder experience than he did going from Thompson's Ferry" to their home site. When they arrived in 1816, the Lincolns were pioneers, part of a totally self-sufficient economy, growing or making almost everything they consumed. Seven-year-old Abraham, big for his age, helped his father build a log cabin and clear the dense forests that covered their farm. "We lived the same as Indians," his cousin Dennis Hanks said, "'cept we took an interest in politics and religion," which says as much about the pioneers' living conditions as it does about their ignorance of Native American culture. Years later, when Lincoln was asked about his Indiana years, he said that a single line in Gray's *Elegy*, "The short and simple annals of the poor," contained the substance of his early life.

Only a few years after the Lincolns settled in Indiana, the tiny community was hit by the scourge of milk sickness, or the "trembles." The afflicted suffered waves of nausea and vomiting, intense dizziness and vertigo, and a rotting odor of the breath, before their pulses became erratic and their breathing irregular. Most often a coma and death followed. The pioneers correctly attributed it to cow's milk but never discovered the cause. Milk sickness, which also afflicted the cattle, is actually snakeroot poisoning. Snakeroot flourishes in the deep shade of the forests, at the verge of the settlers' clearings. In particularly dry seasons, the cows wandered into woods looking for fodder and were drawn to the funereal white flowers of the snakeroot.

First Abraham watched his mother's step-parents succumb to the malady. Then his mother became ill and, within a week, was dead. He and his family prepared his beloved mother's body for burial in the one-room cabin where they lived. She lay thusly for the days it took for Thomas Lincoln to whipsaw the planks for her coffin, and nine-year-old Abe to whittle the pegs that pinned it together. A family horse dragged a primitive sled carrying the coffin up to the knoll above the cabin, where they lay Nancy Hanks Lincoln to rest.

As he grew to adulthood, "Abe looked as if he'd been chopped out with an ax an' needed a jack plane took to him," his father said. He was a raw-boned six foot four inches, renowned for strength. Abe planted, cultivated, and harvested crops; hauled grain to gristmills from Troy to Huffman's Mill; worked as a ferryman and flatboatman; cut timber and spit rails till he had a name for it. But as an acquaintance later recounted to a biographer, "his father taught him to work, but never learned him to love it." Abraham's real love, encouraged by both his mother and stepmother, was books and learning, and he ferreted out every book in the vicinity, from the family Bible to exhoratory books like Weem's *Life of Washington* and *The Autobiography of Benjamin Franklin*. While Abraham Lincoln attended school for only five terms, less than a year all told, it was considered a common-school education for the day. He was considered an educated man, able to read and write and cipher. He also extended his learning to the world around him, absorbing the sermons of the passing preachers and the blandishments of the local politicians. By the age of twelve, he was exhorting his younger cousins from a tree stump as they sat enthralled. Later, Lincoln haunted the three county courthouses that were within riding distance, and eagerly participated in the political debates that flared at the crossroads stores and blacksmith shops.

By 1820 there were still only forty families within a five-mile radius of their farm on Little Pigeon Creek, but by 1822 there were fifty. By the mid-1820s the frontier had moved on, and this part of Indiana was tied into the larger mercantile world—goods and people moving up and down the Ohio in the rapidly growing fleet of steamboats.

It was time for the Lincolns to move on west, as the family had been doing since it arrived in America five generations before, moving from Massachusetts to New Jersey, Pennsylvania, Virginia, through the Cumberland Gap to Kentucky, further west yet to Indiana, and then off to the prairies of Illinois, always looking for a better life. In March of 1830, Thomas sold his Indiana farm, selling the eighty-acre section for cash and trading a horse for the other twenty acres. The Lincoln family loaded their belongings into a cart and rolled west on the Troy-Vincennes Road, the wooden axles of the cart squealing and squeaking into the woods as they trundled off. "I understand why Lincoln did the things he did to keep the Union together," Lincoln interpreter Mike Capps has said. "He learned his determination here."

In 1844 Abraham Lincoln returned once to Spencer County, Indiana, on a campaign trip for his Whig hero, Henry Clay. He spoke at the courthouse in Rockport, and he spoke from stumps and storefronts and front porches in the region. He visited with boyhood friends and poked around the haunts of his youth. And at some point in his visit, he excused himself and returned to his father's old farm, and he made the long climb up through the autumn forest to the knoll of his mother's grave to pay his respects.

Mileage

200.0 **Grandview** sits at a wide bend in the river, affording a fine view. The town has a gas station, a bar, and a good B&B. The tiny town dates back to settlement in the early 1800s and was incorporated in 1872. The Lincoln family lived nearby, and Abe hauled hoop poles for barrels through the town with an ox team en route to the river. The **Abraham Lincoln Marker** notes the event. Lincoln himself immortalized Grandview with a satirical story entitled, "The Chronicles of Reuben" after he and his family were not invited to a fancy double wedding in town. The story, written in biblical style, has the grooms confusing their bedrooms and nearly spending the night with the wrong wife. David Turnham was a local farmer who loaned Lincoln the first law book he ever read, *The Revised Laws of Indiana*. In 1860 Lincoln wrote to Turnham, recalling their times together, wishing to be able to visit the old home, "but I feel the chance of doing so soon, is not very good."

203.5 Route 231N is an **alternate route** from the Ohio River Scenic Route, leading in fifteen miles to the crossroads hamlet of Gentryville. Route 231 follows, for a large part, the old **Yellow Banks Trail** that ran from Rockport to the Delaware Indian town at the forks of the White River. For several decades, Gentryville has been most famous for the creative antique clutter of the **Antique Shak,** housed in an old general store and other buildings at the junction of Route 162. But it was at this crossroads, located at the junction line of the portentously named Jackson and Clay townships, that Abe Lincoln began his political education, absorbing the banter and bluster of the days' issues at Gentry's Store as the Whigs of Clay Township debated the Democrats of Jackson Township. A local merchant, William Jones, burnished Lincoln's nascent Whig loyalty that he learned from his father. From the local blacksmith, John Baldwin, Lincoln learned many of the homespun stories that became his stock-in-trade as he joined the debate.

Turn east on Route 162. A marker for the site of the **James Gentry Homestead,** the founder of Gentryville, pioneer entrepreneur, and friend of the Lincoln family is down the road .1 miles. The front yard shrines of the German area are replaced by Hoosier yard art of an astounding variety.

Proceed another 1.5 miles east through a leafy tunnel, past split rail fences and field stone walls to the **Lincoln Boyhood National Memorial and Living Historical Farm.** The 196-acre complex encompasses the hundred-acre farm that Thomas Lincoln sold when the family moved to Illinois in 1830. The Memorial Building houses a museum dedicated to the life and times of Lincoln, a visitor center, and auditoriums. The **Memorial Building** was designed with the esthetics and culture of the Lincolns in mind. The Abraham Lincoln Hall is paneled with cherry, Thomas Lincoln's favorite wood. The rostrum and pews are typical of early churches and courthouses. The Nancy Hanks Lincoln Hall is beamed and columned with yellow poplar logs, the wood of choice for pioneer cabins. The huge sandstone fireplace is an outsized version of one that could have heated a lonely wilderness cabin, and the enormous braided rug is a pattern that Nancy Hanks Lincoln would have known. The nearby gravesite of **Nancy Hanks Lincoln**, Abraham's mother, is the focus of the park. She died of milk sickness in 1818 and was buried on a knoll above the Lincoln cabin.

Concern over the lack of maintenance of the grave in 1907 precipitated the Indiana legislature to create a board to oversee the site. The memorial park development continued in 1926 when the newly formed Indiana Lincoln Union hired New York's Central Park architect Frederick Law Olmstead to submit plans for a Lincoln Memorial. In 1932 the state separated the memorial grounds from the adjoining state park. In 1935 the perimeter of the Lincoln cabin was marked with bronze logs, and the original hearthstones were returned from the schoolyard of Lincoln City where they were found. When the Memorial Building was built in 1943, it anchored thousands of acres of state land, with extensive landscaping throughout.

In 1962 Indiana relinquished control of the memorial to the National Park Service, which developed the Living Historical Farm in 1967, one of only two in the park system. The farm is a well interpreted working pioneer farm, giving visitors a sense of life on the Indiana frontier. Self-sufficiency was the rule, with nearly everything consumed on the farm needing to be grown or made. A simple linen shirt, for instance, took several operations from seed to shirt. Flax was planted, grown, and harvested, after which the fibers were left to rot through the winter, and then the fibers broken. Only then could the laborious spinning and weaving process begin.

Across the road, **Lincoln State Park** is an extensive seventeen-hundred-acre recreation area, with an eighty-five-acre swimming and boating lake, cabins, hiking trails, a nature center, and two hundred campsites. Many of the park's original structures and trails were constructed as part of the Depression-era CCC program. The park is also the site of the Noah Gordon Mill, a horse mill where the horse went round and round in a circle, grinding the corn while Abe Lincoln sat intently reading yet another book. Looking up from his book one day and seeing the slow progress of the milling, Lincoln remarked that "his dog could eat the meal as fast as the mill could grind it." When Abe's turn came to hitch his horse to the grindstone, he evidently urged it on a bit too much, and the horse retaliated with a swift kick. According to the reports, Lincoln was "apparently killed for a while," before coming to and uttering the last half of the "cluck" he was saying when he was kicked. From mid-June through mid-August on Tuesdays through Sundays, the 1,514 seat **Lincoln Amphitheatre** rings to theatrical performances such as *Young Abe Lincoln* and, in 1998, Roger and Hammerstein's *Oklahoma!* Nearby, a historic reproduction of the log-construction **of Little Pigeon Primitive Baptist Church** is erected on the site of the church that served the Lincolns as a spiritual haven. Thomas Lincoln was a trustee of the church, and Abraham acted as sexton. Many years after the original church was abandoned, a faded memorandum book was found in a crack between the loft logs. It read in a spidery hand:

> *Dr. To 1 broom*
> *To 1/2 doz tallow candles*
> *Abe Lincoln, Sexton.*

The **Gravestone of Sarah Lincoln Grigsby,** Abe's beloved older sister is in the church cemetery. Sarah died in 1828 during childbirth, a common occurrence on the frontier. She and her stillborn child are buried together.

The theme and water park of **Holiday World & Splashin' Safari** at Santa Claus, Indiana, are five miles to the east on Route 162. Besides the amusement rides, wax museum, and toy and doll museum, Holiday World has a collection of Lincoln memorabilia. See Chapter Five for a fuller description of Santa Claus, Indiana.

Return west on Route 162 to Gentryville. Turn south on Route 231 to the next road west, CR 1575N, and proceed .7 miles to the **Colonel William Jones House.** Jones was a contemporary of the Lincoln family and, while a storekeeper at the Gentryville store, Jones fanned Lincoln's enthusiasm for the Whig cause. The Whig party of Henry Clay were strong believers in internal improvements, high tariffs to protect budding American industries, and a national bank. Jones later bought out the Gentrys and ran a store at Gentryville before moving his operation to Jonesboro, the village that surrounded his house. When the house was built in the 1830s, the road in front was a major highway between Troy and Vincennes. The 1834 Federal-style brick home reflects Jones' economic position; his neighbors were housed in log cabins. Its grand staircase to a nonexistent second floor gives a clue as to Jones' aspirations as well as his financial limitations.

In 1844 Lincoln returned to Indiana from Springfield, Illinois, where he was by that time a young, ambitious attorney, to campaign for presidential candidate Henry Clay. Lincoln gave several speeches in the county and spent the night with his old political mentor at the Jones home. In the 1850s Jones moved back down the road to Gentryville, which was prospering at the more advantageous junction of the north-south highway. He served a term as a member of the Indiana Legislature, as well as a lieutenant colonel in the Union Army during the Civil War, dying at the Battle of Atlanta.

"Jones had ambitions, ideas, ideals," historic site director Peggy Brooks said. "That's why he built this Federal house here. There was a burgeoning economy, a growing middle class. They had literally hewn a community out of the wilderness in a few decades, and refined it." By the time Jones built the house in 1834, this was no longer the frontier. The self-sufficiency of the pioneer years gave way to a bustling mercantilism, tied to the larger economic patterns of the region. In 1816, when the Lincolns crossed the Ohio, there were only seven steamboats on the entire Western river system. By 1825 there were 143 bustling between the river towns. Jones the mercantilist could buy in Louisville and have his goods shipped on schedule to his general stores scattered through the region, doubling the price in the process. By the 1830s, the region was a long way from the 1819 "wild and desolate" country Lincoln's stepmother, Sally Bush Johnston Lincoln, described.

In 1976 Bloomington preservationists Bill and Gayle Cook purchased the Colonel William Jones house and totally restored it. In 1990 it became the latest Indiana State Historical Site. It is listed on the National Register of Historic Places.

Further north 4.6 miles, the town of **Dale,** founded in 1843, has **Windell's,** a 1940s town cafe that looks like a scene from an Edward Hopper oil painting. The streamline formica tables and wraparound counter aren't the creation of a hip Los Angeles retro designer; they are just lovingly cared-for parts of the town history. For decades, the cafe served as the local Greyhound terminal. Today, farmers in faded overalls sit next to local lawyers at the horseshoe counter, wolfing down the daily blue-plate special. Windall's famous pies take you back to another time. To the east 3.7 miles on Route 62, **The Chateau** at Mariah Hill is famous for catfish.

Two miles further north of Dale on Route 231, **Dr. Ted's Musical Marvels** is a vast compendium of one man's devotion to restored musical instruments, including music boxes, nickelodeons, street organs, and orchestrations, along with the posters and ephemera of America's vaudeville years.

To return to the Ohio River Scenic Route, drive south on Route 231 through Gentryville toward Route 66, about twenty miles. The twin 1,040-foot towers and boiling vapors of the **AEP** (American Electric Power) generating plant and the seemingly endless line of coal cars lining the tracks are substantial reminders that we belong to an industrial century. South of Crisney looms the mammoth **AK Steel Plant,** which has had a dramatic economic impact on the county. Turn west on Route 66 1.2 miles through the haze of the river valley's flat, deep bottoms. A sign for the **Energy Information Center** is located on the highway, a relic from when the power plant was part of Indiana Michigan Power Company, a tool to educate consumers about the power industry and lobby for the construction of the plant. Once the controversial plant was built, there were no more funds available for the center and it was closed.

Proceed west to the river port town of **Rockport**.

204.7 The original settlers of Rockport clustered at the bottom of the bluff on which Rockport now sits. The name of the settlement was Hanging Rock, in honor of the two landmark columns that hung from the face of the bluff, named George Washington and Martha Washington. One column fell during the New Madrid earthquake of 1811, and the other eventually had to be dynamited. About 1818, when Rockport became the county seat of Spencer County, the village relocated to the top of the bluff. The incline at the end of Main Street leads you down to the 1.5-mile long, hundred-foot high bluff. The cave in the bluff is allegedly where town founder James Langford and his family lived in 1808.

The riverside bluff is also where Abraham Lincoln cast off on his fateful flatboat journey to New Orleans. An **Abraham Lincoln Marker** at the end of Bluff Road commemorates his trip to the South. The story goes this way: In 1828 James Gentry decided he had enough trade goods to send down the river to New Orleans, and he contracted with Abraham Lincoln to help man the boat along with his son, Allen Gentry. The boat was probably similar to the one William Jones contracted for a few years later: sixty-five feet long by eighteen feet wide with the side boards four and a half feet high in the middle, constructed of good poplar boards two feet in width and nine inches thick. It included a cabin constructed of gum or oak, one and half inches thick and seven inches wide. The vessel cost Jones $97.

Lincoln's craft probably carried the same sort of merchandise that was part of the flatboat flotilla that floated down the Wabash in 1826. In the spring of 1826, twenty-four flatboats from Vincennes and Terre Haute took 57,250 bushels of corn, 20,550 pounds of bulk pork, 2,273 bacon hams, 1,501 barrels pork, 280 barrels of corn meal, forty-one live cattle, seventy chickens, 160 barrels beans, and 410 venison hams down the river.

It was a round trip of three months, one in which the impressionable Lincoln saw slavery first-hand, first along the plantations on the Mississippi where they stopped to trade (including one just below Baton Rouge where they were attacked by slaves but escaped with their lives). In New Orleans, Abe saw the slave markets and the placards and advertisements of the slave sales. "Thirty-seven slaves for sale; two coopers, one shoemaker, and one tanner, two hands at whipsaw. On board transport at the Levee," one commercial notice read. "24 North Carolina slaves to be sold cheap for cash or on a short credit," read another. A traveler, who arrived in New Orleans the same year as Lincoln, noted, "I observed in walking through the streets several large rooms fitted out as slave markets, and generally filled with unhappy blacks, dressed up for the occasion. The men and women are ranged on opposite sides of the apartment, where they may traffic for human beings with the same indifference as buying a horse. New Orleans, I conclude, is a good market for this type of human stock . . . ."

To return to Indiana, Lincoln and Allen Gentry churned back up the rivers on one of the steamboats making their way through the West. If their trip was like most, it probably took about nine days.

In October 1844 Lincoln returned to Spencer County to give a speech for Henry Clay in Spencer County's third courthouse. The current courthouse, built in 1921, is the county's fifth. It features a large interior stained glass dome. A marker at Second and Main streets denotes the site of the **Rockport Tavern** where Lincoln spent the night. Just south of 9th and Main, the **Lincoln Pioneer Village** is located in the city park. The Depression-era WPA project gathered or reproduced buildings significant to Lincoln in his lifetime. The four-acre plot has an inn, church, school, law office, store, and homes of friends and family. A museum was added in 1950 that includes among the diverse holdings one of Thomas Lincoln's cherry inlaid corner cupboards, his specialty as a frontier craftsman. The Pioneer Village was listed on the Indiana Register of Historic Places in 1998, the first step toward national designation.

The 1867 **Mathias Sharp House**, 319 S. 2nd, is listed on the National Register of Historic Places. The interesting 1859 **Crooks-Anderson** octagonal house is located at 419 Walnut Street. The Federal-style **Rockport Inn** at 130 S. Third was built as a private residence in 1857. South of Rockport on Route 231 and several eras away, the nostalgic **Holiday Drive-In Movie Theater** screens the latest in Hollywood films on five huge screens every night in the summer and on the weekends in the fall. (No making out in the back seat. I want to see two heads through that rear window.)

In the late 1880s Spencer County teenagers Clarence H. Kennedy and Arthur C. Veatch began a systematic archeological dig of some of the many prehistoric Native American mounds that dot the Ohio River shore. Nearly a hundred years later, a noted scholar wrote that they were the "first Indiana archeologists since Lesueur [a renowned 1820s New Harmony naturalist] to correctly record materials, attempt artifact comparisons and show interest in internal features of the site they examined, rather than excavating relics for display." The boys both went on to successful academic careers.

The Ohio River Scenic Route continues west on Route 66 through rich bottom land. In the forever thrifty nature of the rural Hoosier, a tiny 1930s gas station straight out of a Frank Capra movie has been recycled into a pizza place on this stretch of road. In the summer a damp blanket of humidity rises from the ground, and the air becomes so moist it's as though the catfish and perch and bass of the river could just swim right on past your car windows.

Visitor Information

Spencer County Visitors Bureau, P.O. Box 202, Santa Claus, IN 47579-0202, 812-937-2848, 888-444-9252.

Recommended Reading

Lincoln's Youth, Louis A. Warren, Indiana Historic Society, Indianapolis, 1991.
Abe Lincoln Grows Up, Carl Sandburg, Harcourt, Brace and World, Inc., New York, 1926.

Recommended Regional Dining

Windell's Cafe, 6 W. Medcalf, Dale, IN, 812-937-4253, is place for Hoosier food and famous pies.
The Chateau, Highway 62, Mariah Hill, IN 47556, 812-937-4386, is revered locally as the place for fried catfish.

Recommended Bed and Breakfasts and Cabins

The River Belle B&B, Route 66, P.O. Box 669, Grandview, IN 47615, 800-877-5165, has rooms in three town houses: a steamboat gothic Victorian house, a late-nineteenth-century brick Italianate, and "the little house under the pecan tree" Victorian cottage. All are scrupulously maintained and decorated with period antiques.
Lincoln State Park, Highway 162, Lincoln City, IN 47552, 812-937-4710, has cabins for rent, along with an array of recreational activities.
The Trails Inn B&B, Highway 45, Rockport, IN 47635, 812-649-9579, is three miles west of Rockport, located at the Ramey Riding Stables.
The Rockport Inn, 130 W. 3rd St., Rockport, IN 47635, is an antebellum inn that serves breakfast on the weekends. Local lore has it that Lincoln stayed here in his 1844 visit to Rockport. The inn also boasts a resident ghost.
Lake Rudolph Outdoor Resort, Route 245, Santa Claus, IN, 812-937-4458, has cabins for rent, as well as an array of other visitor services.

Camping

Lincoln State Park, Highway 162, Lincoln City, IN 47552, 812-937-4710, has a camping sites for both tents and RVs, as well as swimming and boating.

Lake Rudolph Outdoor Resort, Route 245, Santa Claus, IN, 812-937-4458, has a complete camping facility, including miniature golf and horseshoes. They also have cabins and RVs for rent.

The boyhood portrait of Abraham Lincoln most admired at the Lincoln Boyhood Home.

Photo by Lloyd Ostendorf

The Lincoln Boyhood National Memorial and Living Historical Farm is home to the hundred-acre farm once owned by Thomas Lincoln, Abe's father.

Photo courtesy of Paula Werne

The Delta Queen floats majestically down the Ohio River.

The First Settlers

Rockport to Evansville 53 miles

I was deep into adulthood when I stood gaping at the gargantuan earthen mound at Cahokia, Illinois, just east of St. Louis. I was a guy who had a lifelong interest in Midwestern history and what I thought was at least a passing understanding of the major themes. But as I stood at the base of this immense structure, it was very clear my education had skipped over a very important part of it. I felt in good company when I read the 1811 dispatch Henry Brackenridge sent back to Thomas Jefferson when he first encountered the mounds. "When I reached the foot of the principal mound," Brackenridge wrote, "I was struck with a degree of astonishment, not unlike that which is experienced in contemplating the Egyptian pyramids."

Built by Native Americans from 900 A.D. to 1200, Monk's Mound at Cahokia is the largest earthen structure in North America, one hundred feet high and covering fifteen acres, larger by far than the great pyramid at Giza. It was the central focus of Cahokia, the preeminent center of polity, trade, culture, and religion in the vast basin between the Appalachians and the Rockies, from the Great Lakes to Florida—the largest and most powerful center north of the Mayan and Toltec civilizations of Mexico. At its peak around 1200 A.D., Cahokia was home to more than twenty thousand Native Americans spread over four thousand acres, the largest city in North America until Philadelphia in 1820. More than a hundred giant mounds could be seen from the top of the Monk's Mound. A palisade stretched over the rich bottomland, protecting the sacred precincts. To the west, an astronomical calendar made of massive timbers stuck out of the ground like a tall linear sundial, segmenting the sun and stars into predictability.

Subordinate satellite towns and satrapies, allied by trade and culture, stretched up and down the tributaries of the Mississippi from the Missouri to the Tennessee, including the fertile shoreline along Indiana's Ohio River shoreline. Shells and barracuda teeth came up from Florida and the Gulf of Mexico, copper from Lake Superior, silver from Ontario, obsidian from the Rockies, mica from the southern Appalachians, and salt from the Wabash. Mines in Missouri and on the Upper Mississippi sent iron oxide and galena, a lead sulfide ore, for the priests' use in ceremonies atop the great mounds throughout the vast mound building region.

Craftsmen wrought fine objects of metal, wood, fabric, and clay as the commoners tended their fields of corn, beans, and squash. Presided over by the ultimate leader called the Great Sun, the Mississippian mound builders stratified their society into classes below him into noble allies and honored people who lived in thatched houses at the top of the flat mounds, and the common folk called "stinkards," who clustered in wattle and daub structures both inside and outside the walls. The priests and geomancers ministered the tenuous connections between Earth and the heavens, managing the links between astronomy and agriculture.

Upstream on the Ohio shore at Angel Mounds (near present-day Evansville, Indiana), more than one thousand mound builders lived behind a high six-thousand-foot-long palisade, constructed of forty-five hundred logs. On the flat terrace above the Ohio, the daily ritual life pulsed atop and around the eleven mounds, while townspeople and people from the surrounding villages crowded the plaza below, trading supplies, offering obeisance, and betting on their favorite game of chunkey. The players rolled the chunkey stone, a round disc beveled in the center for a hand-hold, into the plaza and then hurled their spears to the spot where they thought the chunkey would spiral to a stop. The closest to the stone won.

For twelve thousand years, Native American culture has evolved in a dynamic interplay of culture and changing environment, in an unending pattern of birth, prosperity, and decay. The Mississippian mound building culture that flourished from 1000 A.D. to 1500 A.D. was only the latest in this tradition that stretched back five thousand years, which in turn emerged from culture that has existed in America for twelve millennia. When the Mayan calendar opened with a mythic date in 3372 B.C., the people of the Mississippi Valley were already creating monumental earthworks.

In Indiana alone, there are eleven thousand recorded sites of Native American inhabitation over ten thousand years, with literally hundreds of mounds scattered through the state. Native Americans lived in rock shelters and seasonal camps, complex towns and bustling villages. They hunted, they harvested the wild provender of the valleys and hills, they farmed, they traded, they fought wars—they lived their busy and productive lives. Quite obviously, they were the first explorers and settlers of the heartland, not the Europeans who came so long after them.

When the first Americans migrated from Asia across the Bering Land Bridge, they lived a nomadic hunting-and-gathering existence south of the immense Ice Age glaciers that covered much of North America. They specialized in group hunting of large herbivores like the mammoth and mastodons that also roamed Indiana. Paleoindians, as the archeologists call them, lived in Indiana from 10000 B.C. to 8000 B.C., tending to hunt along the rivers and lakes. One of their prime Indiana industrial centers was in Harrison County, where they quarried the Wyandotte blue-gray chert that was ideal for chipping into characteristic fluted spear points. The first Hoosiers hunted and traded their Harrison County spear points as far as a hundred and fifty miles from the quarry site.

The Paleoindian culture gave way to the Archaic culture that prospered in Indiana for seventy-five hundred years. The Archaic Native Americans adapted to the receding Ice Age and the warming climate by becoming more settled in their habits and hanging out in seasonal camps much longer than the Paleoindians. All that stable domesticity over the millennia, and the resulting rubbish from their favorite food of shellfish, left vast midden piles of shells and other detritus behind, some ten feet deep and covering several acres, grand places to begin one of their other characteristic traits—ceremonial burials. Midden piles on which the Archaic people built their camps were convenient spots to bury their loved ones, wanting them to be close. Along with Mom and Dad, they also buried their refuse and their dogs—the Native Americans' only domestic animal until the arrival of the Europeans.

The Archaic people became more sophisticated technologically, developing the atalatal, a spear-thrower that leveraged their arm strength and increased the velocity of the weapon. The hunter attached a drilled stone, called a bannerstone, to the atalatal that further increased the power. Bannerstones began to exhibit the clear markings of art, elegantly simple shapes hewn into diverse styles to suit the hunters' fancy. The Archaic peoples' subsistence base broadened as they utilized more of the flora and fauna, and the accompanying surpluses led to an increase in inter-regional trade. There are hundreds of Archaic sites in Indiana in fifty-five different counties, with towering midden piles along Indiana's streams, rivers, and lakes.

The funeral habits of the Archaic people were elaborated upon by the Woodland people who dominated human culture in the central part of the continent from 500 B.C. until 500 A.D. The simple burial rituals of the Archaic period evolved into the elaborate earthworks of the Woodland period—circles and mounds and effigies of diverse animals from snakes to falcons to bear claws. The mound building was an effort sustained over many generations to construct a complex of architecture that binds the sky to the earth, the sacred to the mundane. Part calendar, part charnel house, part burial ground—all sanctified sacred space—the mounds were a divine prism used to peer into the unseeable.

Early in the Woodland period, archeologists say that the culture is "Archaic with pots," as the Native Americans learned the transubstantiation of pliable clay into fire-hardened impermeable vessels. The earliest ceramics are called Marion Thick, ponderous hunks that resemble our common flower pot. As the Woodland people continued to evolve, they improved their food base through horticulturally selecting the best seeds of their wild foods to assist in grain development. They also tilled a tropical variety of corn from Mesoamerica in their fields, ritually cultivating it for ceremonial use making the change from horticulture to agriculture.

In their great flowering in the Middle Woodland or Hopewell period, the tribesmen built thousands of monumental earthworks with millions of basket-loads of soil—vast structures that memorialize them across the middle of the continent. The five-foot-high, thirty-foot-wide Serpent Mound in Ohio, for instance, writhes a quarter-mile in sinuous symmetrical curves, holding an egg in its mouth—perhaps an immense memory of the comet that streaked across the sky when the mound was built around 1066 A.D., the same comet that is woven into the Bayeux tapestry.

The Serpent Mound and great circle mounds in Ohio, the remnant mounds at Mounds State Park, in Anderson, Indiana, and the Nowlin site in Dearborn County, all share religious and material culture with towns that stretch from New York to Florida, Minnesota to Louisiana—trade and ideas moving up and down the waterways and across the high trails. Much of the trade related to ritual objects and materials that were needed for the ceremonies that bound the Hopewell people together. Broad trails, sometimes in boulevard-like sacred ways, followed pilgrimage paths between the Middle West's ceremonial mounds that were often oriented in startling macro-patterns across hundreds of miles, and aligned with each other and the heavens.

Remnants of mound builder life are found across Indiana, but particularly in the valley of the Ohio. At the Mann Site in Posey County, at the southwest corner of Indiana, the Woodland people adorned themselves with shark's teeth and fresh water pearls, sculpted clay figurines, and crafted fine ceramics in a village that sprawled for four hundred thirty acres along a high river terrace. A panther carved into a ceremonial pipe stared into the eyes of a Native American almost seventeen hundred years ago. A shaman danced with a deer-eared helmet fashioned from Great Lakes copper and topped with antlers from the animal he hoped to conjure. A ritual hand, made of sparking mica from the Appalachians, shared the site with a copper bracelet ornamented with a bird effigy.

In Wyandotte Cave, prehistoric spelunkers crawled a mile into the cave with fiber torches to mine the aragonite they used to sculpt their statues fifteen hundred years ago. The residents of the Yankeetown Site on the Ohio in Warrick County witnessed a remarkable transition in the twelve hundred years of inhabitation, from its founding in the early centuries of the Woodland culture in 300 B.C. to the first glimmerings of the next great era of mound building—the Mississippian—when the town finally declined. The archeologists see in the steamy shoreside site a revolutionary place that they term emergent Mississippian.

Historians have isolated the preconditions for the emergence of a mound building culture. An elite needs to organize and mobilize the society across generations. There needs to be a sustained abundance of food, as well as domesticated plants. And importantly, the population needs to be free of infectious diseases to maintain the dense urbanism that accompanies mound building. Prior to European contact, there was an absence of infectious diseases in North America. Most of the infectious diseases that plagued Asia and Europe evolved from domesticated livestock. Since Native Americans domesticated only the dog, they were relatively free of infectious disease, and, as we shall see, free of resistance to the diseases when they arrived.

The Woodland culture's decline is yet in debate. Some attribute it to a change in climate, causing the priests and geomancers to lose their hegemony. Others contend that war was the cause, citing the rise of defensive palisades and the charred remains of wooden structures. Like most human eras, technology may have gotten out of hand. The decline of the Woodland culture follows in time the arrival of the bow and arrow from the Southwest to the Heartland.

Eastern flint corn, an improved variety better suited to the cool, moist conditions of the Mississippi Valley, arrived from Mesoamerica in 700-800 A.D. It precursed the rise of the last mound building culture, the Mississippian. As the mound building societies began to emerge in the Mississippi Valley, they were based on a sedentary, agricultural society which produced abundant resources. Ironically, the Mississippian dependence on corn, as opposed to the Woodland peoples' dependence on wild foods, cost the Mississippians vigor and health. The Woodland people had healthy teeth, though well-worn from their coarse diet. The Mississippians' carbohydrate-rich maize diet gave them major dental decay. On average, the Mississippians were two inches shorter than their Woodland counterparts.

Cahokia peaked in 1200 A.D., Angel Mounds prospered in the fourteenth and fifteenth centuries. By this time, overuse of the land for agricultural and urban needs was well underway. Thousands of people could not be supported in these cities. But the Mississippian culture continued well into the European contact period. Spanish conquistador Hernando de Soto encountered mound building tribes along the Mississippi in the sixteenth century, in one case fending off an attack by a virtual "armada of galleys" manned by hundreds of bowmen, shield carriers, and oarsmen, presided over by a war lord sitting under a canopy. The Natchez tribe in Mississippi were still busily constructing their mounds in the eighteenth century when the Spanish and French encountered them. The Natchez met the fate of many American Indian tribes; they were wiped out in a battle with the French in 1731.

Archeologists find brass objects among the remains of the mounds, signs of European trade contacts. But most of the mound building towns were bare shadows of themselves by the time the European explorers made it into the valleys of the Mississippi drainage. European diseases unfortunately preceded the explorers, brought into the region through inter-tribal trade that spread the plagues throughout the interior far in advance of actual European contact.

It is vital to remember the role of disease in the European conquest of America. Infectious diseases like smallpox and influenza devastated tribe after tribe. When the Black Death hit Europe in the fourteenth century, it killed one-third of the population—a horror. When the diseases of the Europeans cut through the Americas, eighty percent of the Native Americans were killed, a pandemic unparalleled in human history. Prior to 1450, there were seven million Native Americans living north of the Rio Grande—more than four million in the Mississippi Valley alone. By 1600, after the microbes of the Europeans had done their work, there were only a scant remainder left. "The Great Dying," historians call it.

The surviving populations were further disrupted by the avaricious land grabs of the Europeans, and the internecine warfare resulting from the fur trade. The resulting furor from the European colonial period sent many tribes into flight over the Appalachians, searching for a haven in the interior of the continent. In Indiana, for instance, the tribes the first European settlers encountered were all recent arrivals—the Miami from Wisconsin and Illinois in the late seventeenth century, and the Potawatomi from the Lake Huron area and the Delaware from the east in the mid-1700s. Recent estimates indicate there were as many as two hundred thousand Native Americans living in Indiana in the fifteenth century. By the late 1700s, the number was reduced to twenty thousand.

When the flood of white settlers began percolating over the mountains into the valley of the Ohio, the Native Americans that they found were literally refugees—dispirited, culturally bereft refugees—bravely trying to rebuild their societies in the face of further incursions of the Europeans who pushed them west. The frontier wars were nothing more than two different cultures battling for turf—the Native Americans to continue their traditional lives; the Europeans for farms and empire. Obviously, the Native Americans were here first, but with their diseases and superior numbers, the Europeans   won.

Even so, the country's founding fathers, including Washington and Jefferson, understood the connection between the monumental mounds that the early European explorers found and the Native Americans. They harbored no fantasies that Welshmen or Vikings or the Lost Tribes of Israel or some mysterious culture of mound building savants or anyone else built these structures. They knew ancestors of the Native Americans that they saw around them built the mounds. In many ways, the European settlers mirrored the mound builders' choice of sites. Pittsburgh, Marietta, Cincinnati, the Falls Cities, Evansville, Vincennes, St. Louis, Nashville, Natchez, Mobile were all (among many others) the locations of thriving towns centered on mounds, long before the Europeans arrived.

But somewhere in the nineteenth century, in the interests of Manifest Destiny and greater jingoism, it became convenient to portray Native Americans as primitive people, incapable of such grand schemes as mounds and urban culture. The wild myths of the disappeared mound builders became common currency, attributing the mounds to increasingly implausible groups, culminating in the recent books that contend aliens from outer space made the Peruvian earthworks. No, the mounds of the Mississippi Valley and Indiana were developed by our fellow men, constructed by our fellow Americans who also loved this part of the earth and built a life here so many centuries ago. It is good for us to understand and remember. After all, it gives us a lot more history to celebrate.

It seemed an appropriate part of the Scenic Route to cover the prehistoric legacy of Indiana and the Midwest, given that Angel Mounds State Historic Site is just down the road outside of Evansville, a great place to stop and commune with our predecessors. Naturally, there is a variety of contemporary adventures to be had in this stretch of the route, from the charming river town of Newburgh to Evansville's urban pleasures and casino riverboat.

Mileage

231.1 Route 231S junction leads in 5.3 miles to **Owensboro, Kentucky.** Owensboro was chartered as a city in 1866, the second biggest port between Louisville and Paducah. Originally, its growth came from the rich tobacco land that surrounded it, but whiskey and wagon-making soon joined tobacco as mainstays of the economy. The city has a large German population, which is the mainstay of a culinary tradition. Owensboro modestly declares itself the "Bar-B-Q Capital of the World," and celebrates with a giant festival every May. Scattered throughout the town, sprawling restaurants and tiny shacks specialize in barbecue, particularly mutton. The tradition began when nineteenth century politicians realized they had ready-made crowds at the German parish barbecues and used them for stem-winding political speeches. It became a part of the political culture, and gastronomic as well. The sprawling **Moonlite-Bar-B-Q Inn** on Parrish Street is famous for its hickory smoked ribs and desserts. **George's-Bar-B-Q,** 1326 E. Fourth, specializes in the Kentucky mainstay, burgoo, a heady pottage of diverse meats and vegetables that originated in Wales.

The International Bluegrass Music Museum, 111 Daviess Street, is in the River Park Center. It offers interactive exhibits, rare photographs, films, and the memorabilia and personal effects of some of Bluegrass' most famous performers. **The Inter Tribal Indian Fest** is held in early October, a celebration of Indian culture that all are welcome to attend. A gnarled old sassafras tree at the corner of Frederica and Maple is a local landmark. The three-hundred-year old behemoth is a hundred feet high and more than sixteen feet in diameter. Except for doughty old Mrs. Rash, the tree would be kindling, taken down by the state highway crew. Mrs. Rash gathered up her shotgun and sat under it until the governor issued a reprieve and had a retaining wall built around it and a lightning rod installed.

239.7 Little Pigeon Creek, the stream on which Abe Lincoln lived to the north, is the boundary line between Spencer County and **Warrick County.** Named after yet another hero of the Battle of Tippecanoe, the county was organized in 1813. The topography ranges from the rich Ohio bottoms to rolling hills to hilly uplands. Coal is the primary natural resource.

241.0 **Yankeetown** was founded in 1858 by New Englanders, said to be named by the relatives of Ralph Waldo Emerson. Today, it is the site of the mammoth **ALCOA** aluminum plant, built in the 1950s, which feeds on Warrick County's coal reserves. The county's population jumped almost fifty percent in the 1970s after the plant's coal needs expanded. **The Yankeetown Archeological Site** was the location of an emergent Mississippian village that existed from 300 B.C. to 900 A.D., straddling the Woodland and Mississippi mound building cultures. It was listed on the National Register of Historic Places in 1979.

245.0 Turn on Route 662. **The Newburgh Lock and Dam** was opened in 1975, built at a cost of $104.4 million. The main lock is twelve hundred feet long. There is an overlook on Route 662. **The Roberts-Morton House** was built by a local businessman, Gines Roberts, in 1833-34. It is located .3 miles to the west of the overlook on the north side of the road. The Federal-style sandstone house sits on Indian Bluff with a fine view of the Ohio Valley. The two-story structure sports a grand, arched, central entrance and paired chimneys. Not quite a mile further west, the **Newburgh Presbyterian Church** is the site of the first coal-mine shaft in Indiana. A half-mile further west, the **Old Dam and Lock No. 47**, which opened in 1928 and cost $4.4 million, was replaced by the current dam.

Newburgh, perched on a high elevation above the river, began life as Sprinklesville. The hamlet got its beginning in 1803 when the Sprinkle family was evicted from their squatter's shack across the river in Henderson, Kentucky. They repeated their mistake by squatting in what came to be Newburgh, though they managed to prosper on the Indiana side. The town was platted in 1829 and incorporated eight years later. By the mid-nineteenth century, the town prospered with the Newburgh Pork House and the first shaft coal mine, which drew fuel-hungry steamboats.

In 1862 a noted Kentucky guerrilla leader, Adam Johnson, led thirty Confederates in a raid on Newburgh, Indiana, terrorizing the town with fearsome-looking cannon across the river. In subsequent years, Johnson acquired the nickname of "Stovepipe," because stovepipe was what constituted the fake cannons. The Confederates succeeded in briefly seizing the town. They commandeered sabers and pistols from a Union warehouse, along with hospital supplies from the hospital that was nursing eighty-five Union soldiers in the 1841 **Exchange Building** on State Street. The raiders quickly retreated across the river with all of the plunder they could carry. A plaque at Water and State streets commemorates **Johnson's Raid.** It was the first town taken north of the Mason-Dixon line, captured without a shot. The raid precipitated a frenzy of retribution by Union soldiers, who terrorized the Kentucky counties across the river until they were declared cleansed of guerrillas.

As with many river towns, the failure to tie into the railroads ultimately cost the town its prosperity. Neighboring Evansville, though not as well sited, either in elevation above the Ohio's flood waters or in proximity to the mouth of the Green River, boomed through its railroad connections. When historian Reuben Gold Thwaites floated down river in 1894, he found Newburgh to be a "ragged little place that has seen better days." Newburgh did tie into Indiana's extensive interurban system—a light-rail, electric trolley network. The trolley to Evansville initiated service in 1889 and extended to Rockport and down to Henderson by 1907, crossing the Ohio on a trolley car ferry. The hourly service continued until 1930, when a trundling bus replaced it. **The Evansville, Suburban, and Newburgh Railroad Company** terminal still stands on Water Street. The 1912, glazed brown brick depot was converted into a residence in 1952.

Nearby, at 700 Jefferson, John Kuebler and his family ran the **Kuebler's Gardens,** a popular turn-of-the-century recreational site, with a lake, picnic grounds, and gardens. There were facilities for horse racing, baseball, stage shows, and performances by Kuebler's Band. Many of the vacationers came via the traction railroad.

The **Original Newburgh Historical District,** bounded by Route 662 and

Water, Monroe, Main, and Middle streets, was added to the National Registry of Historic Places in 1983, the culmination of a historic preservation battle that **Historic Newburgh, Inc.,** and other concerned citizens and groups waged to save the little town. By the 1970s Newburgh was pocked with empty storefronts and fire-gutted buildings. A rough motorcycle gang made the town their hangout, a 1970s remake of *The Wild Bunch.* Today, Newburgh is a well-restored place with dozens of historic markers denoting the history of the town. Historic Newburgh, Inc. is located at the corner of Route 662 and State Street in the 1837 **Phelps-Sargeant Block.**

One block north on State Street, the 1853 **Newburgh Town Hall** was originally a Presbyterian Church, converted from ecclesiastic to civic uses in 1966. The **Phelps-Hopkins House**, next door at 208 State Street, was built in 1850 by A. M. Phelps, a local tycoon. It was surrounded by a full block of gardens, servants' quarters and outbuildings. The iron work is said to have come from New Orleans. Five generations of Hopkins lived in the family house before it was sold.

The quiet little town boasts an inordinate number of suicides and hauntings, and Historic Newburgh has capitalized on it. Each Halloween they sponsor an increasingly-popular "Ghost Walk" that combines a tour of historic houses with spectral tales of each home's ghosts. At 224 State Street, an elderly, depressed woman hung herself in the stairwell of the **Corneal McCormick House.** At 211 State Street, a tiny spirit haunts the **Pepmiller House,** the supernatural vestige of a nineteenth-century Breach of Promise suit against local brewer and house owner Louis Pepmiller. At the house at 217 State, **Samuel Weed,** the fifth husband of "Marrying Polly," Mary Ann Castle, lived. Depending on accounts, Ms. Castle married eight to seventeen times. She married the same man two or three times—a particularly powerful case of hope triumphing over experience. Her fourth and sixth husband, George Boyden, killed himself by jumping in the house cistern and drowning, reportedly because Ms. Castle refused his hand a third time. In the 1840s Greek Revival **Garwood House,** at 221 State, a local blacksmith accidentally shot himself (or hung himself, according to other reports). Whatever the cause of his passing, it is said his spirit lingers still in the lovely old home.

The **Weis House** at Jennings and Market is the oldest standing house in town, with nothing supernatural to recommend it, only its age and dignified charm. It was built in 1839 by Joseph Weis who was a saddle and harness maker. The house framing was constructed with unsquared timbers, with the twigs and branches left on in some cases. The bricks were brought to the site by flatboat. The Mediterranean Restaurant is now in the house. The nearby **Country Store** has purveyed sachets and candles and all things "country" since the 1950s, when the refurbished store opened in the old 1865 St. John the Baptist Church, the parish for the local German Catholics. At 612 Jefferson, a block to the northwest, the building housed the **Delaney Academy**, which was a popular seminary from 1843 to 1867. The academy was located in the structure from 1857 to 1867.

247.0 **Angel Mounds State Historic Site** is a 103-acre Middle Missisippian village that prospered in the fourteenth and fifteenth centuries on a palisaded bluff above the Ohio. One thousand Native Americans erected eleven significant earthen mounds, the largest rising forty-four feet and covering four acres. In 1938 Indianapolis industrialist and philanthropist Eli Lilly purchased the site from the Angel family and others, and donated it to the Indiana Historical Society. The site was excavated from 1939 to 1942 by an archeology team led by Glenn A. Black from Indiana University, which included 277 formerly inexperienced WPA workers. Until 1960 the self-taught Black was the only professional archeologist in the state. The workers collected over 2.3 million objects during the project, most of which are stored at Indiana University's Glenn Black Museum. The state of Indiana took over the site in 1945, with the Historical Society and Indiana University retaining excavation rights. Angel Mounds was declared a National Historic Landmark in 1966, the nation's highest designation. An interpretation center was opened in 1972, which offers exhibits, an informational slide show, and a simulated archeological excavation. A replica village gives the visitor a sense of urban life in America while Robin Hood harvested the surplus of the rich and Joan of Arc rallied her people in the Old World. This is, as they like to say at Angel Mounds, Medieval Evansville.

The historic site is adjacent to the **Warrick-Vanderburgh County Line.** Vanderburgh County was incorporated in 1818 after the requisite political intrigues of early Indiana, when county boundaries and seats moved at the whims of the legislators and business leaders. Evansville, located in a wooded horseshoe bend of the river, was declared the county seat.

Like the Falls Cities area, Evansville can be a little tricky to navigate on the Ohio River Scenic Route, until signage is complete. The official directions through the Pocket City and onto the next leg of the route are as follows: Take Route 662W to Interstate 164. I-164W turns into Veterans Memorial Parkway and the Riverside Drive in Evansville. Turn left (west) on Route 62 (Lloyd Expressway) in Evansville and proceed west through Mount Vernon to the Indiana-Illinois border.

Thanks to excellent rail connections and progressive business and civic leaders, **Evansville** is the preeminent city in the tri-state region. The corners of Indiana, Kentucky, and southeastern Illinois adjoin thirty twisty river miles downstream where the Wabash flows into the Ohio in a slurry of half land and half water. Indeed, Evansville is the largest city on Indiana's entire Ohio River shore, 126,000 people in 1990, the third largest city in Indiana.

Culturally, the city boasts two universities, an outstanding regional museum, both a philharmonic and symphony orchestra, a clutch of theater and dance groups, and a bustling downtown with fine and funky restaurants and attractions for the visitor. The city has several outstanding parks, as well as the vintage Ellis Park horse racing track. The calendar is crowded with festivals, from the thrilling Thunder on the Ohio hydroplane racing festival and the Teutonic charm of the Volksfest at the one-hundred-fifty-year old Germania Maennerchor to Native American Days at Angel Mounds. There are six historic districts and eighty-six individual structures on the National Register of Historic Places. Evansville is a prosperous place with industrial parks, large manufacturing facilities, regional shopping centers, and affluent suburban neighborhoods.

The town's early days were fraught with the frontier state's political capriciousness. Initially, the wooded bend in the river was to be the seat of a vast Warrick County, but that county was carved up and, suddenly, Evansville no longer was centrally located. In 1818, after some political logrolling, Warrick County was pared down again, with Spencer County to the east and Vanderburgh County to the west carved from it. Evansville, at last, was a county seat, though the county was one of the state's smallest.

Through the 1820s and 1830s, the village suffered through cholera, milk sickness, flood, financial panic, and a winter so severe that the river froze more than twenty-two inches thick, disrupting navigation for the duration of the season. In 1834, however, Evansville was declared to be the southern terminus for the Central Canal that would link Fort Wayne with the Ohio. "Every male citizen of town—also every one of the invited guests from abroad, was over-set, upset, and reeling, staggering, whooping in the streets as a result of too much wine and whiskey mixed," one commentator wrote of the grand opening. Evansville's first industries arrived—a canal boat business and a cabinet maker.

The mammoth Internal Improvement Bill of 1836, a massive program of roads, canals, and other improvements, unleashed Indiana's canal boom and brought prosperous times to the Crescent City. By 1837 the townsfolk "went mad on lot speculation," one visitor said. Newcomers arrived and began a flurry of business-building—foundries, sawmills, and a flour mill to name a few. But the canal boom was short-lived. The state went bankrupt in the ensuing financial panic, and defaulted on its debts. The Wabash and Erie Canal, which incorporated the Central Canal, eventually opened in 1853, but only a handful of boats ever made it down the entire 464-mile-long ditch to Evansville. By 1860 it was abandoned, victim of the rise of railroads and bad financial timing. Fortuitously, the same year the first keelboat floated in from Petersburg, so did the first train from Princeton. Evansville eventually became a major junction point for north-south rail connections, further connecting them to markets in both the North and South. The trans-regional trade has always lent an air of the provincial South to the town, as Evansville was the link between the farms of the North and the markets of the South.

With 2,121 people in 1848, Evansville was chartered as a city just in time for the floods of cultivated and trained Germans displaced by the European Revolution of 1848. Rapidly, the foreign-born population swelled, particularly in the westside area of Lamasco, where scores of businesses began—wholesale houses, mills, breweries, furniture factories, potteries, and tobacco houses. The towns merged in 1857. The Civil War was a boon to the city, as Evansville became a provender and manufacturer for the Union. One local boomer in the 1870s rhapsodized that "the smokestacks of industry at countless points form a forest of progress." By 1890 there were fifty thousand people in Evansville; by 1910, three hundred factories.

Evansville, like much of Indiana, has a sad legacy of intolerance. The black population of Evansville boomed in the post-Civil War era, topping out at over thirteen percent of the population in 1900, the highest in Indiana. However, racial tensions culminated in a 1903 race riot that killed eleven and injured fifty, accelerating a migration from the city in the ensuing decades. The eventual Grand Dragon of the Ku Klux Klan and powerful state political leader in the 1920s, D. C. Stephenson, got his start in Evansville while working as a coal salesman. He formed the first Indiana klavern in Evansville. World War I unleashed a torrent of anti-German hostility. German language was taken out of the schools and churches, and Evansville's German daily, the *Taglisher Demokrat*, was suspended. Even German Township in the northern part of the county was renamed.

The town's industrial and commercial might continued to grow through the twentieth century, refrigerators and auto manufacturing replacing buggies and sawmills. The town called itself Ice-Box City and, for many years the Chamber of Commerce sponsored the football Refrigerator Bowl reigned over by Miss Refrigadorable. But the 1950s caught Evansville with outmoded factories making unfashionable goods. The town floundered until a far-seeking citizen commission in the 1960s put the town back on track. Today, it is again the bustling entrepôt of the lower Ohio.

The river has been a mixed blessing. The town severely flooded in 1832, again in 1882 and in 1884. During the great flood of 1884, Red Cross founder **Clara Barton** directed the Ohio Valley relief efforts from a building at the corner of Mary and Iowa streets that was virtually an island. A plaque commemorates the organization's first disaster-relief effort. The disastrous flood of 1937 inundated more than forty percent of the city and displaced thirty thousand people.

But the city never turned her back on the river, celebrating the river heritage with a riverfront promenade along the levee built after the 1937 flood. **The Evansville Convention and Visitors Bureau** is located in a whimsical 1913, tile-roofed, Japanese-styled pagoda overlooking the Ohio and the **Casino Aztar** gambling boat. The Casino Aztar was Indiana's first gambling boat. It offers thirteen hundred slot machines and forty-eight blackjack tables along with a plethora of gaming options. Nearby, the **Evansville Museum of Arts and Science,** 411 S. E. Riverside Drive, is a cultural mainstay of southwestern Indiana, exhibiting more than twenty-five temporary exhibits annually, along with their fine permanent collection, covering everything from a cabinet that Abe Lincoln built to an Edward Hopper oil, Ch'ing Dynasty ceramics, sixteenth-century paintings, and a collection of locomotives and train cars.

The magnificent mansions of the nineteenth-century timber barons rise like giant wedding cakes across Riverside Drive in the **Riverside Historic District,** a neighborhood of nabobs. The **Reitz Home Museum,** 224 S. E. First Street, is the centerpiece of the neighborhood. Mercantilist John Augustus Reitz built the French Second Empire Home in 1870-71 to display his wealth and prestige; he succeeded quite well. The three-story, seventeen-room mansion still reflects his power. The elaborate inlaid parquet floors, stained glass, and Moorish detailing give the visitor a sense of life among the well-to-do in the Gibson Girl era.

The **Watkins F. Nisbet House,** 310 S. E. First, is considered the finest example of the Second Empire style in Evansville. It took two years and a fortune to build in 1878-1880. The **Stockwell/Wheeler Double House** at 313-315 S. E. First is the oldest house in the downtown area, built in 1836-39. The **Cadwalader Griffith House** and the **Crawford Bell House** at 506 and 534 S. E. First are 1840s examples of the Federal style. The Bell house has thirteen-foot ceilings and six fireplaces, with three in operation. The **John H. Fendrich House,** 827 S. E. First, was built by a local cigar magnate in 1916-17. In the early part of this century, the Fendrich Cigar Company was America's largest independent cigar company, supplying pool hall and cigar shops coast to coast with their famous La Fendrich cigar. The **Benjamin Bosse House,** 813 S. E. First, is a respite from the overwhelming Victoriana of the neighborhood. Built in 1916-17, the house utilizes the Prairie style of Frank Lloyd Wright, melding the house into the landscape with a low-slung structure of horizontal planes.

The **Willard Carpenter House,** 405 Carpenter Street, is one of Evansville's oldest structures, built in 1848-49 by local investor Willard Carpenter. The severe Greek Revival structure is the home of the regional public broadcasting station. Carpenter prospered with his speculations in land, canals, and railroads, along with a wholesale dry goods business. In the 1870s he turned his attention and profits to philanthropy, starting a home for homeless girls and endowing the **Willard Library,** 21 First Avenue. Until the completion of two Carnegie libraries in 1913, the Willard was Evansville's only public library. The brooding, ornately adorned Gothic pile is still in operation, specializing in genealogical and regional subjects.

The library has a ghostly patron. Stories and sightings of the "Lady in Gray" have abounded since the 1930s, when a worker saw a ghostly, veiled woman, dressed in period gray clothing, vanish before his eyes. Since then, scents of heavy perfume and a "presence" have alerted the Willard's librarians and patrons to another visit of the Lady. The Willard's no-nonsense librarians, starched exemplars of rationality, methodically list incidents of supernatural occurrence. Reportedly, Willard was somewhat of a skinflint and spent most of his money on the library and its collections. The librarians theorize that Willard's daughter, Louise, unhappy with her father's choice of charities, haunts the library searching for her lost bequest.

Evansville's downtown has an outstanding collection of historical architecture from the Neo-Baroque treasure of the **Old Courthouse** at Fourth and Vine (built on the terminus of the Wabash and Erie Canal), to the 1930s Art Deco sleekness of the **Greyhound Bus Terminal**, Third and Sycamore streets, with the only running neon dog left in the country. The 1913 **Alhambra Theatre,** 50 Adams Avenue, is a Moorish Revival fantasy that fairly sings with the memories of Rudolph Valentino days. The **Old Vanderburgh County Jail and Sheriff's Residence** was designed to intimidate, a crenalated Gothic Revival interpretation of Lichtenstein Castle. The **Old Post Office Place**, 100 N. W. Second St., housed the federal offices and the customs office as well as the post office when it was built in 1875-79. After an extensive restoration, it houses the Chamber of Commerce, offices, and a restaurant.

The Old Courthouse is perhaps the only pure example of Beaux-Arts architecture in the state. Built between 1888 and 1890, the structure reflects the esthetic ideals that culminated at Chicago's 1893 Columbian Exposition. Note the imperial figures of economic activity on the roof: goddesses of commerce and transportation, ships, trains, and scales weighing coins.

Evansville is a warren of leafy older neighborhoods, close-knit districts that are centered on their churches and neighborhood gathering spots. **The**

Hilltop Inn, for instance, has served beer to their crowd of burly westside Germans since stage-coach days in the 1840s, when it was an inn for travelers. It's still one of the anchors of the westside neighborhood.

They're proud of their brains there and they should be—they serve enough of them. Deep-fried brain sandwiches are a big seller in the area. "Our brains are big," Hilltop manager Janet Trautvetter said, holding her hands out to about the size of a small frisbee. "You always serve them with onion and pickle, catsup or mustard. Mayo sometimes. At the Fall Festival, the West Side Nut Club sells a lot of brains. They'll be lined up for an hour."

The Rosenberger Building, 2100 W. Franklin, is considered one of the German westside's historic linchpins. Built in 1890, the building housed August Rosenberger's grocery and farm store. Rosenberger helped start the German St. Boniface's Church and was an influential local businessman. His house is still standing at 409 N. Wabash Avenue, centering the Independence Historic District, yet another site on the National Register of Historic Places.

The University of Evansville's Olmstead Administration Building is the original building on the campus. Built in 1917 when Evansville lured the Moore's Hill College from Dearborn County, the rubble-stone building has broken, rather than sawn, limestone facade faces, giving the building an air of ancient rusticity. The Methodist institution offers both bachelors and masters programs at the eastside campus. West of town toward Angel Mounds, the **University of Southern Indiana** has a considerably more contemporary feel. Originally, it was founded as a regional campus for Indiana State University, but it has evolved to become the seventh independent state-supported institution of higher education. The university's **Bent Twig Outdoor Education Center** is a collection of historic structures, several of which are pre-Civil War, which are used for a variety of educational and public uses.

A wide range of recreational facilities enlivens the city. **Wesselman Woods Nature Preserve** is a unique urban forest, located at 551 Boeke Road. It encompasses a National Landmark forest and a recreation area offering tennis, ball parks, picnic grounds, and a playground. Until a violent windstorm in the 1980s, the forest was the densest in Indiana, a mature forest of more than twenty-five species. **Burdette Park and Aqua Center,** Nerrenbern Road, has one of the largest swimming pools in the Midwest, two water slides, and a lagoon-sized kiddie pool, along with a BMX track, batting cages, pavilions, and party houses. **The Mesker Park Zoo,** Bement Road, was Indiana's first when it started in the late 1920s with a few small animals, a couple of ragtag lions retired from the circus, and Kay, the elephant purchased in 1929 after a citywide fund drive. Today, more than seven hundred animals cavort and congregate on the zoo's seventy acres, making it one of the state's largest.

Evansville and Vanderburgh County have embarked on a remarkable outdoor project that encompasses recreation and healthy living. The **Pigeon Creek Greenway Project** will eventually include more than forty miles of walking/biking/nature trails that will link parks and neighborhoods through the city in a linear park. Eventually, the greenway will encircle Evansville and connect to the American Discovery Trail, an interstate system of trails that crosses America. The first phase of the greenway begins near the Heidelbach Avenue canoe launch.

On the southside of Evansville, a thousand acres of low floodplain remains where the Ohio lurched southward after the official border was set between Indiana and Kentucky, leaving the only slice of Kentucky north of the river—an area where law enforcement was sporadic at best. Many of the activities legal in Kentucky and illegal in Indiana, and others that were illegal in both states, congregated in this no-man's land.

Built behind an enormous earthen levee, Dade Park opened in 1922 as a legal thoroughbred racing track on two hundred acres, only to ingloriously go bankrupt the following year. It reopened in 1924 under the ownership of James C. Ellis, who operated the track until his death, at which time the track was renamed **Ellis Park Racetrack.** Today, the horses still streak past the original grandstand as they have for the last seventy-five years, and the bettors still crowd the pari-mutuel windows, a horse apple's throw from the Hoosier state.

In the adjoining areas of north-of-the-river Kentucky, a collection of shacks that housed speakeasies and saloons arose in the area that came to be known as "Little Chicago," including the Commando Club, Pearson's, The 101 Club, Kentucky Club, Happy Hour, Midway, and Cloverdale, nearly every one having a "game room" and slots.

Evansville's industrial war boom brought a "swarm of prostitutes and gamblers," according to writer John Bartlow Martin. Since there were no bridges between Evansville and Kentucky till 1932, the club zone was already well established. The best known of them was the elaborate Trocadero, which opened in the 1940s, where big name entertainers like Benny Goodman, Cab Calloway, Duke Ellington, Harry James, Ozzie Nelson, and Gene Krupa helped draw crowds for the crap tables and other gaming. It boomed through the 1950s and 1960s till campaigns by the local ministry finally closed it down. The building operated as an antique store until it burned in the 1980s.

Down in the bottoms on the Old Henderson Road, catfish fiddlers are the specialty of the old wooden **Dogtown Tavern.** The place was built in 1889 as the Cypress post office, situated on the Red Banks Trail, an early buffalo trace. It served as a tavern and post office until 1915 when the postmaster died, and has been a local watering hole since. It's said that the tavern got its name from the hunters' dogs left outside while their owners cel-

ebrated or commiserated on their hunting luck. The packs of pooches eventually gave Dogtown its name. Today, crowds of Hoosiers still come to sit at
the scrupulously clean, vintage, formica tables under fleets of inflatable beer
dirigibles, and drink beer and chow down on some of the best catfish in the
Midwest. "Check out that tartar sauce," my pregnant Madonna-faced wait-
ress said. "The owner, Susie, makes it herself."

Five miles south of Evansville on U. S. 41, the **John James Audubon State
Park** honors the great naturalist-artist who lived here from 1810 to 1820.
While partnering in a general store, Audubon prowled the river banks,
sketching the avian life that became his life. The newly renovated museum
houses a trove of his oil paintings, sketches, and family memorabilia, as well
as the full elephant folio of 435 of his famous bird portraits. The museum
also has a rare daguerreotype of elderly Audubon shot by the Civil War pho-
tographer Matthew Brady.

Visitor Information

Owensboro-Daviess County KY Chamber of Commerce, 335 Frederica St., Owensboro, KY 42302-0825, 502-926-1860.

Historic Newburgh Tourist Information Center, 9 W. Jennings, Newburgh, IN 47629, 800-639-9489.

Evansville Convention and Visitors Bureau, 401 S. E. Riverside Drive, Evansville IN, 47713, 800-433-3025, (www.evansvillecvb.org)

Henderson KY Chamber of Commerce, 201 N. Main St., Henderson, KY 42420, 502-826-9531.

Recommended Reading

An Introduction to the Prehistory of Indiana, James H. Kellar, Indiana Historical Society, Indianapolis, 1973.

Recommended Bed and Breakfasts and Cabins

The Historic Newburgh Bed & Breakfast, 224 State St., Newburgh, IN 47630, is located a refurbished Italianate home with three rooms decorated in period furnishings.

Coolbreeze Estate Bed and Breakfast, 1240 S. E. 2nd St., Evansville, IN 47713, 812-422-9635, offers four guestrooms in a rambling 1906 Prairie School-styled home.

John James Audubon State Park, U.S. 41, Henderson, KY 42420, 502-826-2247, has cabins along with camping sites.

Recommended Regional Dining

Moonlite Bar-B-Q Inn, Parrish Street, Owensboro, KY 42302, 502-684-8143, is a cavernous local institution, famous for hickory-smoked barbecue.

George's Bar-B-Q, 1326 E. 4th, Owensboro, KY 42302, 502-926-0276, specializes in the Kentucky mainstay, burgoo, a thick, pungent stew of diverse meats and vegetables.

The Mediterranean, 3 Market St., Newburgh, IN 47629, 812-858-7383, serves Italian and Greek food in a historic downtown structure.

B's Coffee House Cafe, Jennings Station, Newburgh, IN 47629, 812-858-3885, is a great place to grab a restorative cup of coffee and a pastry after a hard day of fun.

Lorenzo's Bread and Bistro, 972 S. Hebron, Evansville, IN 47714, 812-475-9477, is located on the eastside of Evansville. Owner Larry Minor is a world traveler and has brought back the flavors of Europe with forty different European breads. The bistro serves seasonally based daily specials and various types of Italian sandwiches.

The Jungle Mornings Restaurant Coffee House and Bar, 415 Main St., Evansville, IN 47713, is located in a well-restored nineteenth-century downtown building, and is one of Evansville's premier dining spots, serving a fine variety of New American food.

YWCA Tea Room, 118 Vine St., Evansville, IN 47708, 812-422-1191, is a pink table cloth-ed, pink-geraniumed ladies' place, as it has been since it started in 1925. If you are in a Jane Wyman mood, this is the place for finger foods and fruit plates.

Wolf's Bar-B-Que, 1414 E. Columbia Way, Evansville, IN 47711, 812-423-3599, is in the third generation of family ownership. The Wolfs have served two million people in the last ten years alone. It was the first restaurant in Indiana to have curb service and a drive-up window.

Hilltop Inn, 1100 Harmony Way, Evansville, IN 47712, 812-422-1757, was established in 1839 on the westside of town. Brain sandwiches are one of their specialties, though they serve a variety of Hoosier fare like fried chicken and catfish fiddlers.

Dogtown Tavern, Old Henderson Road, Evansville, IN 47712, 812-423-0808, serves the best fiddlers on the Ohio River Scenic Route.

Camping

John James Audubon State Park, U.S. 41, Henderson, KY 42420, 502-826-2247, has a seventy-one-site campground along with cabins and a lake with a swimming beach.

Harmonie State Park, R.R. 1, Box 5A, New Harmony, IN 47631, 812-682-4821, is about forty-five minutes to the west, and has two hundred campsites, a swimming pool with a water slide, six hiking trails, and a bike trail, as well as a naturalist who presents nature programs.

The Mississippian-era stockade at Angel Mounds State Historic Site was a Native American town that thrived in the fourteenth and fifteenth centuries. It is now a part of the tour taken by hundreds of students each year.

Photo by Richard Fields

Courtesy of Indiana Department of Commerce Tourism Division

The Willard Library was Evansville's only library until 1913. It now specializes in genealogical and regional subjects. Reportedly, a ghost wanders the stacks and halls.

The design of New Harmony's Roofless Church encompasses the faiths of all the world's religions.

Frontier Utopians

Evansville to Illinois Border 29 miles
The Road to New Harmony Alternate Loop 25 miles

Quietly basking on the banks of the Wabash a few miles north of the Ohio, New Harmony is another small Hoosier town with its basketball hoops and Victorian main street and Kiwanis Club meeting on Thursday. But turn down a leafy street and another Indiana emerges. Austere unpainted frame houses with kitchen gardens of remarkable order sit primly beside hulking Germanic brick buildings. Log cabins cluster together. At the edge of the flood plain, clots of people stream into a gleaming porcelain structure, as modern as a spacecraft ready to lift off. Sounds of Tibetan chanting drift down the street.

Early in the nineteenth century when most of Indiana was still a vast, untamed forest, New Harmony was the site of two remarkable utopian experiments—"a chimera in the wilderness," historian Anne Taylor called it. "There were other communities that were utopian," bookseller and local idealist Bob Brooks said at his Golden Raintree Bookstore, "but none that were both sacred and secular. The first, the Harmonists, were waiting for the Second Coming. The second, the Owenites, rejected religion entirely. The Harmonists left the legacy of the buildings and town layout. But the real survival is the scientific and intellectual legacy the Owenites left 170 years ago. I really revel in the intellectual history here."

In 1814 eight hundred German Swabian millennialists arrived on the frontier at New Harmony. Led by a charismatic leader, Father Joseph Rapp, the celibate communalists intended "to make of the wild country fertile fields and gardens of pleasure," as Rapp wrote. The Harmonists, as they chose to be known, were one of the Pietist sects that arose in the ferment of the Protestant Reformation, when people sought a direct connection to the divine without the intervention of the clergy or deadening ritual. "Belief fled from the cold churches with their arid practices into the country parlors," as Taylor wrote. They believed in communal property, celibacy, and the imminent Second Coming of Christ, and they refused military service. All of it was unsettling to the authorities, but the refusal to accept conscription was the final straw. Many Pietist groups fled to the New World to await the End. The Harmonists considered their home in Indiana to be merely a way-station to perfect themselves as they awaited the arrival of the New Jerusalem— the end of the world as we know it.

"There's a Swabian saying," Dr. Don Pitzer, a tall, white-haired expert on American communal societies told me, "'Work, work, work, and die.'" In ten years, the Harmonists cleared and planted thousands of acres and built 180 buildings, including two immense churches. When Indiana was virgin forest and canebrake, operating a bare subsistence economy, an immaculate brick and frame town—a bastion of art, culture, and capital—rose from a surround of tended fields and vineyards on the Wabash. Lemons, oranges, and figs thrived in portable greenhouses. The Harmonist library was the most extensive west of the Alleghenies, and Harmonists were critical to the formation of the state of Indiana. They had the only steam engine in the region, six mills, a printing press, as well as a distillery, brewery, and winery, though they themselves seldom drank. They made shoes, brick, rope, and textiles, including silk from their silkworms.

While most on the day's seventy thousand Hoosiers barely had money for the coarsest goods, a thousand identically clad German communalists marched to field and workshop to the sound of French horns and Swabian hymns. "There was lots of music here," Pitzer said. "I think music got them through." Indiana's first community orchestra was here. Mozart and Beethoven interchanged with the Harmonists' hymns, played on pianoforte, flutes, horns, violins, and bassoons. In their workplaces, vocal groups passed their day in song. One traveler wrote, "They are great musicians, and many of them study music as a Science, using music both as a respite from their harrowing work and as a call to harmony, creating a shared brotherhood as they sang."

Far from the corruption of American society, the Harmonists labored to achieve perfection as they awaited the Second Coming of Christ. In the process, they built a town that was the marvel of the young republic. They did business with twenty-four states and ten foreign countries, trading from a region that was considered one of the wildest places in the country. A Liverpool bell tolled seven miles into the forests, startling travelers thrashing through the canebrake. "They made the wilderness smile," one visitor, Willliam Hebert, wrote. It is the great irony that a group that renounced all worldly possessions for the eternal salvation of the souls, ended up amassing a fortune from commerce.

"It was the cheap land that drew them here," Pitzer said. "In those days, Indiana was the frontier, and frontier land prices and freedom of thought and action have always appealed to alternative religious groups and reformers. That and isolation. Groups like these are out of synch with the general society, and they want isolation. It's still that way." He went on to talk about contemporary communal groups from Hutterites to hippies, from guru-run ashrams to Benedictine monasteries.

Undoubtedly, celibacy focused the Harmonists' energies on the Second Coming, and, of course, the work that prepared them for it. They believed that Adam was a dual person who possessed both genders (as did God), prior to the arrival of Eve. From this starting point, they noted the biblical injunction that "He that is unmarried careth for the things that belong to the Lord, and how he may please the Lord." In 1807, in their first American home in Pennsylvania, the Harmonists followed the Bible again, and declared, "all who were married should live as brother and sister." Don Pitzer said, "The Harmonists were different from the Shakers and other celibate groups, in that the husband and wife continued to sleep together, but as 'brothers and sisters' in Christ. They used the phrase 'eunuchs in Christ.'"

Germans, I thought. *Germans could do that.*

By 1824, when the work on the town was essentially finished and the Second Coming appeared to be less imminent than predicted, the Harmonists grew restive, and Rapp determined to relocate in a virgin spot. His adopted son, Frederick Rapp, the financial genius behind the community, prepared an inventory for sale of the town, providing both an advertisement and a summary of what the Harmonists had accomplished on a material plane. In 1824 he wrote, "Town of Harmony with 20,000 acres of first-rate land adjoining, situated on the east bank of the Big Wabash, seventy miles by water from its mouth, only fifteen miles by land from the Ohio River. Two thousand acres of highly cultivated land, fifteen of it in vineyard, thirty-five in apple orchard, containing 1,500 bearing apple and pear trees. Considerable peach orchards and pleasure gardens with bearing and ornamental trees.

"One large three-story water-powered merchant mill; extensive factory of cotton and woolen goods; 2 sawmills, 1 oil and hemp mill, a large brick and stone warehouse, 2 large granaries, 1 store, a large tavern, 6 large frame buildings used as mechanic's shops, 1 large tanyard of 50 vats, 3 frame barns 5 X 100, with one thrashing mill; 3 large sheep stables, 6 two-story brick dwellings, 60 X 60; 40 two-story brick and frame dwellings; 86 log dwellings; all houses have stables and gardens; 2 large distilleries, 1 brewery."

The Harmonists had not found the banks of the Wabash to be without problems. River transport was erratic, as periodic low water disrupted shipping. Indiana markets and population had not grown as fast as anticipated, and their relations with their Hoosier neighbors were less than harmonious. Their neighbors were naturally jealous of the Harmonists' prosperity. There were numerous complaints to the state capitol about the milling price the Harmonists charged at the area's only gristmill. At one point there was a small riot by backwoodsmen on the streets of New Harmony, probably fueled by Harmonist whiskey. The Harmonists' communalism and pacifism also caused substantial mutterings, particularly when Rapp succeeded in getting a reduction in the taxes the Harmonists paid in lieu of military service.

The Harmonists' celibacy was a particular source of gossip, especially the rumor that Rapp's own son died in Pennsylvania in 1812 after Father Rapp himself castrated him. The validity of the story has been a source of dispute since then. The castration and resulting death was said to have happened after twenty-eight year old John Rapp succumbed to sexual indulgence. The recent revelations about the voluntary castrations by the Heaven's Gate communards in California gives us up-to-date examples of a very old tradition. Human castrations were well known in the early nineteenth century, sometimes prescribed for mumps and other diseases, sometimes meted out as punishment for sexual excess. It is known Father Rapp studied the nineteenth chapter of Matthew that concludes, "for there are some eunuchs, which were so born from their mother's womb; and there are some eunuchs, which were made eunuchs of men; and there be eunuchs, which have made themselves eunuchs for the kingdom of heaven's sake." And it is known that in spite of the Harmonist practice of leaving graves unmarked and unmounded, the only headstone in the Harmonist cemetery in Harmonie, Pennsylvania, lies against the wall to the side of John's grave. It reads after his name and date of birth and death:

> *Here lies a clay upon the potter's wheel*
> *Until decay unlock*
> *The precious salt to a new body*
> *Which is the joy of life will then arise*

Father Rapp declared New Harmony to be "fat and bountiful" when they arrived, but malaria was a constant problem in the low-lying land. Malaria plagued the river settlers all through the Midwest, an inescapable part of life, and it plagued the Harmonists also. Two-hundred and thirty Harmonists who died of malaria lie buried in unmarked rows in the old New Harmony cemetery, interred at night in unmounded graves beside the ancient Hopewell burial mound.

In essence, the Harmonists wanted to deal the Old Maid. They wanted a healthier location, closer to their Eastern markets. They found a willing buyer in Robert Owen, a wealthy Scottish industrialist known for progressive labor practices. For $150,000 Owen bought the town—lock, stock, and barrel. When the day arrived for the Harmonists to turn over their town and move to their new untamed town near Pittsburgh, they marched onto the waiting steamboats, once again to the silver tones of French horns and sounds of their favorite Swabian hymns. The only written record they left behind was scrawled by an anonymous Harmonist under a staircase in Dormitory No. 2, which still can be seen on the rough wood: "In the 24th of May, 1824, we have departed. Lord with thy great help and goodness, in body and soul, protect us."

Robert Owen tirelessly promoted his utopian New Moral World—a world where love and liberal education in communities of social and economic equality would create superior humans. He declared that human nature was less pre-ordained than shaped by environment, which could be ameliorated by the correct surroundings and direction. One of Owen's contemporaries described him as an enthusiast, "one believing things to be miracles where they are not." Unable to garner support in Britain's Parliament—"very woolly," they termed his ideas—Owen was determined to execute his plan in the American hinterlands and purchased the town from the Harmonists.

Owen preceded the Socialist, and even Karl Marx, in the development of his reformer ideas. He believed that the developing industrial society had to improve the conditions of the working class with education and a more equal distribution of wealth. He saw New Harmony as the first of a global network of Agricultural and Manufacturing Villages of Mutual Co-operation, where progressive education and equality could create superior human beings, the vanguard of what he called his New Moral World.

President John Quincy Adams thought Owen was "crafty crazy" and a "speculative, scheming, mischievous man." Journalists described Owen as having the "air of a schoolmaster and quack doctor mixed" and "a delightful bore." Another, less kind commentator termed him an "intolerable bore." But he fired the imagination of a remarkable group of East Coast and European intellectuals, some of the leading educators, naturalists, and geologists of the day. Intent on building a new world and flattered by their presumed high position in it, scientists and educators joined Owen's scheme. In a fraternal bliss of shared intellectualism, they keelboated down the Ohio from Pittsburgh on the *Philanthropist,* sketching and classifying the birds and fish they caught, and reveling one another with their utopian dreams. After a voyage of many weeks, slowed by river ice, they arrived at present-day Mount Vernon and traipsed overland to New Harmony. The rough wooden vessel came to be known as "The Boatload of Knowledge."

It was an eminent group, many from Philadelphia, the cultured heart of the East. Among others, the group included William Maclure, celebrated geologist who was a co-founder of the Philadelphia Academy of Natural Sciences. He had a particular interest in the Pestalozzian method of teaching in which children learned from observation in an environment of common sense and kindness, in contrast to Owen's belief in classical education. He also invested heavily in New Harmony, becoming a partner with Owen. Thomas Say was a brilliant naturalist, the most eminent entomologist the United States had ever seen. His mutton-chop whiskers and bristly cockscomb hair hid a face alight with boyish enthusiasm. Charles Alexander Lesueur was also a renowned naturalist, later famous for his classification of the Great Lakes fishery. Parisian Madame Marie Louise Duclos Fretageot was the schoolmistress of the most highly regarded school in Philadelphia. Robert Dale Owen, twenty-four years old, was joining his father on the frontier.

They joined other intellectuals like Dutch geologist Gerald Troost, and Robert Owen himself, who already arrived in town. They all shared the overcrowded town with a flood of backwoods rustics and eccentrics who were drawn by Owen's call for participants in his New Moral World, where all would share equally. It was as though a band of hippies took over a Shaker town and invited the locals in to share.

Brits tend to get a bit barmy in the hinterlands, all dancing eyebrows and loquacious circumlocutions. Owen was no different, modestly declaring in his first speech to his new community, "I am come to this country, to introduce an entire new state of society: to change it from the ignorant, selfish system to an enlightened social system, which shall gradually unite all interests into one and remove all cause for contests between individuals." Like Rapp, Owen saw the town as interim shelter. "New Harmony, the future name of this place," he said, "is the best halfway house I could procure for those who are going to travel this extraordinary journey with me, and although it is not intended to be our permanent residence, I hope it will not be a bad traveler's tavern."

Owen planned to build the first of his global network of Agricultural and Manufacturing Villages of Unity and Mutual Co-operation nearby. A few miles south of New Harmony, between Solitude and Springfield, where today serpentine rows of green corn twist around old red barns, the Owenites planned to erect an enormous, thirty-acre, multi-story quadrangle, a phalanstery as Owen called it, where the New Moral World could begin. It was to be a hive of industry and self-improvement, overseen by a highly sensitized community. "Owen—he had a prescriptive happiness," Bob Brooks said. The Village was a cross between a Skinnerian rat lab and a Maoist commune, with every action noted by a neighbor, each "cooperating" to produce the best possible human. Owen intended "to place the conduct of the people at all times before the eye of the community."

The reality is that Owen shared a fear of the poor classes with his fellow industrialists. He just thought his plan of mutual cooperation would teach them what was best for them—good habits and industrial skills. When Owen spoke and wrote of human happiness, he often confused it with bovine docility. He wanted a placid work force doing their jobs harmoniously for him. They weren't people; they were lumpen to form into his ideals. Like many entrepreneurs, then and now, Owen suffered a towering ego that caused him to micro-manage disastrously and surround himself with yes-men. The sound of his own pontificating voice was both a salve and a tonic for him. One waspish observer said that Owen had a "vacant spot in his mind where other men may have a political response."

Robert Owen himself spent little time in the town after he purchased it. Eventually, the Owenites fired a few bricks for the quadrangle, but little else— other than wild ideas. If political discourse can be considered an art, the Owenites excelled at it. In two and a half years, the squabbling Owenites promulgated seven different constitutions to govern the fractious community. In general, much of the discord revolved two issues: the economic expectations of the two groups who populated the town—the haves and the have-nots—and differing views of education among the luminaries. The Boatload of Knowledge intellectuals saw knowledge as an end in itself. Owen saw it as a means to an end—a society free of strife with the lower classes trained in "useful" occupations. Split into various factions, the Owenites and fellow travelers formed competing villages. One, Feiba-Peveli, based its name on a system of translating latitude and longitude into letters, which, if universally applied as planned, would make New York Otke Notive. New Harmony never did become a true communal society. The best it ever got to be was a cobbled-together cooperative. Owen himself fled for the calmer environs of East Coast salons, where he could continue his proselytizing in relative decorum. After a brief few years, the dream of the New Moral World was gone, collapsed in a flurry of misplaced expectations and recriminations. "It's a daunting task, re-inventing civilization," Pitzer said.

When they weren't arguing, the Owenites held elaborate balls in the seven-hundred-seat theater building, where sets by the New Orleans painter, Peter Duclos, decorated the enormous stage. The theater was the second-largest in Indiana till the era of the 1920s movie palaces, though there were never more than a thousand people in New Harmony. The Owenites formed one of the first thespian societies in the state, performing plays like *William Tell* and *The Magpie*, as well as original works like *Pocahontas*, which also played New York. The thespian group grew so adept they built a floating theater and took it on the road, or river, in this case. They sailed halfway down the Mississippi before their ingrained discord kicked in, and they abandoned the enterprise. The naturalist artist John James Audubon visited often from his store in Henderson, Kentucky. Swiss artist Karl Bodmer, who documented the life along the upper Missouri, was another artistic visitor, wintering over in 1832-33 with his patron, Alexander Phillipp Maximillian, Prinz zu Wied-Neuwied.

A remarkable group of intellectuals stayed in New Harmony after Robert Owen departed, and broadly influenced the scientific and progressive climate of Indiana and the young republic. "Scientifically, this was the hub of the United States," Pitzer said. New Harmony was the center for the Geologic Survey of the United States for several decades. The first systematic weather bureau was here. Progresssive education of both infants and adults was pioneered in this little town on the Wabash. Natural sciences historian Donald Peattie wrote, "Yet in reality it was the most brilliant asemblage of original intellects in the field of natural history that the western hemisphere has ever witnessed, and in proportion to the poverty and physical disadvantages of the time and places, it gave to birth and to print more pioneering work than the great cities of today."

Among the many brilliant scholars who stayed on after Robert Owen left town, William Maclure stands out. Arthur Beston, the grand old man of American communal studies, declared, "In the long perspective of time, Maclure's contribution to New Harmony was more enduring than Robert Owen's." Maclure was a tall, opinionated Englishman, often called the "Father of American Geology." He and Owen suffered a fatal rupture of interests not long after New Harmony began, which culminated in a highly publicized law suit that had the community, and the republic, atwitter. Maclure himself only visited New Harmony sporadically after 1827—spending much of his time in a geologic survey of Mexico. But at his death in 1840, he still owned thirty buildings and ten thousand acres in the New Harmony area. His brother, Alexander, managed his many interests before he too passed away in 1850.

Maclure had a long-lasting effect on New Harmony in two ways. First, he was a major influence on two of Robert Owen's sons who chose to settle in New Harmony. David Dale and Richard Owen both became respected geologists with long careers. Second, he continued his support of New Harmony progressive education, funding public schools as well as the Workingmen's Institute and Library which was dedicated to adult education. Through his will, he left $500 for a reading and lecture room and a library of at least one hundred volumes to any club or society which established themselves, resulting in 144 Workingmen's Clubs sprouting up around the country.

The French naturalist Charles-Alexander Lesueur plucked and painted and classified his collections until he left for France in 1837. For many years, he sent back to France specimens and curiosities from the American West, including what his French biographer described as "un *pool-cat,* un skung qui n'a encore jamais été vu vivant en Europe."

Lesuer's naturalist compatriot, Thomas Say, followed Maclure to Mexico for some of his trips. But unlike Maclure, he remained a resident of New Harmony much of the time. His work culminated in the ground-breaking *American Conchology,* which classified and illustrated the shell life of American waters. Upon his death in 1834, he was buried in the lawn of the Rapp-Maclure mansion. In 1850 Alexander Maclure joined him.

David Dale Owen was named the state geologist of Indiana and, later, chief geologist of the entire United States. From 1839 to 1856, New Harmony was the U.S. Geologic Survey headquarters with Owen at the helm. Twelve states were surveyed from here, opening the Midwest to industrial development. He assisted in the organization of the Smithsonian Institution in Washington, and some say that the "Castle," the original Smithsonian building, is modeled on David Dale Owen's turreted, towered, and gabled laboratory that still stands in New Harmony, which was in turn inspired by the Owen family seat in New Lanark, Scotland.

His brother, Richard, succeeded David as state geologist and was a longtime professor of natural sciences at Indiana University in Bloomington. He was also the first president of Purdue University but had the good sense to not move to Lafayette, preferring to preside from Bloomington and New Harmony. The trustees dismissed Owen because he proposed that the graduates should have student government and a liberal education along with a technical one.

Robert Dale Owen championed many of his father's progressive thoughts at Purdue and in other areas. He served as a member of the Indiana Legislature, where he unsuccessfully introduced legislation to win property rights for women. His progressive legislation earned him the title of "Father of Indiana's Free Public School System." As a member of Indiana's 1850 constitutional convention, he added widows' property rights and the rights of women to hold separate property to the constitution. He was also instrumental in liberalizing divorce laws to protect women from drunken or abusive husbands. In gratitude, the women of Indiana placed a bronze bust of Richard Dale Owen at one of the entrances to the Indiana State House in 1851 after presenting him with a silver pitcher.

In spite of his father's seeming intolerance for African-Americans (there were none in New Harmony), Robert Dale ardently pressed their rights. In 1862 he sent a letter to Lincoln arguing for emancipation, which Secretary Chase said heavily influenced the President to declare the Emancipation Proclamation. "Can you look forward to the peace of our country," Owen wrote, "and imagine any state of things in which, with slavery still existing, we would be assured of permanent peace? I cannot . . . "

The followers of the elder Robert Owen, both in New Harmony and those who left the state, had a wide-ranging effect on movements for labor unions, feminism, abolitionism, cooperative organizations, and progressive education. It is the conundrum of communal life: groups like the Harmonists and Shakers, who fixate on communalism, ultimately atrophy and die; but groups like the Owenites, who are broadly conceived, often see their ideas radiate out like ripples from a cast stone.

The Owenite experiment placed equality between the sexes at the center of the philosophy. Women were promised social and civil rights, as well as educational opportunities. The symbol of the new equality between the sexes was the costume that Robert Owen prescribed for his "Community of Equality." Men were encouraged to wear extremely full, white pantaloons with a broad belt and a collarless boy's jacket, giving local wags some good material. Sarah Pears said she saw "A fat person dressed in the elegant costume I have heard appropriately compared to a feather bed tied in the middle." Women wore pants that were a cross between pantaloons and harem pants, worn under a knee-length skirt. Ms. Pears dryly noted, "It is rather difficult to distinguish the gentlemen from the ladies." While certainly less restrictive than the dress of the day, the costume quickly lost favor except among the most ardent of the communards.

For young single women, New Harmony was an opportunity to get an education with lots of eligible swains around for entertainment. The reality for working-class, married women was somewhat different, as they often had additional domestic burdens put upon them, along with work that previously had been done by men. Not surprisingly, married women were vocal with their complaints. Modern feminist historian Carol Kolmerten has suggested that dissonance between the Owenite dream and the New Harmony reality created "a 'woman problem' that consumed the Owenite community and helped lead to their early demise."

A remarkable early feminist, Frances Wright, was part of the community. By the time she arrived in New Harmony in 1825, she had already made a name for herself as an outspoken advocate of women's rights and emancipation of slaves. While accompanying General Lafayette on his triumphant 1824 tour of America, she heard of the radical experiment on the Wabash and joined the community. Besides editing the *New Harmony Gazette* with Robert Dale Owen, she organized an early women's society, the Female Social Society. After the community self-destructed, she and Owen moved the newspaper to New York in 1829, where it became the influential progressive publication, the *Free Enquirer.* She also founded Nashoba, a communal society for free slaves based on Owenite labor principles, where slaves could work off the price of their freedom. The community operated near Memphis, Tennessee, from 1826 to 1830. Wright spoke and wrote widely on progressive causes until her death in 1850.

Madame Marie Louise Duclos Fretageot was a Frenchwoman who oversaw the Pestalozzian school for infants in New Harmony. It was she who inspired William Maclure to become partners with Robert Owen in the New Harmony project. Fretageot arrived on the Boatload of Knowledge and went on to become one of the most influential community leaders. She attended to Maclure's business affairs, as well as his publications and schools on Pestalozzian education. In 1831 she died of cholera in Mexico while visiting Maclure.

One of Robert Owen's daughters, Jane Dale Owen Fauntleroy, organized the Minerva Club in 1859, another early women's group, replete with the standard regalia of the modern variety—motto, pledge, by-laws, programs, officers, and pretensions.

One of her nieces, Rosamund, youngest daughter of Robert Dale, returned to New Harmony early in the twentieth century after a particularly exotic round of adventures. Twice she married Englishmen, consummating neither bond. After both husbands summarily died, she spent the balance of her life litigating with the Turkish government over land near Haifa, Israel, that allegedly was the site of biblical Armageddon. It is unclear why she had or wanted to keep this particular property. Rosamund spent much of her life writing particularly overwrought poetry and tales, including her autobiography, and vividly expressing her distaste for men.

The Owenites left a lasting legacy, both in Indiana and the larger modern world. Indiana's free public school system, codified by Robert Dale Owen into the state constitution, reflects the educational ideas of his father and William Maclure. Maclure's concern for the education of the working man, culminating in his bequests for Workingmen's Institutes, presaged the nationwide funding of the Carnegie libraries early in the twentieth century. The geologic research that was done here challenged the theological concepts of geologic time, moving creation into the far nether world of prehumanity. The surveys mapped the immense mineral resources of the Midwest, providing a road map of development.

In the social realm, the Owenites ideals live on as well as their flawed realities. While a center of abolitionism, New Harmony barred African Americans. The Owenites made equality between the sexes a cornerstone of their philosophy, agitating for women's rights and birth control, but women, particularly married women, were doubly burdened with increased domestic responsibilities as well as community work.

Robert Owen promised shared wealth but could never bring himself to actually pull it off, compromising with a makeshift cooperative. In North America and the British Isles, there were eventually twenty-nine Owenite communities. They began here in New Harmony in 1825 and lasted until 1863, when Josiah Warren closed his Modern Times community on Long Island. But the core of the cooperative philosophy lived on in a thousand labor unions and workers' organizations and cooperatives in America and Europe.

The Owenites' real contribution was not in the fixed communities, but the rapidly moving ideas that changed the world. Public education, women's rights, emancipation of African-Americans, the rights of the working class—all were tested and tempered here on the Wabash. Late in the nineteenth century, Karl Marx's collaborator, Friedrich Engels, stated that "all social movements, all real advances made in England in the interests of the working class were associated with Owen's name."

After all of the hullabaloo in its first quarter century, New Harmony drifted quietly for almost a hundred years. Civic-minded preservationists and small town mercantilists catering to the surrounding farm families replaced wild-eyed millennialists and social radicals. Through the somnolence, local descendants of Owen and Maclure helped preserve the town's heritage. The Workingmen's Institute carefully catalogued and defended the Harmonist and Owenite records and artifacts. The town's centennial in 1914 reawakened an interest in the town's remarkable history and helped revive community pride. In a classic Hoosier tradition of nicknames, the local basketball team played as the New Harmony Rappites for many decades. Recognizing the extraordinary history here, Indiana set up the New Harmony Commission in 1934, the state's first historical commission, though it disbanded in 1955.

As the decades rolled on, many descendants from the town's burst of brilliance slowly dispersed from their hometown. Kenneth Dale Owen was one, taking his geologic training to Texas where oil wealth beckoned. He always maintained a home in New Harmony and, in the 1940s, began returning with his bride, Jane Blaffer Owen. She immediately recognized the possibilities of the sleepy little town. In 1959, inspired by the town's intellectual and spiritual history, she set up the Robert Lee Blaffer Trust and embarked on the next Utopian journey, the longest to date.

Jane Blaffer Owen envisioned New Harmony as a place of spiritual awakening, where the mystical and spiritual could commune with a well-nurtured built environment. The town became the destination for assorted clergy, writers, and artists, co-evolving in an atmosphere of seminars, think tanks, liturgical ceremony, and secular expression—kind of a macro-salon.

Construction began on a series of contemporary additions to the town. The first was the Roofless Church designed by renowned modernist architect Phillip Johnson, with gates and sculpture by Jacques Lipchitz. The nearby wooded park, more an environmental piece of art, was dedicated to theologian Paul Tillich in 1963.

The establishment of the second New Harmony Commission in 1973 augured the arrival of Ralph G. Schwartz, a professional urban planner. Schwartz designed the town plan that integrated the planned contemporary architecture into the extant historical fabric. Historic New Harmony, Inc. was formed to carry out the plan. Under the aegis of a determined group of preservationists and town molders, the sleepy town was transformed. Assisted by private funds and federal, state, and Lilly Endowment grants, they carted historic buildings to sites where newer houses stood and toted the newer ones elsewhere; restored Harmonist buildings to their original appearance and painted other ones colors scarcely imaginable to the ascetics. They installed historic dioramas and exhibits and instituted a successful interpretation program. New construction raised medical buildings and middle-income housing. Infrastructure improvements gave the town sewers, freshly paved streets, and parking lots to handle the tourists that began arriving in greater numbers. Outside of town, Harmonie State Park opened along the Wabash.

More modern architecture that had the townsfolk rubbing their eyes began rising at the edge of town. The New Harmony Inn opened to visitors, designed by Evans Woollen to express the spare beauty of the Harmonist structures. A Richard Meier-designed ceramic studio was built in 1978. Construction began in 1979 on the monumental porcelain Atheneum visitor center that Richard Meier designed to visually hover on the edge of the Wabash bottoms like a spacecraft poised for the future.

The changes were not without controversy. As small town Hoosiers are not the most adaptable of creatures, there was consternation as their town was literally picked up and hauled around. There are tales of fiery public meetings and sullen mutterings. One local homeowner, previously not a gardener, felt obliged to raise corn in front of her house after it was decreed that only appropriately ambient flowers could be grown in front lawns.

By the early 1980s the town morphed into what the visitor sees today. In 1982 Historic New Harmony, Inc. won the coveted American Institute of Architects award for blending the original Harmonist buildings into the work of contemporary architects. "New Harmony is a peaceable kingdom," the award read, "a continuum of past and present that gives new meaning and added luster to its name. " Today, New Harmony is still a center for spiritual and intellectual inquiry, with retreats, conferences, and artistic performances throughout the year in historic sites and the award-winning contemporary structures. Like some eerie cultural magnet, New Harmony continues to draw dreamers and visionaries to the shores of the Wabash. "We're all hopeless romantics here," bookseller Bob Brooks said. "Oh, New Harmony is the cemetery of former radical thinkers," weaver and charmingly reprobate idealist Nancy Reichen added.

Mileage

251.0 Continue west on Route 62. Route 41 in Evansville leads ten miles south to **John James Audubon State Park**, honoring the great naturalist-artist who lived here from 1810 to 1820. See Chapter 7 for more details.

258.0 The **Posey County Line** is just past the University of Southern Indiana. The county was carved from parts of Gibson and Warrick counties in 1814, and the county seat ricocheted around the county before settling in Mount Vernon in 1825, taking advantage of its river port. "Everything is near the river in Posey County," state tourism official and Posey County native Marianna Weinzapfel said. "We've got two to pick from." The Ohio curls along the southern border and the Wabash (that's pronounced "Wall-bash" by the locals, with the accent most distinctly on the first syllable) writhes down the western side. The road is through a flat lowland with the industrial sprawl of Evansville alternating with prospering farms tilling the rich soil. Small oil wells pump endlessly like giant grazing insects.

259.0 The road to **St. Phillips** turns to the north. The little German hamlet is a few minutes up the road. There are Wednesday night clabber tournaments at the Weinzapfel Tavern. Clabber is a card game unique to the area, perhaps migrating from Alsace-Lorraine along with the folks who settled here in the nineteenth century. The St. Phillips Inn reportedly has good fried chicken.

270. There are several prehistoric archeological sites scattered along the route, none open to the public. Four archeological sites in Posey County are listed on the National Register of Historic Places, including the **Mann Site** just east of Mount Vernon, which was the largest Hopewell town in Indiana, probably a satellite town of Angel Mounds to the east.

In the 1980s there was a furor when pot-hunters were discovered tearing apart a Posey County mound with construction equipment to loot the artifacts for a collector who hired them. The mound was located on land owned by GE, and after a multi-party wrangle that included the corporation, state law enforcement, FBI, representatives of Native American tribes, archeologists, and collectors, the loot was given a cursory archeological examination that was never promulgated, and then returned to the site and re-bulldozed. "That was a fiasco," IU archeologist Noel Justice said.

271.0 Route 69 leads to **New Harmony**, approximately twelve miles north. This is an **alternate loop** off of the Ohio River Scenic Route. In the growing season, the road north is a nostalgic route, passing golden hay fields and rising hills of corn, with old Greek Revival structures along the way. Oil wells and tract houses keep you from getting carried away. The location of Owen's proposed thirty-acre **Agricultural and Manufacturing Village of**

Mutual Co-operation is just north of **Solitude**, about five miles from Mount Vernon. Except for a few loads of brick, construction was never started.

Harmonie State Park is another five miles down the road. The park stretches along a series of rapids in the Wabash that gave the original Harmonie the reason for its location.

New Harmony is 2.5 miles further down the road. Most tours begin at architect Richard Meier's **Atheneum**, Arthur and North streets, where visitors can orient themselves with a seventeen-minute informational film, *The New Harmony Experience,* and pick up maps and literature. The multi-level building offers exhibits on the town and great vistas of the Wabash and the town. When the visitor center opened, the contemporary structure was hailed as an architectural expansion of the prevailing modernist canon. *The New York Times* architectural critic Louise Ada Huxtable wrote, "One can make the point that the creative spirit of this building is not far from the pioneering heritage of New Harmony. Frontiers are where you find them."

Across North Street from the Visitor Center, **Cathedral Labyrinth and Sacred Garden** is based on the sacred geometries of Chartes Cathedral in France. The exterior wall is identical to the outside of the cathedral, and the brick piers at the perimeter are identical in spacing to that of the main columns at Chartes. The labyrinth at the center is virtually identical to the one at Chartes. The path through the maze operates on a deep psychological foundation, allowing walkers to untangle their own distresses in the knot of the labyrinth. This labyrinth is somewhat different from the hedgerow maze planted by the Harmonists, which was replanted south of town in 1939. That one was seen by the Harmonists as a confusing path through life, until finding the lushness at the center. The Cathedral labyrinth has only one path.

The brick wall next to the labyrinth encloses the **Harmonist Cemetery**, where 230 Harmonists are buried in unmarked graves alongside a ninth-century Hopewell burial mound. The wall was built by Harmonists who returned in 1874 to raze the original Harmonist church that had deteriorated; they used the bricks to build the wall. Proceed down North Street past austere frame houses that the Harmonists left unpainted, since the Second Coming was imminent. The **David Lenz House** at West and North streets is typical of the Harmonist period. A cluster of **log cabins** across the street speak of the structures lived in by Harmonists' neighbors in the hinterland. They are not original to the site but were moved in from the county. The **Barrett-Gate House** at Main and North streets is one of only two existing log and frame Harmonist structures. Behind the house is the **wooded park** dedicated to the theologian **Paul Tillich.**

The **Roofless Church**, across from the Barrett-Gate House, is Phillip Johnson's interdenominational paean to spirituality, designed with the thought that only the sky is a big enough roof to shelter all faiths. The church includes sculpture and gates by Jacques Lipchitz and the recently installed *Pieta* by Stephen de Staebler. Next door to the church on North Street, the small white building is the Richard Meier-designed **Pottery Studio**, completed in 1978. The corner of North and Brewery streets is the site of the **Harmonist Distillery**, where the industrious Harmonists made five hundred gallons of beer every other day, and thirty-six gallons of whiskey a day. A small log still with a dog-powered pump produced another twenty gallons daily. Almost all of it was for export, as the Harmonists seldom tippled. New Harmony's premier restaurant, the **Red Geranium**, and the **New Harmony Inn** are further east on North Street.

One block south at Granary and Brewery streets, the 1823 **Salmon Wolf House** contains an entrancing diorama of New Harmony as it appeared in 1824. The house was moved from another site in 1975, and the original bricks were rotated so the unweathered side was exposed. Nearby, the fieldstone Harmonist Granary is in a state of intense re-construction. Because the upper windows were mistakenly thought of as gunports, old accounts of New Harmony call it the "Rappite Fort." David Dale Owen used it as his geology laboratory and museum. It was the headquarters for the U.S. Geologic Surveys during his tenure as chief geologist.

On Main between Church and Granary streets, the mammoth brick **Dormitory No. 2** was built in 1822 to communally house both men and women. During the Owenite period, the building housed a Pestalozzian school and a tavern. It later served as a newspaper office for the *New Harmony Register*. The Rapp-Maclure House at Main and Church, was built in 1844 after a fire destroyed Father Rapp's 1816 Georgian home. William Maclure owned the home and used it as his office and a school. Eventually it became the home of David Dale Owen, who remained in Indiana. It reflects a transition from the spare Harmonist style into a more fashionable mid-nineteenth-century esthetic.

The greensward on Church Street is the site of the two **Harmonist Churches**. The brick church that later formed the cemetery wall was built in 1822 and was a marvel to travelers of the day. The free-standing doorway in the park is a reproduction of the church door. At Church and West streets, the **Fauntleroy House** is an original Harmonist structure that grew with additions to be grand enough to house Jane Dale Owen Fauntleroy, the only daughter of Robert Owen to migrate to Indiana. This is the site of one of the first modern-style women's clubs, the Minerva Society, which Fauntleroy founded in 1859.

The **Workingman's Institute** at Tavern and West streets is a remarkable holdover from the era of endowed public libraries, like the Willard Library in Evansville, before Andrew Carnegie dispersed his library buildings throughout the land in the twentieth century. William Maclure bequeathed the money for the library upon his death in Mexico in 1840. It is Indiana's oldest public library. The building itself was given to New Harmony by Dr. Edward Murphy, who was taken in as a waif by the Owenites. Today, it is a repository of manuscripts and artifacts relating to the communalist days, as well as a quirky town museum. Where else are you going to store the Civil War horse skeleton and the sideshow Siamese twin calves? They also have a good collection of Harmonist crafts and Owenite natural specimens.

The gingerbreaded brick house across the street is the 1867 **Schnee-Ribeyre-Elliott House**, built by a saddle maker who made his fortune in the Civil War and who sold the home to "Corn King" Captain Alfred Ribeyre. He was known locally for his extensive land holdings in the county. The bright-yellow field-hand houses that marked his domain also still stand. President Taft came to tea at the house in 1914 during the New Harmony Centennial.

The corner of Tavern and Brewery streets has a clutch of historic houses, including the brick Georgian **1830 Owen House** that was built by Robert Dale and David Dale Owen. The other three corners include a National Register Harmonist shoemaker's house, now used for historic exhibits, and the **Keppler House**, now used for geology exhibits.

New Harmony's Main Street reflects Indiana's boom time in the Victorian era. Several interesting shops, galleries, and cafes grace the tidy street. **The New Harmony Maximillian-Bodmer Collection** at the Lichtenberger Building on Main Street showcases artist Karl Bodmer's depiction of zoologist Prince Maximillian's exploration of the Upper Missouri in 1832-34, when nature was still wild and the life of Native Americans was still intact. Bodner and Maximillian spent the winter of 1832-33 in New Harmony. "Here," Maximillian wrote, "I derived much instruction and entertainment from my intercourse with two highly informed men, Thomas Say and Mr. Lesueur . . . ."

On Church Street, **Thrall's Opera House** was important to New Harmony through the decades. Originally built by the Harmonists as Dormitory No. 4, it served as a singles dorm and boarding house during the Owen period. By 1828 the building began its life as a theater, opening with a thespian society headed by William Dale Owen, another of Robert Owen's sons. The famous 1880s thespian family, the Golden Troupe, used the theater as their home base as they traveled the country. In 1888 the facade was given an up-to-date look and operated as a theater and cinema until 1914, when it became a garage. The state of Indiana bought the opera house in 1964 and restored the structure to its 1888 splendor. It reopened as a theater in 1968 and operates today under the management of the University of Southern Indiana.

The town also hosts yearly retreats for writers and media professionals. The **Ropewalk Writers Retreat** is a week-long conference focused on creative writing, with respected professional writers from around the country as faculty. **The New Harmony Project** is a conference for media writers who are dedicated to work that nurtures the dignity of the human spirit in the face of contemporary pap and exploitation. Each summer **Music at Marymount** presents a week of chamber music for the town.

Walking down New Harmony's lanes today, it's easy to hear the echoes of the Harmonist horns and the Owenites voices as they steam up the meeting hall with their wrangles. You can imagine Karl Bodmer and John James Audubon comparing field notes, and can almost see Father Rapp bent over a table at the old Yellow Tavern with Robert Owen, discussing the bright utopian future awaiting all of them, though somewhat in disagreement about what it will be. But today's idealists add to the story—young people considering deep questions, writers crafting tales of human courage and dignity, theologians sharing the commonality of their faiths. The sounds of contemporary artists add to the reverie: the clack of the looms, the whine of the saws, chamber music drifting down from a window. New Harmony was an amazing place on the frontier in the nineteenth century, and as it moves into the twenty-first century, it still is.

Return to the Ohio River Scenic Route via Route 69.

272.0. **Mount Vernon** is the home of the **Southwind Maritime Center**, Indiana's second-largest port. It was dedicated in 1979 to handle cargo traveling the inland waterway system from the Great Lakes to the Gulf of Mexico. The center includes a mile of river front designed to handle mooring, fleet assembly, and dry-dock repair. The adjacent industrial park serves a grain terminal, coal transfer point, timber export company, and shippers of bulk commodities.

Mount Vernon is a throwback to the Hoosier small town of yore with its courthouse square surrounded by rococo Victorian homes and turn-of-the-century neighborhoods. The summer evening I was there, neighbors chatted from their porches, bike-riding kids flitted like dragonflies, and a large man circled his lawn on a tiny lawn tractor wearing a dago-T and a Sony Walkman. Many of the town's public structures and fine homes are relatively unchanged from the turn of the century.

Andrew McFadden moved his family to Mount Vernon in 1805, the first of many settlers crossing from Kentucky to the riverside town. It grew rapidly after it was named the county seat in 1825. The **Courthouse Square** and its 1876 courthouse is a historic district on the National Register of Historic Places, as is the **Welborn Historic District** bounded by 9th Street, Locust, 2nd Street, and the alley between Walnut and Main streets. The 1895 **William Gonnerman House**, 521 West 2nd, is on the National Register of Historic Places, a fine example of the period.

At the foot of Main Street, **Shelburne Park** provides public access to the Ohio River. Nearby at College Avenue, a marker on a boulder memorializes the site of McFadden's first store and second home. A high water mark from the 1937 flood is also nearby.

Follow Route 69 South out of town nine miles to **Hovey Lake State Fish and Wildlife Area.** The Nature Conservancy calls the pristine environment one of the "Last Great Places." The enormous wetland, 4,298 acres in all, is redolent of the Deep South, a slurry of sloughs and swamps in the pocket of southern Posey County where the Ohio joins the meandering Wabash. In the wetlands, bald cypress trees poke their bony knees from the swamp water as blue herons stalk, somber as priests, among the water lilies. Turtles plop from their basking spots, as warblers and gnat catchers flit amongst the wild grape vines. Hanging moss frames the deer who peer shyly from the cottonwoods and wild pecans. Bald eagles nest, joined by double-breasted cormorants and great blue herons who hunt the waters.

The Twin Swamps Nature Preserve and Gray's Woods complex is an unsullied 890-acre wetland with some of the Midwest's most intriguing flora and fauna, including America's northernmost stand of bald cypress. The rise in the Ohio's water level following the construction of the Uniontown Locks and Dam near the confluence of the Ohio and the Wabash has caused the death of some of the stand, as the cypress need to have their distinctive "knees" sticking out of the water at least part of the time. Some of the old stand remains—massive trees, hundreds of years old, stately among the buttonbush and swamp rose. Moonseed, chanterelles, rare feather foil and spider lily are scattered though the swamp, with wild blue orchids flaring here and there. More than fifty thousand visitors come yearly to re-create amidst the quiet beauty and to witness the spectacular arrival of the migratory birds.

Hovey Lake is also a magnet for hunters. Six thousand hunters, the majority of them waterfowl hunters, used the park in 1996.

Three miles further down Route 69, the **Uniontown Locks and Dam** is at the lowest point in Indiana. The first boat passed through the locks in 1970. This is considered a high-lift dam, raising vessels an average of eighteen feet. Four to five million tons of cargo move through the locks monthly.

Return to Route 62 via Route 69. Continue west 7.4 miles on Route 62 to the **Illinois Border.** You just completed the Ohio River Scenic Route.

Visitor Information

Historic New Harmony, P.O. Box 579, New Harmony, IN 47631, 800-231-2168.
Mount Vernon Chamber of Commerce, P.O. Box 633, Mt. Vernon, IN 47620-0633, 812-838-3639.

Recommended Bed and Breakfasts and Cabins

New Harmony Inn, P.O. Box 581, New Harmony, IN 47631, 812-682-4491, architecturally reflects the intellectual and spiritual traditions of New Harmony with spare Swedish-meets-Shaker decor. It is an refined piece of architecture with courtly service.

The Raintree Inn, 503 West St., New Harmony, IN 47631, 812-682-5625, is an elegantly restored Victorian home with four rooms.

The Old Rooming House, 812-682-4724, is an interpretation of Mannie Rickert's 1948 boarding house. The owner, Jim Stinson, is a magpie with a focus, lavishly decorating with 1940s and 1950s ephemera and kitsch.

Wright Place Bed and Breakfast, 515 S. Arthur St., New Harmony, IN 47631, 812-682-3453, is housed in an 1840s saltbox house. It's the place if you are traveling with small animals, as the owners are vets and offer a "Kennel and Kibble" to go with the B&B.

Recommended Reading

The Angel and the Serpent, William E. Wilson, Indiana University Press, Bloomington, IN 1964, is the most readable of the New Harmony histories, written by one of the deans of Indiana literature.

America's Communal Utopias, edited by Donald E. Pitzer, University of North Carolina Press, Chapel Hill, 1997, is a collection of essays on the American communal experiments, past and present.

Visions of Harmony: A Study in Nineteenth-Century Millenarianism, Anne Taylor, Oxford University Press, NY 1987, is a well-written revision of New Harmony and, particularly, Robert Owen.

Women in Utopia: The Ideology of Gender in the American Owenite Communities, Carol Kohlmerton, Indiana University Press, Bloomington, IN 1990, is an incisive study of nascent feminism in the Owenite experiment.

Recommended Regional Dining

The Bayou Grill, North St., New Harmony, IN 47631, 812-682-4431, offers New American fare in an atmosphere of sponged walls and contemporary art.

The Main Cafe on Victorian Main Street, New Harmony, IN 47631, 812-682-3370, offers Old American fare in a vintage pressed-tin decor hung with local Kiwanis Club banners. Blue-plate specials with three sides can set you back almost four bucks.

The Red Geranium, North Street, New Harmony, IN 47631, 812 682-4431, is New Harmony's top restaurant. The Tillich Room is a pleasant atrium environment for dining.

The Yellow Tavern, 521 Church Street, New Harmony, IN 47631, 812 682-3303, is a favorite among locals for bar food and pizza.

Aunt Sallie's Soda Fountain, 515 Main St., New Harmony, IN 47631, 812-682-3383, is a great place to take a rest and grab an ice cream soda in a nostalgic, soda-fountain atmosphere.

Camping

Harmonie State Park, R. R. 1, Box 5A, New Harmony, IN 47631, 812-682-4821, forty-five minutes to the west, and has two hundred campsites, a swimming pool with a water slide, six hiking trails, and a bike trail, as well as a naturalist who presents nature programs.

Evening falls on a Harmonist house.

Courtesy of the Indiana Department of Commerce Tourism Division

Courtesy of the Indiana Department of Commerce Tourism Division

The Atheneum is a contemporary exclamation point in the heart of the New Harmony historic district.

Appendix

Ohio River Scenic Route Information

The Ohio River Scenic Route of Southern Indiana, Inc., 315 Southern Indiana Ave., Jeffersonville, IN 47130, 800-552-3842, is dedicated to the preservation of the history, scenery, natural features, and recreational opportunities of the Ohio River Scenic Route. They are a great source of information.

Indiana Tourism, 1 N. Capitol St., Indianapolis, IN 46204, 800-289-6646, is a font of southern Indiana recreational information. Call for info or see their website at indianatourism.com.

Indiana Historical Society, 315 W. Ohio, Indianapolis, IN 46202-3299, 317-232-1882, is the grandaddy of all of the state organizations, established in 1830. They are a forward-thinking old-time organization, well worth a membership for all of the literature and programming they deliver.

Historic Landmarks Foundation of Indiana, 340 W. Michigan Street, Indianapolis, IN 46202-3204, 800-450-4534, (www.historiclandmarks.org) is considered the premier architectural preservation organization among all of the states. If you have an interest in historic architecture, this is definitely a group to contact. Among their many programs, they preserve and maintain historic homes and structures throughout the state, including the monumental West Baden Springs Hotel. Their southern regional office is located at 113 W. Chestnut St., Jeffersonville, IN 47130, 812-284-4534.

Historic Southern Indiana, a division of the University of Southern Indiana, 8600 University Boulevard, Evansville IN 47712-3597, 800-489-4474, has been instrumental in the establishment of the Ohio River Scenic Route, as well as a number of other heritage programs throughout southern Indiana.

Hoosier National Forest, 248 15th St., Tell City, IN 47586, 812-547-7051, 800-280-2267, has information on their extensive holdings along the Scenic Route.

The Indiana Department of Natural Resources, has organized the state recreational facilities into three divisions: Division of State Parks and Recreation, 204 W. Washington St., Room W298, Indianapolis, IN 46204,

317-232-4124; Division of Fish and Wildlife, 204 W. Washington St., Room W273, Indianapolis, IN 46204, 317-232-4080; Division of Forestry, 204 W. Washington St., Room W273, Indianapolis, IN 46204, 317-232-4105.

The Nature Conservancy, 1330 W. 38th St., Indianapolis, IN 46208, 800-YES-LAND, has been quietly preserving some of Indiana's most natural land since 1959. They have saved more than twenty-six thousand acres of Hoosier land preserved in 146 nature preserves, including a number in the region of the Ohio River Scenic Route.

Heartwood, P.O. Box 1424, Bloomington, IN 47402, 812-337-8898, is another conservation organization, this one with a strong focus on the forests of the central hardwood region, particularly the National Forest land.

The U. S. Army Corps of Engineers, P.O. Box 59, Louisville, KY 40201-0059, 502-582-5613 has information on the eight locks and dams that tame the Ohio, as well as maps to the river from Pittsburgh, PA, to Cairo, IL.

Visitor Information for individual counties and cities are listed at the back of each chapter.

Festivals

Aurora

July, Firecracker Festival & Craft Show, Lesko Park & Water Street. 812-926-2625. Music, dances, crafts, refreshments, fireworks, contests, along Ohio River. Hillforest Mansion open for tours.

August, 5th Annual Civil War Re-enactment, U.S. 50 at Aurora, 812-744-3288. Over 150 re-enactors involved in re-enactment of Morgan's Raid through Dearborn County. Also, find settlers selling wares and clothing.

September, St. Mary's Riverfest, Lesko Park, 812-926-0060. Church festival featuring food, drink, entertainment, games, raffles and a country store.

October, Farmers' Fair, downtown. A town tradition since 1908. Free stage shows, street parade, games, rides, food. Many booths.

Bethlehem

October, Autumn on the River, Town Commons, 812-256-6111. Taste this town's famous steamboat stew and flatboat bean soup. Pioneers and Indians re-create the founding of Bethlehem in 1812. Reconstructed village, arts, crafts and folk music.

Bristow

October, Hoosier Heritage Fall Tour, various locations, 812-547-2385. A different part of Perry County featured each weekend: Bristow on the 10-11; Derby/Rome 17-18; Tell City/Troy/Cannelton 24-25. View fall foliage along the Ohio River. Enjoy local music, live entertainment and local artists.

Clarksville

September, Falls Fossil Festival, Falls of the Ohio State Park, 812-280-9970. River yields fossils and minerals that are for sale. Also lapidary, jewelry, and other crafts. Enjoy educational workshops, exhibits, hikes along fossil beds.

Corydon

May, Harrison County Popcorn Festival, Courthouse Square, 888-738-2137. Parade, contests involving popcorn, arts and crafts booths, demonstrations on aspects of popcorn, food, and more.

May, Old Capitol Traditional Music Festival, Corydon Presbyterian Church, 812-738-2137. Featuring a dulcimer band, jam sessions, music lessons, workshops and sale of rare sheet music.

October, Halloween on the Square, Old Capitol Square, 812-738-4890. A frightful-friendly fun time with a Halloween parade, costume contests, music, food booths, games, pumpkin painting, and more.

Harrison County Fair, July-August

Elizabeth

October, Rebirth of the Buffalo Festival, Needmore Buffalo Farm, 800-752-4766. See life in the late 1800s; visit a frontier Indian village; see authentic pioneer skills; tour the farm in a wagon. Rodeo. Buffalo burgers served.

English

Oktoberfest, various locations, 812-338-3214. Celebrate fall with arts and crafts, wood carving, continuous entertainment, hot air balloon rides, parachute jump, antique car show and more.

Evansville

March, Maple Sugarbush Festival and Pancake Breakfast, Wessellman Woods Nature Preserve, 812-479-0771. Learn how maple syrup is made; enjoy tours, tree tapping, evaporator demonstrations. .

March, Springtime at the Old Courthouse, Old Vanderburgh County Courthouse. 812-423-3361. All four levels of this historic building are occupied by art and craft vendors from tri-state area.

May, Pioneer Days Festival, Wesselman Woods Nature Preserve, 812-479-0771. Travel back in time to the 1820s; try your hand at throwing tomahawks, dipping candles, and grinding corn.

June, Classic Iron, 4-H Center, 812-963-3731. See working antique machinery. Displays, demonstrations, large flea market, craft show, and more.

June, Reptile Invasion! Wesselman Woods Nature Preserve, 812-479-0771. Tri-state's greatest reptile and amphibian show, with 150 live, touchable animals from around the world. Educational programs.

June-July, Evansville Freedom Festival/Thunder on the Ohio, downtown riverfront, 812-464-9576. See the world's fastest boats race. Carnival, three stages of live entertainment, parade, fireworks and more.

July-August, Evansville Riverfest, Riverside Drive, 812-424-2986. Four stages of entertainment, wide variety of food, carnival rides, children's activities, car show and more.

August, Rainforest Festival, Mesker Park Zoo, 812-428-0715. Learn about endangered habitat of rainforest. Rainforest games, hands-on crafts, displays and animals.

August, Evansville Iron Street Rod Frog Follies, Vanderburgh 4-H Center, 812-477-3225. One of biggest car shows and swap meets in the Midwest. Souped-up hot rods galore, concessions, and craft fair.

September, Children's Art Fair, Mesker Park Zoo & Botanical Gardens, 812-428-0715. More than fifty art and craft activities throughout the zoo. Clowns and costumed characters.

September, Native American Days, Angel Mounds State Historic Site, 812-853-3956. Educational, hands-on events highlighting the Mississippian and modern Native American cultures. Demonstrations including flintnapping, dancing and arts.

October, West Side Nut Club Fall Festival, West Franklin Street, 812-985-9459. Sample incredible food from many nationalities—over 115 booths. Nightly entertainment, carnival rides and more.

October, Boo at the Zoo, Mesker Park Zoo and Botanical Gardens, 812-428-0715. Halloween extravaganza including spooky trails, safe trick-or-treating, games, activities and frightful fun.

October, Haunted Hay Rides, Wesselman Woods Nature Preserve, 812-479-0771. Warm yourself by a friendly bonfire before taking a mildly spooky ride through a haunted field. Roast hot dogs and marshmallows afterwards.

November, Christmas at the Old Courthouse & Coliseum, Old

Vanderburgh County Courthouse & Soldiers and Sailors Memorial Coliseum, 812-423-3361. Handmade arts and crafts are housed in this 107-year-old courthouse.

December, Holiday Zoo Festival, Mesker Park Zoo & Botanical Gardens, 812-428-0715. Celebrate the magic of Christmas with joyous carols, dazzling lights, live entertainment, and a special guest appearance by Santa.

December, First Night Evansville, various locations, 812-422-2111. Alcohol-free, family-oriented New Year's Eve celebration. Children's activity area, all types of entertainment: Big Band sounds, magic, juggling and much more.

Ferdinand

June, Ferdinand Heimatfest, 18th Street Park, 812-482-9115. Celebrating town's German heritage. Food concessions, games, tractor pulls and special performances.

October, Primitive Corn Shredding Festival, 1.5 miles north of Ferdinand on S.R. 164, 812-367-1206. Mules and horses work the fields. Horse-drawn power take-off equipment from the 1800s grinds corn and bales fodder. Corn shucking competition.

French Lick

September, Orange County Pumpkin Festival, Downtown parking lot, 812-936-2405. Fun crafts and booths revolve around this seasonal symbol. Carnival rides, Big Pumpkin parade on Sunday.

Grandview

September, Grandview Fall Fest, Civic Center, 812-649-4046. BBQ chicken, pork chop dinners, short-order foods. Car show, quilt show, bingo, line dancing, and more.

Guilford

July, St. John's Annual Festival & Chicken Dinner, 25743 S.R. 1, 812-576-4159. Home-cooked chicken dinner; raffles, bingo, and country store with locally made crafts, homemade quilts, baked goods, and produce.

Huntingburg

September, Old Fashioned Bargain Days, business district, 812-683-5699. 4th Street merchants roll back the prices on clothing, gift-shop items, produce, crafts. Old-time prices; priceless treasures.

October, Herbstfest, City Park at First & Cherry streets, 812-683-5699. German harvest festival featuring a parade, carnival, food and game booths, pageants, flea market, and farmers' market. Entertainment inside League Stadium.

Jasper
May, Four Rivers Spring Arts & Crafts Show, Dubois County 4-H Fairgrounds, 812-354-6808. Over two hundred quality crafts booths.

June, Lions Club Strawberry Festival, Riverview Park, 812-482-4609. Strawberry shortcake, strawberry sundaes, fresh strawberry bulk sales, and recipes. Live band and vocal group.

July, Dubois County Fair.

July-August, Strassenfest, downtown, 812-482-6866. Celebrate Jasper's German heritage with authentic music, delicious food, beer tent, talent show, arts and crafts fair.

October, Harvest Home Festival, Dubois County 4-H Fairgrounds, 812-354-6808. An extraordinary craft show: approximately 330 booths of high-quality, unique crafts made in the area.

Jeffersonville
September, Jeffersonville Steamboat Days, Riverside Drive, 812-288-9295. Celebrate importance of steamboats and early inland waterways. Arts and crafts, children's rides, food booths, free entertainment and exhibits.

Lawrenceburg
May, Tri-State Antique Market, Lawrenceburg Fairgrounds, 513-738-7256. Over three hundred dealers show and sell a wide variety of antiques and vintage collectibles.

June, Intergalactic Bead Show, Top Hat Reception Center, 704-669-1949. Modern, historic, and ancient beads. Demonstrations of glass bead making, wire wrap. Beads and supplies for sale.

June, Tri-State Antique Market, Lawrenceburg Fairgrounds, 513-738-7256.

July, Dearborn County Fair.

August, Tri-State Antique Market, Lawrenceburg Fairgrounds, 513-738-7256.

September, Intergalactic Bead Show, 704-669-1949.

September, Tri-State Antique Market, 513-738-7256.

September, Arts & Crafts in the Park, Newtorn Park, 812-537-2735. Over two hundred spaces with artists and crafters from the tri-state area selling handcrafted items.

October, Perfect Autumn Festival, Perfect North Slopes Ski Area, 812-537-

3754. Chair-lift rides, pony rides, hay rides, live music, children's games, clogging, antique tractors, crafts and more.

October, Extension Homemakers Annual Quilt Show and Craft Boutique, Agner Hall, Lawrenceburg Fairgrounds, 812-537-7025. Gorgeous display of quilts. Crafts, quilting, and various other demonstrations. Crafts and other homemade items for sale.

November, Extension Homemakers Annual Quilt Show and Craft Boutique, 812-537-7025

November, Ski Swap & Sale, Perfect North Slopes Ski Area, 812-537-3754. Swap or sell used ski equipment, clothing. New equipment on display. Proceeds support the non-profit National Ski Patrol organization.

December, Winterfest, Perfect North Slopes Ski Area, 812-537-3754. Ice-sculpture demonstrations, children's games on the snow, carriage rides, holiday entertainment, and many craft booths.

Madison

April, 2nd Annual Hot Luck & Fiery Foods Exhibition, Thomas Family Winery, 812-273-3755. Sample and buy foods, chilies, sauces, peppers. Music, too.

April, Madison in Bloom, Historic District, 812-265-2335. Tour eight private gardens. Enjoy spring colors and various landscape schemes.

May, Madison in Bloom, Historic District, 812-265-2335.

May, Choice Automobiles of Madison-Annual Sock Hop & Car Show, Vaughn Drive at Crystal Beach House, 812-273-4348. Friday night cruise and sock hop; awards for dress, etc. Saturday car show with over two hundred cars on display.

May, Old Court Days, Courthouse Square, 812-273-6226. High quality handmade crafts, art. Some antiques and collectibles.

June, Fete de la Fleur, Madison Vineyards, 888-473-6500. Free wine tasting, wines for sale; live classical music. Food, arts and crafts.

June, Madison Strawberry Festival, on Broadway between 2nd St. and Vaughn Dr., 800-559-2956. Strawberry delicacies; also music, crafts, kids' activities, continuous entertainment.

July, Jefferson County Fair

August, Annual Midsummer Garden Tour, various locations, 812-265-2799. Tour more than twenty residential gardens in Madison's 133-block historic district.

August, The Big Texas Brisket Bash, Thomas Family Winery, 812-273-3755. Outdoor BBQ with Texas-style smoked brisket, trimmings, bluegrass music, contests, activities.

September, Old Court Days, Courthouse Square, 812-273-6226. Large array of high-quality, handmade crafts and art. Christmas—big sellers are holiday items.

September, Harvest Celebration, 123 Mill Street, 800-41-WINES. Artist and craft demonstrations; items available to purchase. Tour the gardens; wine tasting.

September, Madison Chautauqua, downtown, 812-265-2956. Juried fine arts and crafts show with artists from across the country. Music and food add to the event along the picturesque Ohio River.

October, Annual Lanier Days Social, Lanier Mansion, 812-265-3526. Mid-nineteenth century skills are showcased: rug making, candle making, cider pressing, log hewing, wool spinning, quilting, blacksmithing and pottery throwing. Old-fashioned games.

October, Tri Kappa Tour of Homes in Historic Madison, various locations, 800-559-2956. See privately owned, architecturally significant homes that are not normally open to public viewing. Area includes 133-block area on the National Register of Historic Places.

November and December, Nights Before Christmas Candlelight Tour of Homes, Madison Historic District, 812-265-2956. Tour historical sites, various private and public homes that are decked in Christmas finery. Carriage rides, carolers, parade and Messiah concert.

Mauckport

August, Riverfest, Mauckport Park, 812-732-4771. Demonstrations of old-time skills, log saw contest. Arts and crafts booths, street dance, kids' contests, antique vehicles, and parade.

Moores Hill

June, Annual Strawberry Festival, Carnegie Hall, 812-744-4015. Strawberry shortcake; also foods, crafts, children's games and entertainment.

New Albany

October, Harvest Homecoming, various locations. 812-944-1593. Over three hundred craft and food booths anchor this festival. Also a parade, carnival, sporting events, concerts, and fun for the whole family.

New Harmony

April, Heritage Week, 812-682-4488. various locations on North and West streets. See a variety of nineteenth-century craft demonstrations: basket making, candle dipping, wood turning, blacksmithing, and more.

September, Kunstfest, various locations, 812-682-3490. Large German craft festival, featuring-nineteenth century craft demonstrations, German food and German music.

October, Scots in Harmony, North Street, 812-682-4488. A family festival celebrating the town's historic links to Scotland. Traditional music, dancing, entertainment, and more.

December, Christmas in New Harmony with Candlelight Tours, various locations, 812-682-4488. A heart-warming tradition; bundle up for a tour of the town's historic homes. All homes decorated for the holiday season.

February, "Under the Big Top" Arts and Crafts Show, Castle High School, 812-853-7404. Over one hundred fifty dealers featuring a variety of quality arts and crafts.

Newburgh

June, Newburgh Summerfest, Old Lock & Dam Riverpark, 812-853-7111. Beerstube, line dancing, carnival, crafts and food booths.

September, Fiddler Fest, downtown, 812-853-2815. Outdoor festival featuring fiddler—both the eating kind (catfish) and the musical kind! Continuous entertainment; craft, game and food booths.

December, Newburgh Celebrates Christmas & Home Tours, historic downtown district, 812-853-2815. Tour several lovely homes that are decorated for the holiday season. Downtown merchants' open houses. Tree-lighting ceremony at dark.

North Vernon

June, Railroad Days Festival, city parking lot, 812-346-7377. Art contest, railroad events, model train shows, scheduled train events and more.

June-July, Jennings County Fair.

September, St. Mary's Pork Festival, St. Mary's Church, 812-346-3604. BBQ sandwiches and grilled pork chops. Also country store with crafts, baked goods, silent auction, 3-on-3 basketball and more.

Paoli

June, Lotus Dickey Home Town Reunion, Orange County Courthouse, 812-723-4769. Music, arts, crafts, and food on courthouse lawn.

September, Indian Summer Festival, Orange County Courtyard, 812-723-4769. Arts and crafts; music nightly; parade on Sunday.

Rising Sun

April, 18th Annual Quilt Show and Art Fair, 888-Rising-Sun, various historic buildings along S.R. 56. Over one hundred handmade quilts and art on display.

July, 2nd Annual Shiner Pride '98 Car Show, Riverfront & Main Street,

812-438-2438. Pre-1940 to present-day cars, trucks, motorcycles shown
in their classes. Door prizes, flea market, 1950s and 1960s music and food.

July, Ohio County Fair

August, Taste of Southeast Indiana, Front Street, 888-RSNG-SUN. Restaurants, organizations, and individuals showcase their homegrown specialty dishes at a street fair.

October, Navy Bean Festival, Main & Front streets, 812-438-2011. Feast
on bean soup made in an open kettle; watch the horse parade. Craft and
food booths, artists, entertainment and line dancing.

November, Annual Country Christmas Craft Show, Rising Sun Elemen-
tary/Middle School, 812-438-2565. Good quality crafts, good cause.
Handmade items, baked goods and concessions.

December, Holiday Winterwalk, Riverfront, 888-RSNG-SUN. Walking
tour of a turn-of-the-century lighting display along the river. Hot chocolate, cider and caroling add to the festivities.

December, Christmas Home Tour, Ohio County Historical Building, 812-
438-4440. Tour several distinctive homes, each decorated for the season.
Shop Phi Beta Psi sorority craft booths at the museum.

Rockport

October, Christian Education Foundation Craft Show & Flea Market,
St. Bernard School, 812-649-9445. Fine arts and crafts featuring local
and regional artists. Also a flea market and food booths.

Salem

February, Sugarbush Annual Sugar Festival, Sugarbush Farm, 812-967-
4491. Tour a modern maple syrup plant; children's games, Indian teepee;
historical craft demonstrations.

September, Aviation Awareness Days, Municipal Airport, 812-755-4541.
Hot air balloon race; watch parachutists, various aircraft. Entertainment;
fleamarket. Breakfast and lunch served.

September, Old Settlers' Days, Steven's Memorial Museum, 812-883-4500.
Tour the reconstructed Pioneer Village. Pioneer craft demonstrations,
children's games. Juried art show, food entertainment.

October, 4th Annual Crusade for Children Craft Show, Bradie Shrum
Upper Elementary School, 812-883-6920. A pleasant day of shopping:
quality, handmade art and craft items. Unique craft raffle. Goes for a good
cause.

Santa Claus

December, Christmas in Santa Claus & Festival of Lights, various locations, 812-937-2848. Feel the old-fashioned warmth. Music performances, Christmas craft fair, parade. Evening Festival of Lights tour through Christmas Lake Village.

Scottsburg

September, Scott County Courtfest, Scott County Courtyard, 812-752-2475. Over one hundred booths of arts, crafts, food. Continuous live music, dancing programs.

November, A Courtyard Christmas, Scott County Courthouse Courtyard, 812-752-4343. More than seven hundred luminaries cast their glow. Additional light displays, carriage rides, food, entertainment. Santa parade, carolers, children's games.

Starlight, October, Stumler Orchard Applefest, Stumler Orchard & Restaurant, 812-923-3832. Smells of autumn mingle with open kettle cooking. Apple butter making, cornmeal grinding, hay rides, arts/crafts, flea market and antique machinery demonstrations.

Tell City

April, Dogwood Festival, various locations, 812-547-2385. Tour Cannelton, Rome, Tell City, and Troy. Visit local communities along the way for food, arts, crafts; take buggy rides and more.

August, Schweizer Fest, Hall Park, 812-547-2385. Celebrate town's Swiss-German heritage. Authentic food, Brau Garten, nightly entertainment, amusement rides and market.

November-December, Bright Lights of Christmas, various locations, 812-547-2385. Parades, special lighted displays throughout the county. Residential lighting competition; arts and crafts.

Troy

June, Trojan Fest, Burke Park, 812-547-3646. Live bands, mud volleyball and horseshoe tourneys, games of chance, crafts, food and more.

Vernon

April, Springfest in Historic Vernon, streets of Vernon, 800-928-3667. Celebrate spring at this arts and crafts festival.

April, Sassafrass Tea Festival, North American House, 812-346-8989. Heritage artists, period cooking, and evening dance at Blue and Gray Ball. See Civil War living history.

August, Labor Day Antiques & Collectibles Market, various locations, 812-377-6102. Over two hundred quality dealers line streets with antiques, collectibles and crafts.

October, Bittersweet & Cider Days/Fall Tour of Homes, various locations, 812-346-2654. Over fifty booths of arts and crafts. Display of over one hundred fifty antique apple peelers; history-related demonstrations. Historic and unique homes open for tours.

November, Vernon Christmas Craft Show, Vernon Gym, 812- 346-8329 or 800-928-3667. Select from a wide variety of hand-crafted items made by local artists. Great gift ideas.

Versailles

September, Annual Versailles Pumpkin Show, Courthouse Square, 812-689-6188. Carnival, concessions, art displays, contests, entertainment. Parade Saturday at 10:30 AM Giant pumpkin weighing, other pumpkin activities.

Vevay

April, Easter Egg-Stravaganza, downtown, 800-Hello-VV. Egg hunt, lunch with Easter Bunny, kite-flying contest, trees decorated with eggs.

August, Swiss Wine Festival, Paul Ogle Riverfront Park, 800-HELLO-VV. Food, entertainment, wine tasting, arts and crafts, grape stomp, riverboat cruises, parade, amusement rides and athletic events.

October, Legend of Sleepy Hollow Celebration, downtown, 800-HELLO-VV. Bake sales, crafters, contests, fall decorating, quilts, and other items that say "Fall" can be found here.

December, Over the River and Through the Woods Christmas Open House, downtown, 800-HELLO-VV. Luminaries, carolers, tour of homes, puppet show at the historic Hoosier Theater, special merchant discounts, and more.

Zoar

August, Zoar Mosquito Fest! United Methodist Church grounds, 812-536-2920. Food, country store, old-fashioned games, wiffleball tourney, homemade ice cream and nightly entertainment.

Southern Indiana Guild of Artists
(Members along the Ohio River Scenic Route and Alternate Loops)

Traditional
Anderson, Mary. Handwoven Reed Baskets. 3505 E. Old Goshen Road, S.E., Laconia, IN 47135, 812-737-2903.

Etienne, Cindie, L. Handmade Felt Hats. P.O. Box 54, Mackey, IN 47654, 812-922-5714.

Merritt, Billy J. Blacksmithing, Knifemaking. 911 W. State Road 64, English, IN 47118, 812-338-2876.

Murphy, Anita. Ukranian Eggs. 11363 E. Purdue Farm Road, Dubois, IN 47527, 812-678-3702.

Renn, Cathy. Promote & Teach Dulcimer and Traditional Music. 10024 County Line Road, Sellersburg, IN 47172, 812-246-2430.

Schnapf, Mason. Builder of Dulcimers & Tune-rigs. 1900 Vann Avenue, Evansville, IN 47714, 812-477-6104.

Textiles
Gaither, Marlene. Loom Weaving, Rag Rugs, Placemats. 6719 Frank Ott Road, Georgetown, IN 47122, 812-951-2307.

Johnson, Billie J. Ribbon Embroidery, Tatting. 6760 Brookside Drive N.E., Lanesville, IN 47136, 812-952-8802.

Stained Glass
Helming, Joseph. Stained Glass, Metal Work. 408 Main Street, Jasper, IN 47546, 812-634-1379.

Henry, Kay. Stained Glass, Kaleidoscopes. 815 Schutte Road, Evansville, IN 47712, 812-422-9048.

Pottery
Keller, Lori. Wheel & Hand Built Pottery. 7916 S. 750 W., Holland, IN 47541, 812-536-3588.

Rohrbacher, Brigitte. Wheel Thrown & Hand Built Pottery. 6771 S. County Road 150 W., Paoli, IN 47454, 812-723-5992.

Sobek, R. Breeze. Pottery Sculpture. 3100 Blackburn Road, Mt. Vernon, IN 47620, 812-838-4549.

Tisdale, Lavonne. Sawdust Fired Burnished Pottery, Paintings. 730 W. 6th Street, Huntingburg, IN 47542, 812-683-4286.

Fine Arts

Cox, Helen D. Painting (watercolor, acrylic & oil). 1012 N. Fairlawn Circle W., Evansville, IN 47711, 812-476-9870.

Hickman, Pam. Drawing, Painting, Pastels, Papermaking, Jewelry. 614 Main Street, Huntingburg, IN 47542, 812-683-3039.

Johnson, Carl G. Painting, Woodcarving. 6760 Brookside Drive, Lanesville, IN 47136, 812-952-8802.

Jumper, Stephanie. Painting (oil & acrylic). 1514-1/2 Mill Street, Huntingburg, IN 47542, 812-482-7839.

Massie, Juanita J. Painting (watercolor), Gemstone Jewelry. 2459 N. Evans, Evansville, IN 47711, 812-423-2295.

Reshanov, Suzette. Painting (oil & acrylic). 309 Chandler, Apt. 3, Evansville, IN 47713, 812-422-3256.

Reshanov, Yurie. Portraits on spot. 309 Chandler, Apt. 3, Evansville, IN 47713, 812-422-3256.

Steinkuhl, Evelyn. Painting (oil & watercolor). 14700 N. St. Joe Avenue, Evansville, IN 47711, 812-963-6240.

Walts, Cindy J. Painting, Sculpture, Woodcarving. 1831 McDonald Lane, New Albany, IN 47150, 812-945-2401.

Wood

Butler, G. Joseph. Folk Art using Rustic Wood, Paper & Stone. 3918 Claremont Avenue, Evansville, IN 47712, 812-421-1868.

Buttrum, R. Wayne. Wood Turner, Stave Bowls. 100 Pemberton Avenue, Evansville, IN 47710, 812-421-9815.

Hardin, Warren. Wood Turning, Woodworking. 2035 Breckenridge, Corydon, IN 47112, 812-952-3277.

Koressel, Robert. Woodcarver. 3901 Rose Avenue, Evansville, IN 47720, 812-424-2622.

Nicholson, Lucian R. Art Furniture & Accessories (using limbs, twigs, fabric). 3918 Claremont Avenue, Evansville, IN 47712, 812-421-1868.

Slone, Don. Hardwood Stools, Sleds, Doll Beds, Trivets. 3009 Sycamore Drive, New Albany, IN 47150, 812-944-8079.

Miscellaneous

Alley, Nancy. Canvas Floor Cloths, Clay Jewelry, Paintings. 4300 Seven Hill Road, Evansville, IN 47711, 812-983-4497.

Kirkham, Cora. Florals, Small Woodcrafts. 3485 Payton Road S.E., Elizabeth, IN 47117, 812-968-3245.

Coker, Sandra S. Old World Santas, Bears, Dolls. 1213 W. Mulberry Street,

Salem, IN 4716, 812-883-4392.

Scott, Elayne. Cutting & Decoration of Real Egg Shells. 347 E. Phillips Road, English, IN 47118, 812-338-3188.

Wade, Larry. Custom Framing. 207 E. 6th Street, Jasper, IN 47546, 812-634-2787.

All-American Roads and Scenic Byways

The Ohio River Scenic Route is part of a national program administered by the U. S. Department of Transportation that celebrates highways for their outstanding scenic, natural, cultural, archeological or recreational qualities. The program was created in 1991 as part of the Intermodal Surface Transportation Efficiency Act (ISTEA). In 1996, the Department of Transportation named the first twenty recipients of the award, the Ohio River Scenic Route among them. The Ohio River route was cited as being "a model for which all others should be developed," because of the wide spread local support and participation. Then-Lt. Governor of Indiana Frank O'Bannon said, "Being designated a National Scenic Byway allows Hoosiers the opportunity to share the beauty and history in southern Indiana along the Ohio River with the rest of the country."

For more information on the program, contact Federal Highway Administration, National Scenic Byways Program, 400 7th, SW, HEP-10, Room 3222, Washington, DC 20490, 800-4BYWAYS. Their web site is http://www.byways.org/

THE ALL-AMERCAN ROADS are the highest designation, exemplifying overweening national and global significance. The 1996 recipients included:

Selma to Montgomery March Byway, Alabama. The route is a forty-three mile tour through Civil Rights history, following the path of Dr. Martin Luther King's 1965 march. Contact Alabama Bureau of Tourism, 800-ALABAMA.

Route One, Pacific Coast Highway, California. The highway sweeps along the dramatic coastline of California for seventy-two miles past rugged cliffs, and fog-draped cypress and crashing waves. Contact the Monterey Peninsula Visitors and Convention Bureau, 408-648-5360.

San Juan Highway, Colorado. The 233-mile route snakes through the Mesa Verde National Park and picturesque towns of Durango and Telluride. Contact San Juan National Forest Information, 970-247-4884.

Trail Ridge Road/Beaver Meadow Road, Colorado. The two roads connect Estes Park and Grand Lake as they cross the Rocky Mountain National Park. Contact Rocky Mountain National Park, 970-586-1206.

Natchez Trace Parkway, Mississippi, Tennessee, Alabama. This 425-mile trail was traversed by Native Americans, soldiers, fortune-seekers, and flatboat men returning from the long float to New Orleans including the young Lincoln. It created a vital link in the opening of the new Mississippi Territory to the young Republic. Contact Natchez Trace National

Park Service, 800-305-7414.

Blue Ridge Parkway, North Carolina. The parkway winds through spectacular mountain and valley vistas, past waterfalls and bucolic scenery. The route is 252 miles long. Contact Blue Ridge Parkway Information, 704-298-0398.

In 1998, three additional All-American Roads were announced:

Historic Columbia River Highway, Oregon. On bluffs high above the Columbia, visitors can thrill to the breathtaking scenery. The large number of waterfalls outside of Yosemite are along this thirty-eight mile road. Contact USDA Forest service Columbia River Gorge National Scenic Area, 541-386-2333.

Volcanic Legacy Scenic Byway, Oregon. This 140-mile road sweeps through an expanse of ranchland before skirting lakes and forest under mountain peaks. More bald eagles nest in this area than anywhere else in the lower forty-eight states. Contact Klamath County Department of Tourism, 541-884-0666.

Mather Memorial Parkway, Washington. This eighty-five mile route is the most picturesque crossing of the Cascade Mountains, including a spectacular view of Mount McKinley. Contact Yakima Chamber of Commerce, 509-248-2021.

THE UNITED STATES SCENIC BYWAYS are recognized for their outstanding regional characteristics that reflect our American diversity and heritage. There were fourteen highways chosen in 1996, including:

Tioga Road/Big Oak Flat Road, California. The road crosses mountain meadows and past craggy mountains as it passes through the park for sixty-four miles. Contact Yosemite National Park, 209-372-0200.

Grand Mesa Scenic and Historic Byway, Colorado. The fifty-five mile "playground in the sky" climbs from the dusty canyon floor to the mesa top at eleven thousand feet past diverse wildlife such as deer, porcupines, elk, fox, and mountain lion. Contact Delta County Visitor Information, 800-874-1741.

Connecticut State Road 169, Connecticut. The thirty-two mile, twenty-five town route traverses one of the last unspoiled spots in the Northeast, a tableaux of farms, villages, forests, and historic structures. Contact Connecticut Office of Tourism, 800-CTBOUND.

Merritt Parkway, Connecticut. This thirty-eight mile route is over a talisman of highway engineering, which brilliantly set the tone of evolved highway design. Contact Connecticut Office of Tourism, 800-CTBOUND.

Ohio River Scenic Route, Indiana. A 303-mile traverse is through the lush hills along the Ohio River, a sashay through southern Indiana's history and diverse culture. Contact Historic Southern Indiana, 800-489-4474.

Creole Nature Trail, Louisiana. The 180-mile highway passes four National Wildlife Sanctuaries, natural beaches, prairies, and wetlands. Contact Lake Charles Convention and Visitors Bureau, 800-456-7952.

Edge of the Wilderness Scenic Byway, Minnesota. The route passes through the natural wonder of northern Minnesota's woodland lakes and lowland meadows for forty-seven miles. Contact Grand Rapids Visitors and Convention Bureau, 218-326-9607.

Eastshore Drive, Nevada. This twenty-nine mile drive skirts the edge of Lake Tahoe, affording breathtaking views of the basin. Contact Incline Village/Crystal Bay Visitor and Convention Bureau, 800-GO-TAHOE.

Pyramid Lake Scenic Byway, Nevada. This is the only byway completely in a Tribal reservation. The thirty-seven mile route is around one of the largest desert lakes in the world on the Paiute tribe reservation. Contact Pyramid Lake Paiute Tribe, 702-574-1000.

Kancamgus Scenic Byway, New Hampshire. A twenty-eight mile "living museum" of fauna elaborates the story of ecological development in a New England forest. Contact Saco River District Visitor Center, 603-447-5448.

Seaway Trail, New York. Tracing the eastern Great Lakes, the 454-mile route courses past historic lighthouses as the forces of wind and water are displayed in the landscape. Contact Seaway Trail, Inc., 800-SEAWAYT.

Peter Norbeck Scenic Byway, South Dakota. The sixty-nine-mile tour through the Black Hills includes Mount Rushmore and stirring vistas of forested mountains. Contact U. S. Forest Service, 605-673-2251.

Cherohalo Skyway, Tennessee. The twenty-three-mile route through the southern Appalachians passes historic Cherokee and pioneer sites.

Highland Scenic Highway, West Virginia. The forty-four miles of the highway provides scenic vistas as well as trailheads for renowned hiking in the Monongahela National Forest. Contact West Virginia Division of Tourism, 800-CALLWVA.

There were thirty-three National Scenic Byways chosen in 1998, including:

Talladega Scenic Drive, Alabama. This route is located along the southernmost stretches of the Appalachian Mountains and provides panoramic views of Alabama's highest peak, Cheaha Mountain. The drive winds twenty-nine miles along the upper reaches of Horseblock and Talladega mountains. Contact Shoal Creek Ranger District, 205-463-2272.

The Seward Highway, Alaska. From jagged peaks and alpine meadows to breathtaking fjords and crystal lakes, the Seward Highway offers a concentrated series of diverse landscapes and experiences like nowhere else in the world. Each of these distinctive landscapes can be viewed over the 127 miles between Anchorage and Seward. Contact Alaska Division of Tourism, 888-256-6784.

Crowley's Ridge Parkway, Arkansas. The only known erosional remnant of the Pleistocene Era in North America, Crowley's Ridge is a narrow ribbon of land 198 miles long. The road rises two hundred feet above the Delta topography in a landscape carved into huge glacial sluiceways. Contact Arkansas Parks and Tourism, 501-682-1120.

Kaibab Plateau-North Rim Parkway, Arizona. The Kaibab Plateau is covered with dense ponderosa pine and mixed conifer forests punctuated with huge meadows. Wildlife is abundant across the forty-two-mile road that crosses the plateau. An elevation of over eight thousand feet offers a cool retreat from the surrounding desert heat. Contact Kaibab Plateau Visitor Center, 520-643-7298.

Death Valley Scenic Byway, California. This road provides access to the nation's largest park unit outside Alaska. Death Valley Scenic Byway travels fifty-five miles through ecosystems that include rugged canyons, fragile wetlands, native palm oases, and sand dune environment. Contact Death Valley National Park, 760-786-2331.

Frontier Pathways, Colorado. Frontier Pathways traverses 103 miles, offering views of the Great Plains through Pueblo's Union Historic District and verdant Greenhorn Highway. The visit can traverse the Wet Mountains via Hardscrabble Canyon and then descend into the spectacular Wet Mountain Valley. Contact Frontier Pathways Scenic & Historic Byway, Inc., 719-783-2699.

Sante Fe Trail Scenic and Historic Byway, Colorado. In southeastern Colorado, the Sante Fe Trail travels 184 miles along the historic trade route between Missouri and the Mexican frontier. Discover the magic by retracing the steps of pioneers. Contact Colorado Welcome Center-Lamar, 719-336-3483.

Top of the Rockies, Colorado. Travel seventy-five miles across the spine of the North American Continent and view one of the highest concentration of fourteen thousand foot peaks found anywhere in the Rocky Mountain region. Contact Greater Leadville Area Chamber of Commerce, 800-933-3901.

Ohio River Scenic Route, Illinois. This route in southern Illinois is intimately tied to the Ohio River throughout the 188-mile journey. View the limestone features throughout the byway, including an enormous cave once home to river pirates. Contact Southernmost Illinois Tourism Bureau,

800-248-4373 or 618-845-3777.

Meeting of the Great Rivers, Illinois. Within the fifty-mile stretch of road, the Mississippi, Missouri and Illinois rivers meet to form a thirty-five thousand acre flood plain. This confluence is the backdrop of the Meeting of the Great Rivers rout which starts thirty minutes north of St. Louis, Missouri. Contact Greater Alton/Twin Rivers Convention and Visitors Bureau, 800-258-6645 or 618-465-6676.

The National Road, Indiana. US 40 is the first federally funded highway in the United States. Authorized by Thomas Jefferson in 1803, the road runs from Cumberland, Maryland, west to Vandalia, Illinois. Designed to connect with the terminus of the C&O Canal in Cumberland, the National Road enabled agricultural goods and raw materials from the interior direct access to the eastern seaboard. The Indiana section follows 156 miles of the original road across the central part of the state giving drivers the opportunity to take a step back in time and experience life at a more leisurely pace. Contact Old National Road Welcome Center, 800-828-8414.

The Grand Rounds Scenic Byway, Minnesota. Over 114 years ago one of the nation's most comprehensive park systems linked by boulevards was designed in and around the city of Minneapolis. Today travelers can experience the fifty-two miles of this byway in a lushly vegetated urban environment where vistas of the city skyline appear as frequently as the lakes, streams, and rivers it passes. Contact Minneapolis Park & Recreation Board, 612-661-4800.

White Mountain Trail, New Hampshire. The White Mountain region of New Hampshire has long been known for its national splendor, cultural richness, historical charm, and stimulating recreational opportunities. The trail is important for its varying topography, for mountain and river views, a variety of vegetation from wetlands to forests, and for the eighteenth and nineteenth century structures found along its 123-mile path. Contact White Mountain Attraction, 888-WHITEMTN or 888-944-8368.

Billy the Kid Trail, New Mexico. The byway travels through a region marked by exceptional natural scenic beauty and diversity, and features some of the earliest-known evidence of humans on the North American continent. The sixty-eight-mile route in south-central New Mexico passes through the rough terrain of the land where the outlaw Billy the Kid lived and died. Contact Ruiodoso Chamber of Commerce/Visitors Center, 505-257-7395.

El Camino Real, New Mexico. The Camino Real de Tierra Adentro, or Royal Highway of the Interior Lands, linked New Mexico with New Spain (Mexico) beginning in the Spanish colonial period (1598-1821) and was the first European road in the United States. The 303 miles traversed by the byway is the most historic trail in New Mexico as it follows the path that originally ran from Mexico City to Santa Fe. Visitors can admire the diverse and scenic landscape of New Mexico as experienced by the Spanish Conquistadores. Contact Albuquerque Hispano Chamber of Commerce, 505-842-9003.

Jemez Mountain Trail, New Mexico. The Native American and Hispanic cultures are alive and well along the 132-mile byway. Traveling from the ancient ruins of Bandalier National Monument to the Jemez Pueblo and tribal lands through which the route passes, visitors will be enthralled by the rugged mountain scenery of north-central New Mexico. Contact Sandoval County Visitors Center, 505-867-TOUR or 800-252-0191.

Santa Fe Trail, New Mexico. The trail was the first of America's great trans-Mississippi routes. Visitors traversing the 304 miles in New Mexico can see the most extensive remains of the trail from the original wagon ruts to historic sites and landmarks. The spectacular and rugged scenery is little changed from what the pioneers saw and experienced nearly two hundred years ago. Contact New Mexico Department of Tourism, 505-827-7400.

Cherohala Skyway, North Carolina. Located in the far western part of the North Carolina's Appalachian mountains the twenty mile route links the formerly isolated mountain towns of Robbinsville, North Carolina, and Tellico Plains, Tennessee. As the route skims along and besides high ridgetops in this pristine area, the traveler feels like a soaring bird. Contact North Carolina Travel & Tourism Division, 800-VISITNC or 800-847-4862

Ohio River Scenic Route, Ohio. Traversing 452 miles along the northern shore of the Ohio River in Ohio, the visitor can experience par of what has been called America's "valley of democracy." Examples of the history and culture of people who migrated and settled along the Ohio River and a rich industrial and transportation heritage are found along the route. Contact Ohio River Trails, Inc., 513-621-7737.

Cascade Lakes Scenic Byway, Oregon. Located in the Cascade Mountains of Central Oregon, the sixty-nine miles of the byway treat the viewer to dramatic views of the greatest concentration of snow-capped volcanoes in the lower forty-eight states. Nowhere else in the United States is there such ready access to a diversity of volcanic features both in age and type. Contact Bend Visitor and Convention Bureau, 541-382-3221.

McKenzie Pass-Santiam Pass Scenic Byway, Oregon. The byway takes the visitor eighty-six miles through the High Cascades and two spectacular mountain passes with striking views of black lava in contrast to white snow.

The youngest basaltic volcanoes in the Cascades are found along the byway as well as a grand assortment of wildlife, particularly birds traveling the Pacific Flyway. Contact USDA Forest Service McKenzie Ranger Station, 541-822-3381.

Pacific Coast Scenic Byway, Oregon. The most beautiful coastline in America lies along the 363 miles of US 101 as it traverses high bluffs and low agrarian valleys giving panoramic and framed views of the Pacific Ocean. Visitors will find a rich array of cultural, historic, archaeological, and recreational qualities that fill the byway from border to border and from beaches to mountains. Contact Oregon Tourism Commission, 800-547-7842.

Outback Scenic Byway, Oregon. This route, in southeastern Oregon, captures all the dramatic diversity of the Great Basin Region in a relatively short distance of 165 miles. The scenery changes from the old-growth ponderosa and lodgepole pine stands of the eastern Cascades to the sagebrush steppe and wetlands of the high desert. This area is one of the most important stopovers for migrating birds using the Pacific Flyway. Contact The Lake County Chamber of Commerce, 541-947-6040.

Cherokee Foothills Scenic Highway, South Carolina. High hills and distinct mountain ridges characterize the prominent natural features along the scenic highway which the Cherokee Indians called the "Great Blue Hills of God." The Cherokee Foothills Scenic Highway offers picturesque views along 112 miles of South Carolina Route 11 in the northwest corner of the state near Greenville, South Carolina. Contact Discover Upcountry Carolina Association, Inc., 800-849-4766 or 864-233-2690.

The Native Americana Scenic Byway, South Carolina. Lying primarily in the Savannah River region of rich historic, cultural, and recreational resources, the scenic highway provides a critical link between the sites and outstanding scenery that tell the unique story of life in the South. Situated in the western part of the state beginning at Route 28 at the Georgia/South Carolina border, the scenic highway runs 110 miles north to Oakway, South Carolina. Contact South Carolina Department of Parks, Recreation & Tourism, 803-734-1700.

Flaming Gorge-Uintas Scenic Byway, Utah. The unique geological features of the Uinta Mountains and the Flaming Gorge Reservoir with its 375 miles of shoreline are among the outstanding scenic, recreational, and natural qualities of the Flaming Gorge-Uintas Scenic Byway. Located in the northeast corner of Utah, the byway begins at Vernal and runs north eighty miles into the Flaming Gorge National Recreational Area. Contact Dinosaur Land Travel Board, 800-447-5558 or 435-789-6932.

Nebo Loop Scenic Byway, Utah. In a short thirty-seven miles, the Nebo Loop

Scenic Byway offers a rare spectrum of scenic experiences, wide range of recreational activities, and significant experiences of Native American history. They byway follows Route 12 in south central Utah near Payson and Nephi. Contact Utah Valley Convention & Visitors Bureau, 801-370-8393.

Mountains to Sound Greenway, Washington. Interstate 90 is the primary west/east highway in Washington State. It provides the traveler the opportunity to travel 101 miles from urban Seattle and the lush green forests and marine climate of the Puget Sound through pastoral rural valleys and a dramatic mountain landscape to the arid eastern face of the Cascades. Contact Washington State Department of Trade and Economic Development, 360-753-5601.

The Coal Heritage Trail West, Virginia. The trail is a remarkable legacy to the working-class of southern West Virginia coal mines who produced the abundant and economical fuel which transformed rural Appalachia into an industrial land. The trail travels along the coalfields ninety-eight miles between Beckley, Welch, and Bluefield. Contact Southern West Virginia Convention & Visitors Bureau, 800-VISITWV or 800-847-4898.

An Historic Architectural Guide to Indiana

Vernacular Architecture

Most of Indiana's buildings are vernacular, springing from a long tradition of utilitarian popular construction without a fixed stylistic reference. Barns, cabins, farmhouses, and simple commercial structures are all examples of vernacular architecture. Cultural geographers and historians describe buildings with vernacular forms and details or elements inspired by high-style architectural trends as popular architecture.

Indiana's numerous I-houses are often used as examples of popular architecture. Cultural geographer Fred Kniffen coined the term I-house in 1936 because they were common in Midwestern states beginning with the letter "I." The I-house type is formed by a central hall, flanked by two rooms, on both floors. Typically, builders placed three or five openings across the front, giving houses a balanced, formal appearance with rear wings, called "ells." To this basic form, Greek Revival cornices or Italianate brackets, or both, could be added as the decades wore on to keep with current trends.

The Federal Style

The Federal Style is characterized by its simple proportions, box-like exteriors and roofs, and long narrow multi-paned windows. Builders limited the ornamentation to simple detail around entrances, windows, and cornices. The occasional use of curvilinear forms adds to the lightness and delicacy which is typical of this style. Because the style was popular early in Indiana's history (from about 1810 to 1840), most examples are located in southern Indiana, especially near navigable waterways and early roads.

The 1818 Jeremiah Sullivan House, in Madison, is an exceptionally sophisticated Federal-style house, reflecting the prosperity and Virginia background of its first owner, successful lawyer Jeremiah Sullivan. Most examples of the style were built of wood frame construction—comparatively few were built of brick like the Sullivan House. The entrance is characteristic of the Federal style, with its slender engaged columns and delicate semi-elliptical fanlight above the door and sidelights. The finely ornamented cornice is also typical of the Federal style.

The Greek Revival Style

The Greek Revival style was most popular in Indiana from about 1840 to around 1860. The style uses heavy, temple-like exteriors, rather than the delicate classicism of the previous Federal period. Stylistically, Greek Revival emulated the temple forms of ancient Greece, resulting in the creation of straightforward, box-like buildings. In smaller, domestic structures, carpenters created simple ornamentation. Most Greek Revival buildings have evenly spaced, multi-paned windows and entrances marked by sidelights and rectangular transoms. Substantial cornices often extended into gable ends as "returns." Roofs were low-pitched gables, similar to those of classical temples. Columns and pilasters proportioned to imitate ancient forms appear on larger Greek Revival buildings. The style was used for many different building types, ranging from courthouses to homes to tiny commercial structures to even outhouses. The simplicity of the style made it practical, but it was philosophically attractive also. Many Americans considered their nation heir to the democratic principles exemplified by ancient Athens, to them it was natural that American buildings should look like those of ancient Greece. The Second Presbyterian Church in Madison is an outstanding example of the stark classicism of the era; it clearly follows the ancient Greek temple form.

The Early Gothic Revival Style

During the early 1800s English architects and critics advocated Gothic (medieval) designs as being more natural than those of the classical era creating the Gothic Revival. It was the first nineteenth-century architectural movement to rely heavily on medieval rather than classical forms. Americans, taken with the style, published house-pattern books advocating informal Gothic cottages such as A.J. Downing's *The Architecture of Country Houses* (1850). The Early Gothic Revival style was introduced to Indiana around 1840 and was popular until about 1860 in Indiana. Although not as popular as the Greek Revival style, this mode was quite common for churches. Congregations often chose Gothic Revival designs long after it ceased to be popular for houses. Designers of this style favored the picturesque and irregular above all. Details were inspired by European (especially English) Gothic architecture. Builders used pointed arches and lace-like tracery, borrowed from Gothic architecture. Carpenters reproduced these elements in wood and applied them to windows, doors, gables, porches, and bay windows. Floor plans were irregular, and steeply pitched gable roofs were common. Materials ranged from frame cottages with vertical wood siding (called board-and-batten) to brick and stone structures.

The applied, lacy detailing of this style gives Gothic Revival buildings a delicate appearance.

The Italianate Style

Of all the styles of the nineteenth century, the Italianate style was one of the most common in Indiana. As the name somewhat implies, Italianate architecture was a fanciful reinterpretation of Italian Renaissance architecture. The style was initiated in England in the early 1800s. Italianate buildings were most often asymmetrical in plan, but occasionally owners chose a more formal, balanced plan. A wide entablature with heavy scroll brackets supporting wide eaves identifies most Italianate buildings. Windows were tall, narrow, and often half-rounded or segmentally arched on top. Some were surmounted by ornamental stone or pressed-metal hood molds. Architects distinguished large houses and public buildings with high towers, inspired by the bell towers of the Italian countryside. Walls were built of clapboard siding or brick with stone detailing. Porches were very common on Italianate homes with chamfered posts and bracketed cornices.

In Indiana, the Italianate style was most popular between 1855 and 1890. Unlike other late nineteenth-century styles, Hoosiers selected the Italianate style for all kinds of buildings, including commercial and industrial structures.

Corydon's Main Street shows how builders retrofitted Italianate architecture to a commercial row of Federal buildings. Italianate buildings were especially well suited to commercial areas in crowded downtowns, where citizens could appreciate their showy detail. In this case, the use of cast iron columns allows large storefronts, while the sheet metal window hoods and cornice mimic expensive stone work at a modest price.

The High-Victorian Gothic Style

Unlike the Early Gothic Revival, the High-Victorian Gothic style was mainly inspired by Venetian Gothic architecture rather than English Medieval buildings. English architectural critic John Ruskin was an important figure in advocating the style. Many characteristics of early Gothic Revival are also used in this style. In contrast to the use of delicate applied wood ornamentation of the earlier movement, architects of the High-Victorian Gothic style favored heavy, structural detailing. Buildings of the style are usually irregularly shaped and nearly always of masonry construction. Even the colors of materials were supposed to evoke the sense of craftsmanship associated with medieval buildings. The style was short lived in popularity, lasting only from about 1875 to 1885 in Indiana.

The Willard Library in Evansville is typical of this style. The picturesque outline, pointed arches, horizontal banding and polychromy (use of materials which contrast in color) are common elements of High Victorian Gothic architecture.

The Second Empire Style

Historians named this popular French style for the reign of Napoleon III of France, that country's second emperor. In Second Empire buildings, the most obvious distinguishing characteristic is the mansard roof, called a

"French roof" by American builders. Prominent dormer windows, a wide entablature with brackets and various elaborate window treatments were typical of this mode. The asymmetrical design, convex and concave mansard roofs, elaborate door and window hoods and rich detailing are common Second Empire elements. Architects borrowed many details from the contemporary Italianate style. Plans ranged from balanced, classically influenced types to picturesque designs with prominent towers. This style was used for large public structures as well as mansions. Second Empire homes tend to be large mansions, but smaller cottages were erected in this mode. This style was most common in Indiana from about 1860 to 1885.

The Queen Anne Style

Victorians used this style mostly for residences and occasionally for commercial buildings. By combining motifs from medieval and Early Renaissance architecture, builders created one for the most popular late nineteenth-century styles in America, full of frills and elaborate gingerbread. Inspired by the work of English architects, the style first appeared in the United States in 1876, when the English made several "Queen Anne" display halls for the Centennial Exposition in Philadelphia.

The Neo-Classic Revival Style

In 1890s America's love affair with classical forms was rekindled, and the neo-classic style, also known as Beaux-Artes, was born. It was most often used for large public buildings like the Beaux-Arts Old Courthouse in Evansville.

The Prairie Style

The Prairie Style sprung full-grown from the fertile mind of Frank Lloyd Wright, the preeminent architect of the twentieth century. The flat prairies of the Midwest inspired Wright and all of the devotee architects who followed him. The style favored low rectilinial profiles, overhanging roof lines, and casement windows. The ubiquitous Hoosier Four-Square and Bungalow designs popular in the 1920s and 1930s incorporated many of Wright's ideas

Art Deco

The sleek curviliniar lines of Art Deco was testimony in masonry and metal to the machine and airplane age. The style was popular between 1925 and 1940. The wonderful Greyhound Bus Terminal in Evansville, with its running neon dog, is a fine example of the style.

Special thanks to *Historic Indiana 1997/98: A Guide to the Indiana Properties Listed in the National Register of Historic Places,* published by the Indiana Division of Historic Preservation and Archeology.

INDEX

Unless otherwise noted, cities and towns are all in Indiana.

H

I

J

Douglas Wissing is a writer and world traveler who lives in Bloomington, Indiana. He writes for publications such as the *New York Times*, *National Geographic Traveler*, *Travel Holiday*, *Travel and Leisure*, *ARTnews*, and *Saveur*. A descendant of eighteenth-century French fur traders in Vincennes, Wissing's as Hoosier as you get.

Scenic Route
Ohio River